ESCAPING THE CONFLICT TRAP

MIDDLE EAST INSTITUTE POLICY SERIES

The MEI Policy Series aims to inform policy debates on the most pressing issues that will shape the future of the Middle East. The series publishes manuscripts that provide cutting-edge analysis and recommendations to policymakers in the Middle East and to international actors as they work toward solutions to some of the most searing problems facing the region.

Seeking to contribute to policy debates that will influence the Middle East in the future, the MEI Policy Series promotes innovative and incisive work that focuses on issues that cut across the various countries of the region and span the areas of politics, culture, economics, society, the state, climate, health, gender and any other issue that meets the above policy impact criteria.

ESCAPING THE CONFLICT TRAP

Toward Ending Civil War in the Middle East

Second Edition

Edited by

Paul Salem and Ross Harrison

I.B. TAURIS

LONDON • NEW YORK • OXFORD • NEW DELHI • SYDNEY

I.B. TAURIS

Bloomsbury Publishing Plc

50 Bedford Square, London, WC1B 3DP, UK

1385 Broadway, New York, NY 10018, USA

29 Earlsfort Terrace, Dublin 2, Ireland

BLOOMSBURY, I.B. TAURIS and the I.B. Tauris logo are trademarks of
Bloomsbury Publishing Plc

First published by The Middle East Institute, 2019

This edition published 2023 by I.B.Tauris, an imprint of Bloomsbury Publishing

Series design by Charlotte Daniels

Cover image © Kay Nietfeld/Pool/AFP/Getty Images

A catalogue record for this book is available from the British Library.

A catalog record for this book is available from the Library of Congress.

ISBN: HB: 978-0-7556-4694-4
PB: 978-0-7556-4695-1
ePDF: 978-0-7556-4696-8
eBook: 978-0-7556-4697-5

Typeset by Newgen KnowledgeWorks Pvt. Ltd., Chennai, India
Printed and bound in Great Britain

Series: Middle East Institute Policy Series I MEI

To find out more about our authors and books visit www.bloomsbury.com
and sign up for our newsletters.

CONTENTS

CONTRIBUTORS

Paul Salem is President of the Middle East Institute, Washington, DC.

Ross Harrison is a Senior Fellow and Director of Research at the Middle East Institute and is on the faculty of the Political Science Department at the University of Pittsburgh. Previously he was on the faculty of the School of Foreign Service at Georgetown University.

Jessica Maves Braithwaite is an Associate Professor of Political Science in the School of Government and Public Policy at the University of Arizona.

Gerald M. Feierstein is Senior Vice President and a Distinguished Senior Fellow on US diplomacy at the Middle East Institute. He was previously the Principal Deputy Assistant Secretary of State for Near Eastern Affairs and US Ambassador to Yemen.

Robert S. Ford is a Senior Fellow at the Middle East Institute and a Senior Fellow at Yale University's Jackson Institute for Global Affairs. He previously served as the US Ambassador to Syria and Algeria, and as Deputy Ambassador to Iraq.

Marvin G. Weinbaum is the Director of the Afghanistan and Pakistan program at the Middle East Institute, a former US State Department intelligence analyst for Afghanistan, and Emeritus Professor of Political Science at the University of Illinois at Urbana-Champaign.

Jonathan M. Winer is a Nonresident Scholar at the Middle East Institute and previously served as US Special Envoy for Libya.

Randa Slim is the Director of the Conflict Resolution and Track II Dialogues Program at the Middle East Institute and a Nonresident Fellow at the Johns Hopkins University School of Advanced and International Studies (SAIS) Foreign Policy Institute.

Chester A. Crocker is Emeritus Professor of Strategic Studies at Georgetown University and Distinguished Fellow at its Institute for the Study of Diplomacy. He previously served as Chair of the Board of the US Institute of Peace and as Assistant Secretary of State for African Affairs.

PREFACE

Paul Salem and Ross Harrison

xamining the phenomenon of civil war is like looking through a kaleidoscope: the image can change depending on the angle at which it is viewed. In a similar fashion, this book is an attempt to look at the civil wars in the Middle East from different angles and through varying analytic lenses.

This book project emerged out of the observation that most of the present accounts of the civil wars wracking the Middle East are either too granular and focused on the nitty gritty of the fighting, or too abstract and academic to be of much use to the practitioner looking for answers about the origins of and roadmaps out of these conflicts. There have been excellent attempts to begin building a more analytic and nuanced understanding of these conflicts.[1] We felt that more needed to be done.

This volume is a response to what we saw as the gaps in the existing discourse on civil wars in the Middle East. It includes contributions of three different types. The first are focused accounts of the civil wars in Syria, Libya, Yemen, Afghanistan, and Iraq by practitioners who have had either direct or indirect experience in coping with and mediating the conflicts. The second are contributions that pull back from the individual conflicts and address the broad historical sweep of civil wars in the Middle East (Paul Salem) and the global and regional geopolitical drivers of civil wars in this tumultuous region (Ross Harrison). While the authors of the country-centric chapters are stewards of the particular, the authors of the chapters with a broader focus provide more general insights. The third type of contribution is represented by chapters written more topically, such as the role constructive engagement can play in mitigating and even ending civil wars (Chester Crocker), and how frameworks offered by academics for analyzing civil wars can be applied to the current conflicts in the Middle East (Jessica Maves Braithwaite). Taken together, these three different types of contributions provide the kaleidoscope-like effect we are seeking and that we feel is absent from most other treatments of civil wars in the Middle East.

The reader who doesn't have the stamina or interest to read the entire volume shouldn't despair. This book had a long gestation period because of the painstaking efforts we took to bring the three different types of authors together for symposia and workshops as the project was unfolding, beginning in 2017 as the first edition got underway, and all the way through 2021 as the manuscript was being revised and updated for this second edition. This process engendered a cross-pollination effect, such that a bit of each of the three perspectives will be found in all chapters.

While each of the civil wars covered in this volume is in a way sui generis, there are patterns that we have seen across the cases that are important to point out at the outset. First, while each of the current conflicts under examination erupted over the past decade, they all have long historical tails. The Yemen civil war is really a continuation of a conflict that goes back almost sixty years. The Afghan war, which presumably ended—or at least paused for the time being—with the 2021 victory by the Taliban, is itself the evolution of a conflict that has gone on for several decades. Syria had elements of a civil war in 1979–82, and Iraq has experienced civil conflict—along both the Arab-Kurdish and Sunni–Shi'i axis—for some decades as well. Libya's civil war had its origins in the decades of repression and hollowed-out institutions under Muammar Gaddafi's reign, as well as the divisions of pre-independence Libya.

Second, each of the civil wars had deep and complex domestic drivers and dynamics over issues of governance, political identity, and resources. These domestic drivers of conflict were accentuated by crises of legitimacy in all of the countries that descended into war. All of them had deep regional and international components as well. At the regional level, some of the conflicts, namely Syria, Iraq, and to a lesser degree Yemen, fell along a Shi'i–Sunni fault-line with Iran backing one side and various Arab Sunni states and Turkey backing the other side. Other conflicts, particularly Libya for example, fell along regional and tribal lines, and drew in foreign intervention along a Sunni–Sunni divide with different Sunni states backing opposing sides. Global powers have competed most visibly in Syria, where Russia used its intervention in 2015 to return to the regional and world stages with a bang. Russia also cast its shadow in the conflict in Libya. In Afghanistan, the global and regional levels merged as the United States, prior to its 2021 withdrawal, was directly involved in that war, pitted against local players—for example, the Taliban and ISIS—but also grappling with the influence of regional powers such as Pakistan, India, and Iran.

Third, all of these civil wars have been affected by the presence or entrance of armed transnational non-state actors. While armed non-state militias have been components of civil wars in other regions of the world, their transnational reach and centrality of involvement in the conflicts in the Middle East have rendered them more significant actors on the regional and civil war chess boards. These include a network of radical Sunni jihadi groups, such as recognized terrorist organizations like ISIS and al-Qaeda. They also include a large network of Shiite militias largely backed by Iran, as well as Kurdish armed groups.

Fourth, each of the conflicts will require a mixture of local, regional, and global factors to bring them to an end. The Afghanistan conflict has ended—at least for now—as a result of a negotiation between the United States, a global power, and the Taliban. Marvin Weinbaum examines the denouement of this protracted conflict and considers the potential futures of this troubled country. In his chapter on Libya, Jonathan Winer points to alignment between regional and international actors as the most important determinant of what happens next in Libya, while Gerald Feierstein focuses more on the importance of local dynamics in Yemen, the healing of domestic divisions in the country, and of the necessity of political will among local national actors in redressing power and economic distribution problems. The other cases fall in between the extremes of seeing external versus internal actors as the most critical factor in conflict resolution.

Last, the works by Chester Crocker and Jessica Maves Braithwaite warn us that few of the conflicts are likely to end cleanly through either a negotiated settlement or a clear victory by one party or the other. The outlier in this regard is of course Afghanistan, where the Taliban are—at least for now—consolidating their control over the country. Of the five conflicts examined in this volume, Iraq perhaps has the best chance to build positive traction in ending its latest round of civil conflict and in moving forward toward a more stable future. In Syria, the Assad regime, with help from its allies, has reconquered much, but not all, of its territory, and is being courted by several Arab countries that want to bring Bashar al-Assad in from the cold. But in the absence of any political settlement, and with a cratering economy, Assad's hold on Syria will remain precarious, and the risk of renewed conflict will continue to be high. In Libya and Yemen, a negotiated settlement is a distinct possibility, but the two countries are so fragmented and state institutions so weak that even if a deal can be struck, restoring national order, governance, and security will remain extremely challenging.

But despite this bleak and pessimistic overall assessment, the book emphasizes that policymakers shouldn't throw their hands up in despair. Rather they need to develop and pursue policies aimed at the national, regional, and global levels that help mitigate the worst effects of the conflicts and work toward ultimate resolution. Realistic policies need to aim at different short-term outcomes for each of the countries. In Iraq, the goal, after winning the war against ISIS and trying to move against sectarian and ethnic civil conflict, is to consolidate the peace. In Libya and Yemen, the goal of a negotiated settlement is attainable, and policy should drive at helping generate sufficient political will for all sides to negotiate. But policy toward these two conflicts needs to also address the fact that if and when a settlement is reached, the amount of attention to—and investment in—institution building will have to be significant.

In Syria, the goal might be more modest: to avoid further massive bloodshed and population displacement in the northeast and northwest, while also grappling with the challenge of the al-Qaeda-affiliated Hayat Tahrir al-Sham in the northwest and finding a path forward for the Kurdish and Arab forces in the northeast. Policy will also need to alleviate the conditions of millions of internally displaced persons, address the need for reconstruction, and enable a free and positive return for millions of refugees. In Afghanistan, the choices are bleak for the international community: between isolating the Taliban-led Afghan government and treating it as a rogue state at one extreme, or alternatively engaging with it knowing that without external aid, the country could slide again into failed state status, with all of the implications that has for the Afghan people and the international community in terms of refugee flows and international terrorism. Hence, for global and regional policymakers there, the challenge is to choose among the least bad options, and perhaps to marshal policies and resources to maintain a glass-half-full situation.

Policymakers will also face dilemmas on how to proceed with cases of civil strife that have emerged since the first edition of this book came out. Ethiopia has recently fallen into civil war, and Lebanon is at risk of complete state failure and civil conflict in the wake of the economic collapse that started in 2019, the Beirut Port blast of 2020, and the political paralysis that has ensued.

But it is also important to note that from the longer-term policy perspective, civil wars generally don't go on forever. While attending to the near-term policy goals, which must be realistic and potentially achievable, policy should also keep in mind the long game. This means having an eye toward a regional security architecture that can help secure some gains in reducing conflict levels and preserving those gains if and when they are achieved. While this may seem starry-eyed and unrealistic given the realities on the ground today, policymakers need to remember that other regions of the world, like Europe and Southeast Asia, developed regional architectures out of the crucible of conflict.

This book tries to grapple with this wide array of issues. It was designed to be of value to various categories of readers, including practitioners, policy analysts, academics, and interested citizens. Our hope is that in aggregate, this work provides possible roadmaps for exiting this treacherous and destructive period in the Middle East, and for creating a brighter future for the peoples of the region.

Note

1 For a great example, see Kenneth M. Pollack and Barbara F. Walter, "Escaping the Civil War Trap in the Middle East," *Washington Quarterly* 38, no. 2 (2016): 29–46 provides an excellent combination of both policy and academic perspectives.

1 MIDDLE EAST CIVIL WARS

Definitions, Drivers, and the Record of the Recent Past

Paul Salem

Introduction

The wider Middle East has suffered from numerous civil wars during its recent history. The current civil wars in Libya, Syria, and Yemen and the recently ended ones in Afghanistan and Iraq were preceded by conflicts in Oman, Lebanon, Sudan, Algeria, and Jordan, as well as previous bouts of civil war in Yemen, Afghanistan, and Iraq.[1] Somalia and other countries in the Horn of Africa, including, most recently, Ethiopia, have also seen devastating civil wars. The long-standing Israeli–Palestinian conflict itself started as a civil war in Mandate Palestine and still has many attributes of one.[2] This is in addition to lower-order internal civil conflicts in Turkey, Syria, Egypt, Morocco, and elsewhere. Almost no country in the region has escaped experience with some form of armed internal conflict.

In this chapter, I will examine the patterns, definitions, and dynamics of civil war, and review sixteen cases of civil war or civil conflict in the twentieth-century history of the wider Middle East. Of course, any thorough examination of the many case studies of twentieth-century civil conflicts in the region would be, by itself, several volumes long, so this chapter will only attempt a broad overview to give the reader an appreciation of the complex and varied history of civil conflict in the modern Middle East, and to provide some comparative and historical perspective on the civil wars ongoing today. The chapter will also seek to draw some preliminary parallels or lessons from these past conflicts, to help understand the current civil wars and to consider how they might be brought to an end.

Far more civilians have died or suffered from civil wars in the Middle East since the Second World War than from state-to-state conflict. The Arab–Israeli conflict has killed over eighty thousand[3] and the region's largest interstate conflict, between Iran and Iraq, left more than five hundred thousand dead.[4] By comparison, the Syrian civil war alone has already cost at least as many lives,[5] and Sudan accounts for even more, at around two million. If we add up all the victims of civil war in the region since the Second World War, the total exceeds four million. At present, there is no active direct interstate war in the Middle East, but there are several ongoing civil and proxy wars.

The large footprint of civil wars and the toll they've taken in terms of the dead and wounded since the Second World War is not just a Middle Eastern phenomenon. "Civil war has gradually become the most widespread, the most destructive, and the most characteristic form of organized human violence."[6] "The three hundred years between 1648 and 1945 constituted an era of war *between* states; the last sixty years appear to be an age of war *within* states."[7] This has included internal conflicts in Chad, Rwanda, the Congo, Nigeria, Colombia, Costa Rica, Spain, Greece, India, Burma, China, and Cambodia, to name but a very few. Of 259 wars since 1989, almost 95 percent have been within states.[8] Globally, civil wars tend to last longer—on average four times longer—than state-to-state wars. Also, countries that have undergone civil war have a 50 percent chance of slipping back into one again in the future.

Civil wars also have a fundamentally different impact than state-to-state conflicts. Traditional wars generally have the effect of unifying a nation and strengthening state-society bonds and state institutions. This is typically true whether the state wins (Israel 1967), draws (Iran 1989), or loses (Egypt 1967), provided the loss does not involve the full collapse or removal of the state (Iraq 2003 or the Ottoman Empire in the First World War). But civil wars have the opposite effect: they tear asunder the national fabric, damage state institutions, and weaken the bonds between the society—or at least that portion of the society that rebelled—and the state.

In addition, civil wars hollow out a country from the inside, devastating its social fabric and social capital, destroying its economy, and dismantling its institutions; they also drive people from their homes and businesses, and in many cases, drive them out of the country altogether. Traditional state-to-state warfare is often a nation- and state-*building* pathway; by contrast, civil wars are generally nation and state *destroyers*. This makes civil wars much harder to end, since both national and state cohesion and capacity have been weakened. It also makes the post-conflict period, if and when it comes, much more challenging: Above and beyond reconstructing destroyed physical infrastructure, it requires reweaving the national fabric and standing up national and state institutions.

Questions of Terminology and Definition

Most scholars and political analysts consider civil war to refer to conflicts among members of one national community in which armed civilians are at least one party to the conflict. This includes cases where the state is battling armed civilians (such as Syria today or Oman and Algeria previously) and cases where the war is among various groups of armed civilians (Lebanon in 1975–90, Libya today) with the state playing only a very minor role, if at all.[9]

While this might apply to many Middle East civil wars, it does leave a number of gray areas. For instance, how do we categorize the Arab revolt against the Ottoman state in 1916? From one perspective, it was a civil war within the Ottoman state, but from another, it was an Arab nationalist revolt against a "foreign" Turkish state. Indeed, how do we categorize the various civilian-led anti-colonial revolts against European mandate and colonial states in countries like Syria, Sudan, Libya, and Algeria? Moreover, what about cases in which those fighting are not nationals of the country where the "civil war" is taking place, but are instead part of transnational networks that have entered the country? That is the case with various Sunni jihadi groups engaged in "civil wars" in parts of today's Middle East, or with Shiite fighters recruited from Pakistan, Afghanistan, and Lebanon to fight in Syria.[10]

We need not consider the great anti-colonial revolts to be civil wars per se, but the experience of large numbers of civilians taking up arms against the colonial state might have a bearing later on, when armed civilians took up arms once again—this time against the indigenous state. The patterns of the great Syrian revolt against French rule in the 1920s, for example, bear some similarities to those of the armed revolt that began in the Syrian uprising against the regime of Bashar al-Assad in 2011. Likewise, the ways in which the civilian-led war against the French colonial state played out in the 1940s and 1950s has some relevance to the conflict between armed Islamist civilians and the Algerian state in the 1990s.

Another issue when it comes to defining civil wars is the politicized nature of the appellation: "Naming ... is always a form of framing."[11] Established governments want to call challenges to their rule illegitimate rebellions; recently they have found it useful to describe them more generally as *terrorists*, as the Assad regime has done. Most armed civilians in conflict with a state, colonial or indigenous, usually consider themselves *revolutionaries*; this was the case in the Algerian revolution against the French, the Syrian revolution against the Assad regime, or the Libyan revolution against Muammar Gaddafi. It is typically only outsiders who use the term "civil war." As one keen analyst of civil wars put it: "*I* am a revolutionary, *you* are a rebel, *they* are engaged in a civil war."[12] This terminology matters: a state or regime that considers its opponents illegitimate rebels, or indeed terrorists, is not on a trajectory to contemplate political negotiations. The same might be true of some rebel groups, which define themselves as wholesale revolutionaries (whether ethnic, nationalist, Islamist, or other ideological).

Another definitional matter is that of size and scope. When does a set of armed civil conflicts or skirmishes accede to the level of a civil *war*? Is it a matter of the number of dead (some scholars start counting after the death toll exceeds a thousand[13]); or a matter of longevity (a civil skirmish, even if it leaves many thousands dead, might not be considered a civil war if it started and ended in a few days); or is it about geographic scope. (Can a war that is limited to a very small part of the country be considered a civil war, like the armed conflict in northern Sinai?)

For the purposes of this chapter, I will look at both wide-scale and "long-lived" civil wars, as well as cases of narrower or shorter-lived civil conflicts. It is important to take a broad view of this wide array of conflicts to get a more nuanced understanding of their complexity and to gain a deeper and richer background for examining the current civil wars that are the main subject of this book.

Civil War as Politics

Civil war, like traditional war, is also a continuation of politics by other means.[14] It is the use of violence—in this case taken up by civilians, not professional armies—to achieve a political end. In that sense civil wars are essentially *political* phenomena; and this means that understanding them and finding ways to bring them to an end must take into account not only the elements of armed conflict but also the political demands and ends that the various combatting groups are contending for. Ending civil wars in any sustainable way is a fundamentally *political* challenge. Of course, in many cases, civil wars are resolved by brute force (as in Algeria), and the winning side—whether it is the state or a rebel group—simply imposes its will by force. In some cases the losing party is weakened, decimated, or exiled such that its "political" demands no longer matter. In other cases, ending the civil war by force only represses the political demands, many of which are likely to resurface in the future (e.g., Yemen's recurring civil wars). This is one of the many reasons that countries that suffer a civil war have a 50 percent chance of relapsing into civil war again.

Of course, the spectrum of political ends varies widely, and different "rebel" groups might have very different objectives. In the political sphere, some groups are seeking full secession (like the Southern Hirak movement in Yemen and some Kurdish parties in Iraq), while others are advocating for greater autonomy (e.g., several Kurdish parties or movements in Iraq, Turkey, Syria, and Iran). Some groups might be seeking the overthrow and fundamental redesign of the whole political system (most of the regions' modern civil wars involved groups that proposed a "redesign" of the political system, with many groups proposing an Islamist redesign of some sort and others advocating a more inclusive or democratically representative system); others might only be demanding the removal of a ruler or a particular regime (some contenders in the civil unrest in Syria or Libya can be said to be motivated mainly by a desire to remove and replace the Assad or Gaddafi regimes). Some groups might simply be demanding a lifting of repression; others might be demanding a full role in political life (elements of the current civil wars in Syria and Libya, and unrest in Egypt, in which reacting to excessive repression was virtually an independent motivating force for many participants in the civil conflict or unrest). In the economic sphere, some groups might be demanding more jobs and social justice (e.g., elements of the Dhofar rebellion); others might be demanding a deeper transformation of the economic system of the country (e.g., leftist parties and militias in the Lebanese civil war). This certainly does not exhaust the list of political ends for which contenders in civil wars might be aiming. The fact that these unsatisfied political ends contributed to the outbreak of a civil war usually indicates a prior failure of politics to address them or to keep them within the bounds of the political; and any *sustainable* end to a civil war must grapple with the underlying political and socioeconomic objectives that combatants put their lives on the line for.

Furthermore, a civil war changes the political landscape of a country. The society, institutions, values, and patterns when a country *enters* a civil war are not at all those that exist at the end of it.[15] Civil wars fundamentally change nations.[16] In some cases, like Yugoslavia, the prewar nation ceases to exist at the end of the conflict. In other cases, the war devastates the national and governing fabric so severely that the nation enters a decades-long period of chronic collapse—Somalia might be a case in point.[17] One can also cite the cases of Yemen and Afghanistan, which in earlier times seemed like a kind of "chronic" condition. While Lebanon has managed to avoid slipping back into a major civil war since 1990, the underlying fissures brought about by the 1975–90 conflict are still there and the risk of state collapse has been greatly exacerbated by the recent economic and financial crisis.[18] Syria did not seem particularly prone to civil war before 2011, but it has been so transformed by the conflict that low-level or chronic civil war—or at least extreme fragility—may be part of its future for decades to come.

In contrast to the overwhelmingly negative and regressive effects of civil war, in some cases and aspects they can also represent moments of political progress or evolution. The American Civil War was part of the process of abolishing slavery; the English civil war led to new and more inclusive arrangements of constitutional rule. In the Middle East, the Lebanese civil war undid a longstanding political injustice and led to a wider and fairer power-sharing arrangement. The Iraqi civil war is at least partly an understandable contestation between various parties and communities seeking to secure a place for themselves in a new political order, after decades of absolutist and exclusionary rule. The conflict in Libya is in part an attempt to "hammer out" a new political order after the horrendous despotism of Gaddafi. In Oman, the civil war spurred changes that led to a much-improved development and welfare situation for Omanis.

Some civil wars, however, are simply nightmares, with no political dividend whatsoever. That might be the case in Syria, which even after hundreds of thousands killed and millions displaced might see absolutely no political change or evolution whatsoever, but rather a worse imposition of the terrible status quo ante that led to the rebellion in the first place. It might also be the case in Yemen, where even if peace is cobbled together at some point, it is hard to see how the country would have "learned" from the experience or moved forward in a significant way.

Of course, not all parties to a civil war can be said to be pursuing political ends. In many cases, once the civil war takes hold, and along with it a new wartime economy, what emerges alongside or within contending "political" groups are essentially mafia networks of smugglers, racketeers, and profiteers that have no political ends, but do have an interest in the continuation of the civil war, of which they are major beneficiaries.

Historical and Systemic Drivers

Contested Nationalisms

The transition from a multinational Ottoman imperial system to a system of nation-states, in the context of the aftermath of the First World War, carried within it the seeds of many potential civil wars. Nationalist thought, which blew into the Middle East from Europe during the late nineteenth and early twentieth centuries, proposed a political order built not on imperial power and religious legitimacy but rather on the principle that every national "people" should have its own state.[19] People would no longer be identified in reference to the states they were subject to, but rather states should be erected in reference to the identities of population groups. This wave of political thought gave rise to competing nationalisms. The Young Turks that took power in Istanbul in 1908 promoted a Turkish nationalism to buttress the weakening Ottoman order. Many Arab intellectuals and leaders proposed an Arab nationalism, in juxtaposition to the Turkish and Ottoman one, that would subsume the various Arab lands together in one state. Many Lebanese and Egyptian intellectuals and leaders clamored for separate Lebanese and Egyptian national identities, based on ancient Phoenician and Pharaonic pasts.

Kurdish leaders certainly had a strong nationalist case and advocated for their own state as well. A number of Islamist activists and leaders adapted modern nationalism to refer to the Islamic *ummah* and to echo the unified Muslim state that prevailed in the days of the prophet and the first four caliphs. The redefinition of political order from an imperial to a nation-state system would, in any conditions, have given rise to numerous disputes and conflicts in many parts of the heterogeneous Middle East where communities with different ethnic, linguistic, and religious identities lived cheek by jowl.

The situation was exacerbated, however, by the arbitrary decisions made by European powers after the First World War, to carve out the Arab domains of the defunct Ottoman Empire in ways that served their own imperial interests. Thus, the promises of an Arab state made to the leader of the Arab revolt, Sherif Hussein of Mecca, were broken; the fairly arbitrary borders of "modern" Syria and Iraq were established; the borders of "greater Lebanon" were drawn to join large Muslim-majority districts to the Christian–Druze Mount Lebanon, and the Balfour Declaration's promise was made to the Zionist movement.

The two points that are important to note are that the Western divisions of the post-Ottoman lands set the stage for many ensuing conflicts (e.g., Iraq, Syria, Palestine, Lebanon), but even without those particular decisions and divisions the process of working out the competing nationalisms of this very heterogeneous region would have been contested and prone to conflict.

Low State Legitimacy

Many states or regimes in the Middle East have long suffered from low levels of popular political legitimacy. In some cases it was related to questions of nationalism in which segments of the population simply did not identify with the state they found themselves part of (e.g., Kurds in Iraq, some Muslim communities in interwar Lebanon, or some Hejazis under the Saudi state). For much of the interwar period, the new states that were established were mostly under European domination and control and for that reason they suffered from low levels of legitimacy. After the Second World War, ideological differences became more prominent. Arab nationalists sought Arab unity and considered any "local" states or elites standing in their way to be illegitimate "separatist" entities. Socialists and communists considered states that enabled capitalist elites and created economic injustice as illegitimate and in need of revolution. Islamists considered secular rulers and states illegitimate. In the latter decades of the twentieth century, sectarianism also emerged as an ideology in which political community was increasingly defined along sectarian lines and these fault lines led to civil wars in countries like Lebanon, Syria, and Iraq.[20]

This is not to say that levels of state legitimacy were uniform across the region, or that they did not ebb and flow over time.[21] The Egyptian nation-state enjoys a level of systemic legitimacy, based on centuries of a unified political past, that countries like Yemen, Libya, Lebanon, or Iraq do not. And even in Egypt, some eras or leaders—like Gamal Abdel Nasser in the 1950s and 1960s—had much greater legitimacy than others, such as the latter years of Hosni Mubarak.

And rulers and regimes tried different approaches to create or maintain legitimacy for themselves. Some, like in Saudi Arabia, Jordan, or Morocco, appealed to tradition and religion; Arab nationalist leaders like Nasser appealed to national ambitions and the promise of social justice; modernist leaders like Habib Bourguiba in Tunisia appealed to the promise of creating a modern Western-style economy and society. In few cases was legitimacy tied to a system of electoral accountability and renewal of political leaders and governments. For that reason, even when these rulers or regimes enjoyed significant stretches of legitimacy, the inability of the system to rotate them out of power and bring new leaders to the fore meant that these regimes would age and ossify, inevitably suffering a decline of legitimacy. Indeed, most states in the region eventually had to resort to increasing repression and control as their legitimacy gradually faded away.

This then created new drivers for discontent or rebellion, in that repression itself became a burden on populations. In several recent cases populations have rebelled in part to stop the repression, detentions, torture, and disappearances being carried out by the regime.

Low State Efficacy and Uneven Development

Among the drivers of discontent that have contributed to rebellion and civil war are conditions in which populations are not able to satisfy their basic needs, either because of a lack or failure of public services and public goods, or because of slow or uneven economic growth—or a combination of the two. The uprising in 1960s Dhofar, Oman was partly about neglect and underdevelopment. Elements of Yemeni civil wars in the 1960s were also partly expressions of acute socioeconomic need. So too were parts of the Lebanese civil war in which Muslim communities felt underserved by the central government and marginalized by the economy.

Thus, the political, ideological, and socioeconomic drivers of discontent, which have occasionally spilled over into civil war, are complex and numerous. And perhaps it should not be surprising that a complex and heterogeneous region like the Middle East, going through such fast-paced and fundamental changes as took place during the twentieth century, should have increasingly complex and often competing political currents and contradictions, and that in many cases these might spill over into civil war. But this does not lessen the devastation of these wars and the heavy toll they have taken on their societies and the region.

In addition to these systemic drivers, it might also be useful to look at the effects of external conditions—at the level of the international and regional political order—that also had an impact on either driving civil wars or on avoiding them and/or bringing them to an end.

External Factors

The International Order

The relationship between the international order and the Middle East can be organized into different phases. For several centuries before the First World War, the Arab Middle East was largely part of the Ottoman empire and interacted with the international order of competing imperial domains within that context. There wasn't a regional order of multiple competing states in the Middle East, as there would be in later years, although there was Iran to the northeast and a Saudi kingdom in the desert interior. Even within the empire, there was regional rivalry to Istanbul from the vassal state of Egypt, and European incursions into the Ottoman realm increased beginning in the late eighteenth and nineteenth centuries. The combination of these power struggles between Istanbul, Cairo, and European capitals, for example, partly fueled the first period of Lebanese civil unrest in 1840–60. But by and large, the vast and monocratic Ottoman order discouraged the emergence or persistence of civil wars. While local grievances and rebellions abounded, they could rarely find regional or international succor to develop into sustained armed conflicts.

The second phase in the region's international order is the period of European domination in the interwar years. Indeed, many of the contradictions that contributed later to civil wars emerged during the post–First World War period. This included of course the overarching fact of the defeat and dismantling of the Ottoman empire and the colonial agreements to carve up the "Arab provinces"—an epochal development that left previously Ottoman-governed societies to find fresh pathways forward.

The waves of nationalist sentiment that had blown from Europe into the Middle East were reinforced by Woodrow Wilson's fourteen points, which included the right to self-determination. This of course would fan broader Arab nationalist sentiments, but also aroused various forms of local nationalist sentiment (Egyptian, Lebanese), non-Arab nationalism (among Kurds), and Islamist "nationalism" (the Muslim Brotherhood and the yearning to revive an Islamic caliphate).

This cacophony of aspirations—which in themselves would carry the seeds of several civil wars—was confronted by the decisions taken by the Western powers in Sykes-Picot and subsequent agreements, as well as the Balfour Declaration. These diktats, by imposing new borders and orders in a turbulent region, also carried their own germs of civil war.[22] The "war to end all wars" created conditions that would be fought out in civil wars throughout the region for many years.

The Israeli–Palestinian conflict essentially began as a civil war over the legacy of the First World War in Palestine; ISIS, a century later, is still contesting the borders drawn up by the Europeans; and the Kurds are still trying to achieve the goals they were denied in the Paris peace talks a hundred years ago.

The impinging of global powers into the Middle East would be relevant again in the Second World War and its aftermath. But the two behemoths that emerged after that war, the United States and the USSR, were *imperial*, but not per se *colonial* powers; this would have an important effect. The collapse of British and French (and Italian) power ended the colonial model of direct Western rule; the United States and USSR favored an imperial system in which they would align *sovereign states* in the region with their regional and global alliance systems. Initially, the United States tried to preserve Western hegemony over the Middle East and keep the USSR out, but through the 1950s and 1960s the USSR made major inroads and became a coequal imperial power to the United States in the region. This Cold War contest between the two superpowers ended up fueling several civil wars in the region, either directly or indirectly, and was part of the dynamic of civil war in Yemen, Lebanon, Oman, and Afghanistan to name a few.

The collapse of the Soviet Union in 1991 brought about a more unipolar global order, in which the United States had no superpower counterweight in the region. This should have led to a reduction in global contestation in the Middle East and a diminution of civil war, but two other dynamics eventually took hold. The first was America's hubris and overreach: it is no coincidence that the first major US military operation in the Middle East was in 1991 in the Gulf, as the Soviet Union was in final collapse; but the administration of George H. W. Bush kept its military goals limited to liberating Kuwait and went no further. After the events of 9/11, however, the George W. Bush administration would show no such restraint. All-out invasions of Afghanistan and Iraq left both countries in conditions of full or partial state collapse and civil war.

The second dynamic was that after the end of the Cold War the states of the region either had lost a major global patron or no longer mattered as much in the international game of superpowers; in both cases, it meant weaker states that were more vulnerable to rebellion from within. It is no coincidence that several of the Arab states that succumbed either to foreign attack or internal rebellion and civil war (e.g., Iraq, Syria, and to some degree Libya) were once Soviet clients; and it is also noteworthy that once-essential partners for the United States in the Cold War— Mubarak in Egypt, Zine el-Abidine Ben Ali in Tunisia, and the Al Khalifa in Bahrain—received little concern or support from Washington when they found themselves under siege from their own populations.

It is not clear to what extent the period of American hegemony encouraged the Arab uprisings of 2011. But those uprisings led to wider revolutions that not only brought down the regime and led to civil war in Libya, but also challenged the regime and resulted in civil war in Syria as well. Civil war was averted in Bahrain by strong Saudi and Gulf Cooperation Council (GCC) military intervention; similar conditions of civil conflict were beginning to develop in Tunisia and Egypt as well. Tunisia avoided them by pivoting toward political negotiation and inclusion; Egypt pivoted back to a military takeover of government and a harsh security crackdown.

The period of American dominance in the Middle East ended decisively in 2015, when Russia sent its armed forces into Syria, reversing the course of the civil war there, helping to deny victory to the rebels that had at least partial American support, and favoring a Russian-backed freezing of the conflict.[23] As of 2015, the United States was no longer the only or hegemonic international player in the region. Russia had come back in force. China's economic power was beginning to loom large as well. The return of great power rivalry in the region is likely to complicate the challenge of ending civil wars, with different superpowers backing different sides, such has been the case in Syria.

The Regional Order

These regional dynamics are covered in great depth in the chapter by Ross Harrison later in this volume, but it is nonetheless helpful to highlight some themes in this chapter to better understand the overall context of the region's civil wars. The regional order, like the international order, went through several different phases over time as well. Most of the region's states were established after the First World War, but for the duration of the interwar period their foreign and regional relations were managed and dictated by the mandate powers. As the majority of states gained independence after the Second World War, what emerged from the late 1940s was an Arab order organized loosely under the League of Arab States while the region's three non-Arab powers—Israel, Turkey, and Iran—were looking westward. The Arab states were united in their hostility to Israel and their support for the Palestinian cause, but were otherwise deeply divided by their international alignment—with the United States or USSR in the Cold War—and by their ideological commitment: either in support of Arab nationalist secular revolutionary change led by Nasser's Egypt, or in support of a conservative anti-revolutionary anti-socialist agenda led by Saudi Arabia.

The year 1979 was a turning point at several levels. Egypt signed a separate peace with Israel: This broke a major taboo in Arab politics that had always maintained some modicum of common position among Arab governments; it also sapped the secular "progressive" wing of the Arab world of its Egyptian champion, leading to a rapid collapse of secular, nationalist, leftist movements and a rapid rise of religious and fundamentalist ones. The year 1979 also saw the Iranian revolution, which ended decades of Iranian attempts at Westernization and declared a set of Islamist revolutionary ambitions not only for Iran but also for the new republic's role in the Arab Islamic Middle East.[24] This led to the growth of Hezbollah in Lebanon and eventually other proxy Iranian militias in Iraq, Syria, and Yemen.[25] The year 1979 also marks the Russian invasion of Afghanistan, which led to a US, Saudi, and Pakistani decision to arm and train the Afghan jihadis, a decision that would end up spawning a Sunni armed jihadist movement—including the Taliban, al-Qaeda, ISIS, and other groups—that has become part of the dangerous landscape of the Middle East and has been a dangerous part of the landscape in most civil war countries such as Syria, Libya, Iraq, Yemen, and of course, Afghanistan.[26]

The regional order changed again in 2003, when a US-led invasion toppled the Saddam Hussein regime in Baghdad. The invasion had the unanticipated effect of greatly empowering Iran, which emerged as the dominant player in Iraq, and enabling the rise of ISIS, first in Iraq but then in Syria as well. The Arab uprisings of 2011 and beyond also impacted the regional order. As Syria and Yemen faltered, Iran moved quickly to greatly increase its influence in both countries. Recep Tayyip Erdoğan of Turkey had welcomed the Arab uprisings and hoped that the Muslim Brotherhood, whom he backed, would emerge victorious in Egypt, Tunisia, and Syria, and make significant headway in Yemen, Jordan, Kuwait, and Morocco as well. This did not come to pass, and Erdoğan had to satisfy his ambitions with a zone of influence in northwest Syria, a proxy presence in western Libya, and an outpost in Iraq. The uprisings consolidated the Arab quartet of Saudi Arabia, the UAE, Egypt, and Bahrain, which ended up representing the moderate Arab center, while Iran developed an arc of influence dominating the Levant—through Iraq, Syria, and Lebanon—and with a major foothold in the Arabian Peninsula in Yemen.

The year 2020 also saw a major change, as Israel signed normalization agreements with the UAE, Bahrain, Sudan, and Morocco. After seventy years of isolation—despite earlier treaties with Egypt and Jordan—Israel in 2020 broke through to become a partner with key countries in the Gulf and North Africa.

As we can see from the above, the regional order of the Middle East has gone through many changes. But it has remained a "disordered" system with shifting conflict axes. The regional order has continued to fuel and sustain proxy and civil conflicts, and this includes the case studies under review, particularly in Syria, Yemen, Iraq, and Libya. They all have significant regional proxy components. Until the Middle East arrives at an inclusive and cooperative regional order—that would include the Arab states as well as Turkey, Iran, and Israel—regional conflict will continue to fuel proxy and civil conflict.

There have been some signs of communication and de-escalation between regional powers in the past couple of years. This includes the patching up of the intra-GCC rift between Qatar on one side and Saudi Arabia, UAE, and Bahrain on the other; 2021 talks between Saudi Arabia and Iran hosted in Baghdad; outreach by the UAE to Turkey; as well as the ending of long-standing hostility between Israel and a number of key Arab states. These moves are encouraging and indicate a growing awareness among the region's leaders that regional conflict only creates lose-lose outcomes, and that the region is facing systemic challenges—like Covid-19, climate change, water shortages, and so on—that require regional cooperation. So far, Iran remains the outlier in these attempts, as its national outlook and strategy is still wedded to a long-term militia presence in key Arab states and a permanent state of war with both Israel and the United States. But the more progress is made in intra-regional de-escalation and cooperation, the more chances there are to wind down current civil wars and avoid the outbreak of new ones.

Case Studies from the Twentieth-Century Wider Middle East

In the following section we will review the pre-2001 cases of civil war in the wider Middle East to gain a better understanding of their long-standing drivers and patterns, and to look for clues or lessons that might be of use to understanding and ending the current civil wars. We will also look at a number of lower-level civil conflicts that might not have acceded to what would generally be called "civil wars," but which nevertheless indicate underlying fault lines and dysfunctions that are relevant in understanding the ebb and flow of larger civil wars. This section is by no means a comprehensive review of these complex conflicts, but it does provide significant food for thought about the modern history of civil conflict in the Middle East as we consider the current civil wars afflicting the region. I will divide the sixteen cases into two groups. The first group is that of full-fledged civil wars that meet most analysts' criteria in terms of duration, scope of conflict, and loss of life, while the second group consists of other forms of civil conflict that don't meet all the general criteria of civil wars, but remain significant civil conflicts worthy of examination.

Full-Fledged Civil Wars

Civil Wars in Lebanon

Lebanon has gone through three civil wars in its modern history. The first conflict, in 1860, had socioeconomic roots but quickly became a sectarian bloodletting between Lebanon's Druze and Maronite populations. This conflict led to foreign intervention and an agreement between the Ottoman Porte and several Western powers on a new form of government for the province of Mount Lebanon.[27] The second was a brief conflict in 1958 that pitted the Western-aligned, Maronite-dominated government against a mainly Muslim opposition aligned with Nasser's Arab nationalist project. It was resolved through a combination of internal political change and external pressure. The Western-leaning president was replaced by an army chief who promised to pursue a more centrist policy in foreign affairs, and to prioritize economic and social development—one of the demands of the opposition. The United States also landed Marines on Lebanon's shores to ward off any external intervention from the newly formed United Arab Republic between Egypt and Syria.[28]

The third and much more devastating civil war was between 1975 and 1990. It was caused by a number of convergent factors: a gaping disparity between Maronite domination of the state and the large Muslim majority in the population; opposition demands for greater socioeconomic change; and a growing contradiction between the sovereignty of a weak state and the power of the Palestine Liberation Organization (PLO), which had become a heavily armed state-within-a-state in Lebanon. The long civil war left around 150,000 dead and many more wounded and displaced. It devastated the national economy and infrastructure, as well as the national fabric and state institutions.[29]

The war came to an end for a combination of external and internal reasons. The Israeli invasion of 1982 eventually pushed the PLO out of Lebanon, removing that element from the equation. With the winding down of the Cold War in 1989–90, the great-power-proxy aspect of the conflict was reduced, thus enabling the United States to work with both Saudi Arabia and Syria to create the external conditions for a settlement. While Lebanese parties had been engaged in on-and-off negotiations internally since 1976, these picked up after 1985. As a result, when Lebanese lawmakers were invited to Taif, Saudi Arabia, in 1989 for talks, negotiators already had enough of an agreed political outline for settlement to finalize what came to be known as the Taif Agreement.

The Lebanese case is one of a weak state and a strong but divided society.[30] In this context, recurring bouts of conflict have centered around squabbles over power sharing in the government, all fueled by communal alignments with external powers, and external powers fighting out global or regional proxy contests in the country. The first conflict of 1860 ended based on an international agreement involving the Ottoman state and five European powers. The second conflict of 1958 ended with an external power standoff, but a change in power in the Lebanese central government that promised a centrist foreign policy (enough to satisfy both external camps) and a developmental policy at home that satisfied at least the socioeconomic demands of the opposition. The last civil war of 1975–90 ended based on a renegotiation of power-sharing ratios in the central government—one of the rare instances of that in the Middle East—at a moment when Soviet power was falling away and the United States could work with regional powers (some of which were previously Soviet clients) to help align conditions to end the war. Since 2019, the country has entered a new wave of crisis that threatens the stability of the state and the risk of civil war; this started with the full economic collapse of 2019 and was followed by one of the biggest peacetime explosions in Beirut Port in August 2020 that devastated a third of the nation's capital. Lebanon is currently at risk of full state collapse, which could trigger a return to cantonization, militia rule, and different forms of internal armed conflict.

Civil Wars in Yemen

Yemen also has gone through several civil wars in its modern history. In some ways, the country has been in on-and-off civil war(s) since the early 1960s, as will be chronicled in greater detail in a subsequent chapter by Gerald Feierstein.

The North Yemen civil war (1962–70) erupted after a republican military coup against the ruling traditional imam. The coup followed previous patterns of republican military coups in other Arab countries under the general banner of Arab nationalist, republican, and socioeconomically progressive slogans. The conflict quickly became regionalized and internationalized, with Saudi Arabia, Jordan, and the UK supporting the royalist forces, and Egypt and the USSR supporting the republicans. The republicans eventually prevailed, but not until foreign intervention and support to both sides declined: The British quit South Yemen in 1967, the Egyptians scaled back after their defeat in the 1967 Arab–Israeli War, and the Saudis eventually made their peace with the republicans after fears of a Nasserist Arab national movement on their southern border faded.

The brief South Yemen civil war of 1986 was the result of armed clashes between rival factions of the Yemeni Socialist Party (YSP). It does not necessarily rise to the level of a civil war, as it was quite limited in scope and duration, but it indicates the intensity of division and history of armed conflict even within factions of the same party in South Yemen.

The Civil War of Reunification in 1994 came about after North and South Yemen were unified by negotiated agreement in 1990. The unification was largely the result of the dramatic weakening of the South after the collapse of the USSR, years of internal division in the South, and the discovery of oil on the border between the two sides. But relations between the North and South soured again after the elections of 1993, in which the South did poorly, and tensions spiraled into armed conflict between the two sides. Attempts to mediate and stem the fighting did not bear fruit. Northern forces ground down weaker and more divided southern forces and declared reunification under northern domination in July. Without its Soviet backer, the South had become vulnerable, and although Saudi Arabia and Oman offered limited support to the South fearing a unified Yemen under strong leadership, their help was too little too late.

In addition to the conflicts mentioned above, there were six Sa'dah Wars between 2004 and 2009, in which the central government fought armed Houthi groups in the Sa'dah region.[31] These various civil wars would provide the backdrop for the eruption of the latest round of civil war in Yemen in 2015, which started with a Houthi takeover of the capital, Sana'a, and escalated after Saudi Arabia assembled an external coalition to support the central government and beat back the Houthi rebellion. The current civil war is the main focus of the chapter on Yemen in this volume.

The pre-2005 case of recurring civil war in Yemen is, somewhat like Lebanon, one in which a strong society and a weak state struggle with representation and power sharing, as well as issues of state capacity and delivery of development and public goods. In the Yemeni case, social strength was largely along tribal and regional lines, not sectarian ones, and the weakness of the state also included fundamental conflict over whether Yemen would remain two states or become one. Internal contestation in Yemen, as in Lebanon, got caught up in regional and great-power contestation, which often contributed to the escalation and prolongation of the civil war, but also impacted when and how a round of civil war came to an end.

Civil Wars in Iraq

Iraq has suffered along two lines of civil conflict: Arab–Kurdish and Sunni–Shi'a. Iraq's Arab-Kurdish conflict is a century old, born out of the denial of Kurdish nationalist aspirations in the Treaty of Lausanne in 1923 and the formation of modern Iraq by colonial powers. The Kurds attempted secession in 1919 and declared a short-lived Kingdom of Kurdistan. More attempts at revolt followed in the 1930s and 1940s. The first wide-scale conflict, often called the first Iraqi–Kurdish War, erupted in 1961 and lasted until 1970, leaving around one hundred thousand dead.[32] Negotiations to resolve the tension were attempted, but they collapsed in 1974, and another major round of fighting broke out, resulting in the routing of the main armed Kurdish group. But an armed insurgency continued. During the Iran–Iraq War in the 1980s, the central government launched what can only be described as a campaign of genocide against the Kurds, which left 100,000–200,000 dead. In the aftermath of the first Gulf War in 1990–1, a Kurdish revolt drew US support and the establishment of a no-fly zone; as a result, the Kurds finally achieved an autonomous and fairly secure northern region.

The open armed conflict between Iraqi Kurds and Arabs can be said to have largely ended, or at least turned a positive corner, with the demise of Saddam Hussein's regime and the establishment of an inclusive (at least in law and principle) constitutional order and power-sharing political system. Differences and tensions have continued, but have mainly remained in the political sphere, and central government and Kurdish *peshmerga* forces fought side by side in the war against ISIS.

It is important to note that the Kurdish community of Iraq has had its own bouts of civil conflict, including a serious clash between the Kurdistan Democratic Party (KDP) and the Patriotic Union of Kurdistan (PUK) factions in the mid-1990s that left more than five thousand people dead.[33]

Sectarian Sunni–Shi'a conflict has also been prominent in Iraq. Of course, the very formation of modern Iraq by the British after the First World War planted the seeds of potential sectarian conflict by bringing together a largely Shiite south with a predominantly Arab Sunni middle and west and empowering Sunni factions over others. Sectarian divisions were masked during both the anti-colonial and Cold War periods and were subsumed under more powerful nationalist and socialist ideologies. They began to return to the fore in stages after the decline of Arab nationalism, the collapse of Soviet socialism, and the Iranian Revolution. Following the revolution links between the new power in Tehran and Shiite opposition, clerical and political, in Iraq began to grow.

As regional politics turned more sectarian, so did the fault lines of Iraqi politics. But it took a major international military action, the US-led war to push Saddam's forces out of Kuwait, to create the conditions for a Shiite uprising in 1991. That uprising was forcefully put down by the Saddam regime. And it took another major international operation, the US-led invasion of Iraq in 2003, to overturn the sectarian balance of power in Baghdad in favor of a Shiite majority. Sectarian conflict erupted again around 2006 and again in 2014 with the rise of ISIS. That conflict is now in abeyance, but it is not clear whether Sunni–Shi'a relations are headed toward peaceful coexistence and power sharing or another bout of fighting in the near future.

Unlike the cases of Lebanon or Yemen, the state in Iraq grew extremely strong and indeed used its strength to try to dissolve social capital and primordial social bonds. But this state power and attempt at state domination were what drove much of the internal conflict, whether it was the state's attempt to forcefully subdue the Kurds and deny their identity, or its efforts to decimate the Shiite leadership in the 1970s and 1980s and put down the Shiite revolt in 1991. But Iraq has also struggled with a fundamental national identity contradiction—much more so than Lebanon or Yemen—in which the Kurdish community never wanted or accepted to be part of an "Arab" nation, instead continually seeking its own nation-state. Iraq's sectarian struggle between Sunni and Shi'a Arabs, which is fairly recent, is profound and comparable to that in Lebanon and far more sectarian than the mainly regional and tribal struggles in Yemen.

Of course, Iraq's internal conflicts have been greatly affected by external actions, from the establishment of modern Iraq with its internal contradictions after the First World War through the US-led invasion of 2003 and the subsequent transformation of the Iraqi state's entire power and political structure. Iraq is also an interesting example, a bit like Lebanon, in which peaceful coexistence between the country's three main communities is being attempted through a (new) inclusive power-sharing constitutional order. It will be seen over time whether this new order will endure and be able to build and maintain social peace.

Civil Wars in Palestine

The land of Palestine has known two civil wars. The first is the longstanding conflict between the Zionist and Arab factions in Mandate Palestine—a conflict that has continued between the Israeli state and the Palestinian populations under occupation. The second, of shorter standing, is between the Palestinian parties of Fatah and Hamas. The conflict between Zionists and Arabs in Mandate Palestine was set in motion by the decisions made by the British.[34] This included the latent contradictions between the promises made to the leaders of the Arab revolt in the Hussein-McMahon letters and those made to the Jewish Zionist movement in the Balfour Declaration. Protests and violence began sporadically in 1919–20 and continued throughout most of the mandate period. It erupted into civil war in 1947—a civil war which was won by the Zionist factions and led to the establishment of the state of Israel in May 1948. After the establishment of Israel, the civil war became internationalized and sparked a series of wars between the nascent state and an array of Arab armies, the last of which was in 1973. The United States and USSR were also engaged on opposite sides of the conflict.

In many ways the Israeli–Palestinian conflict still carries many of the characteristics of a civil war. This is especially the case since 1967, as the Israeli state in effect encompasses the large Arab populations of the West Bank and Gaza, none of which want to be under Israeli authority. Attempts at mediation and conflict resolution started in the League of Nations even before the civil war of 1947 and were later taken up by the United Nations

(UN) and subsequently by the US in many repeated efforts—still with no resolution. Reconstruction and development efforts were allotted partly to the UN Relief and Works Agency for Palestine Refugees in the Near East (UNRWA) for the large Palestinian refugee population. After the Oslo Accords and the establishment of the Palestinian Authority (PA), the PA benefitted from a combination of Western and international humanitarian and development aid. The Israeli–Palestinian "civil war" is still very far from resolution.

The Fatah–Hamas Civil War erupted into armed conflict in 2006 and persists today not as a hot conflict, but as an active and deep fault line within Palestinian communities.[35] Egypt and other regional countries have made various attempts to mediate between the two factions, so far to no avail. A resolution would involve the formation of a Palestinian national coalition government, a return of PA authority to Gaza, and the lifting of the siege there. Reconstruction promises for Gaza from Arab countries and the international community have been among the incentives used to try to get Hamas and Fatah to agree on such a resolution—without success.

Like many other civil wars in the region, the Arab–Zionist conflict flowed in large part from decisions taken by colonial powers in and after the First World War. Great Britain had encouraged both Arab and Zionist nationalism, and Palestine was ground zero for that contradiction. After 1948, and especially after 1967, the conflict continued along the lines of a strong state trying to keep down the aspirations for secession or statehood of a national community within the state's boundaries. In some ways, this pattern is not unlike the suppression of Kurdish aspirations in Iraq. Attempts to end this conflict through mediation have failed, and successive Israeli governments have endeavored to settle it using overwhelming power, creating facts on the ground, and preempting any possibility of a negotiated two-state solution. The conflict is likely to go on for years, or decades to come.

The intra-Palestinian Fatah–Hamas conflict is of less consequence, although still significant.[36] While it partly reflects the ideological conflict that has defined much of Arab politics in recent decades between national secularists and Islamists, it also reflects the different physical realities between the West Bank and Gaza. Several attempts at negotiating a power-sharing agreement have been attempted, but so far have not stuck. For now the conflict is frozen by separation, with Fatah holding onto power in the West Bank, and Hamas in Gaza.

Civil Wars in Sudan

As in the case of Iraq, Sudan has faced two axes of internal conflict: that between north and south, and that between the central government and the communities of Darfur, although the internal conflicts in Sudan have led to vastly larger numbers of dead and wounded. The conflict between North and South Sudan erupted in 1955, and continued intermittently until the secession of South Sudan in 2011, leaving over a million dead and many more injured. The conflict has its origins, like some of those in the Levant, in the hasty colonial design of new nation-states. In 1946, the British merged the Arab Muslim north with the non-Arab Christian south, without consulting the south—a similar situation to that of the Kurds in Iraq. In 1953, the UK and Egypt agreed to grant this merged Sudan its independence. This merger created the conditions behind the southern armed rebellion that began in 1955. In its first iteration, the Sudanese civil war continued from 1955 until 1972. This civil war never attracted the level of global attention, and hence interference, that other conflicts in the Levant and Arabian Peninsula did. This raises the question of how and when external intervention escalates conflicts and drags them on, and how and when it can help bring them to an end. In any case, this phase of the war was brought to an end by external mediation—not by great or regional powers, but by the African Conference of Churches and the World Council of Churches. This mediation led to the Addis Ababa Agreement of 1972, which gave a measure of autonomy to the south and marked the beginning of a period of relative calm.

The agreement broke down and war resumed in 1983, when Sudanese President Gaafar Nimeiry abrogated the Addis Ababa Agreement, suspended the autonomy of the south, and declared Sudan an Islamic state. The power grab was not unrelated to the recent discovery of oil fields in the border areas between the north and the south.[37] The fight over this resource would become a major factor in Sudan's politics and conflict in the following years. Nimeiry's actions quickly led to a resumption of armed conflict between south and north that would last until 2005, leaving one to two million dead and millions displaced.

Before the outbreak of the second phase of the civil war in 1983, the United States had become a major arms supplier to Khartoum, largely to counteract Soviet influence in Ethiopia and Libya. After Sudan turned Islamist and waged civil war with the south, however, US support declined and eventually ended in 1987. In 1993, Iran stepped in with support for

Khartoum and China too began to take a larger interest. The Iranians financed a number of Chinese arms sales to Khartoum, and China took an increasingly large share of Sudanese oil fields and contracts. In a bid to attract Iraqi support, Khartoum sided with Saddam in the 1990–1 Gulf War. Meanwhile, the southern rebels, organized under the Sudan People's Liberation Army (SPLA), received support from Eritrea, Ethiopia, Uganda, and Israel.

As humanitarian conditions in the country deteriorated amid war and drought, the United States led a negotiation effort, starting in 2001, with international and regional buy in. A final agreement was signed in Nairobi in 2005, dividing oil revenues equally between the north and south, and giving the south six years of autonomy before allowing a referendum on secession. This brought precarious peace from 2005; secession was approved by referendum in 2011, and South Sudan seceded that same year.

The war with the south also led to civil conflict in the western Darfur region. This erupted in 2003 between Arab and non-Arab tribes and communities. The government was accused of campaigning against the non-Arabs and backing the Janjaweed militia. President Omar al-Bashir was indicted in the International Criminal Court and Sudan came under heavy Western and international sanctions. However, Khartoum was able to maintain and grow its relations with China over oil and defense. Russia and Iran provided limited military support as well. Many attempts at mediation were made by the African Union, the UN, the United States, and Qatar. A cease-fire was eventually reached in 2010. The current crisis in Sudan, which began in 2019, is yet of a different nature, with the population rising up against the thirty-year rule of Omar al-Bashir, followed by his overthrow by the military, a fragile transition to democracy under a civilian-military government, and later, a reassertion of military rule.

The devastating cases of civil war in Sudan exhibit some similarities with Lebanon and Iraq in the sense that the drawing of "national" borders by outside powers set the new polity up for internal conflict. Like the Kurds in Iraq and many Muslims in post-1920 Lebanon, the southern Sudanese had not agreed to the new national boundaries. Sudan has also been beset by deep sectarian and ethnic divisions between a mainly Muslim and Arabic speaking north and a non-Arab, non-Muslim south and southwest. The high toll that civil conflict has taken in Sudan is partly due to the country's precarious resource and socioeconomic conditions, unlike Iraq and Lebanon, but perhaps closer to what Yemen is facing today in terms of the risk of famine and disease. The decades of civil war in Sudan, when contrasted with other civil war cases in the region, present an interesting case study of how external intervention or influence can impact civil conflict—both negatively in terms of escalating and prolonging it, but also positively in terms of creating conditions and leverage to de-escalate the conflict and bring it to an end.

Civil Wars in Afghanistan

Afghanistan has been through many decades of civil war. It suffered a first bout in 1928–9, when tribal forces opposed to the reforms of Amanullah Khan marched on the capital. This led to a power struggle among rival leaders and fighting in and around Kabul. But the second and far more devastating round of civil war started in 1978. While the United States withdrawal from Afghanistan in 2021 promised an end to this conflict, it is still impossible to tell whether this cease-fire is temporary or permanent.

It started with what is known as the Saur Revolution and a communist party military coup in April 1978.[38] The takeover by the People's Democratic Party of Afghanistan (PDPA) led to a series of uprisings around the country. The Soviet invasion the following year was designed to shore up the embattled government, but instead led to a ten-year conflict in which the *mujahedeen*, backed by Pakistan, Saudi Arabia, and the United States, eventually drove out the Soviets in 1989. The communist government fell in 1992.

A host of rebel factions came to an agreement to establish the Islamic State of Afghanistan and appoint an interim government. But rebel concord broke down quickly and what followed was a series of battles for control of the capital and other cities. Pakistan, Iran, Saudi Arabia, India, and Uzbekistan backed different factions and vied for influence in the strategic country. In 1996, the Taliban, an Islamist group originally based in Kandahar with backing from Pakistan and Saudi Arabia, along with the support of a fair number of al-Qaeda fighters from Arab countries, seized Kabul and declared the Islamic Emirate of Afghanistan. Opposition to their rule centered on the Northern Alliance under the leadership of Ahmad Shah Massoud.

After the events of 9/11, the United States led a NATO invasion of Afghanistan that unseated the Taliban and drove out al-Qaeda.[39] It did not put an end, however, to civil war in Afghanistan, which continued until the return of the Taliban and the departure of US troops in 2021, and is the subject of its own chapter in this volume by Marvin Weinbaum.

On one level, Afghanistan is a case of a strong society (with strong tribal, regional, and ethnic groupings) and a weak state (one that rarely was able to extend its writ beyond the capital and a few cities). It is also the case of a country buffeted by strong external competition, both regional and international, and proxy conflict. Thirdly, the country has suffered from the ideological fault line, present in other countries in the region, between hardline Islamists and more secular nationalists. The civil conflict that began in 1978 was ongoing until very recently, and depending on whether the Taliban can govern, could reappear.

Civil War in Algeria

The conflict between the Algerian state and an array of armed Islamist groups lasted for a full decade in the 1990s and left over a hundred thousand dead and many more injured and displaced. The conflict started after the state annulled the results of an election won by Islamists. In the ensuing crackdown, Islamic groups took up arms and a long conflict ensued. Neighboring Egypt and Tunisia, as well as France, the European Union, and the United States, supported the Algerian state. While the Islamist rebels did not have the same level of support, they found backing from Libya (until 1995) and from private Islamist networks and donors from around the region and the world.

The Islamic insurgency in Algeria, led by the Islamic Salvation Front (FIS), was the second major sustained armed Islamist insurgency after that against the Soviets in Afghanistan in the 1980s. Unlike Afghanistan's conflict, however, there was limited regional and international alignment on opposing sides. Furthermore, the Algerian state was able to draw on the country's energy resources to take the lead in postwar reconstruction and development without much need for help from outside.

The civil war in Algeria highlighted three fault lines that would be relevant in other civil wars in the region. The first is between Islamists and secular nationalists, who had fundamentally contrasting world views. This fault line has also contributed to conflict in Syria and Egypt, and threatened conflict in Tunisia. The second relates to demands for representation and electoral democracy—the Islamists won the local elections of 1991, triggering a backlash from an authoritarian state. We have seen the same in Egypt, as well as Syria, Libya, and Bahrain, to name but a few cases. The third fault line relates to the internationalization of the Islamist jihadist movement that gained momentum in Afghanistan in the 1980s and then blew back, first into Algeria, but also later into Iraq, Syria, Libya, and Egypt, among other countries.

The Algerian civil war is a clear case of a civil conflict that was settled by direct use of force, with no negotiations. This is what Gaddafi had hoped to achieve in Libya, and what the Assad regime is hoping to achieve in Syria. In Algeria, one must conclude that ending the civil war by force "succeeded" in the sense that the country regained basic stability and sovereignty and war did not return in the ensuing two decades. The crisis in Algeria now, relating to political legitimacy and reform, is of a different nature.

Civil War in Oman

Oman too has seen its share of armed civil conflict. Fighting first erupted in 1962 in the Dhofar Province, largely driven by grievances related to extreme socioeconomic privation in a still undeveloped Oman. The government enjoyed strong support from the British and Iranians, and the rebels initially received some backing from Saudi Arabia. Later, when Arab politics radicalized after the 1967 war and the British departed from next door Aden, the rebellion drew Egyptian, Soviet, and Chinese support. It turned much more revolutionary and leftist in its rhetoric, becoming part of the regional and international conflict between Western and communist forces and their regional partners/proxies.

The death of Nasser and Egypt's westward turn under President Anwar Sadat dried up Egyptian support. The Chinese established relations with Iran and reduced their support for the rebels. The Soviets too cut back as they pursued détente with the West. The rebellion was finally crushed by the central government with direct armed support from the shah's Iran.

But it is also essential to note that the revolt led to what one can describe as a positive development in governance. The elderly Sultan Said bin Taimur was replaced in a coup in 1970 by his son Qaboos bin Said. The latter took the lesson of the rebellion as a mandate to rapidly develop and modernize the country. He coopted much of the leadership of the rebellion and eventually integrated members of the armed opposition into special units of the Omani armed forces. In other words, the Omani civil war was brought to an end through a combination of significant internal political and socioeconomic reform, as well as changing external conditions. Oman had growing energy resources to lead its reconstruction and development efforts, but also built strong partnerships with the British and other Western interests.

The Omani Civil War is an example of a civil conflict that was generated by acute socioeconomic grievance, became regionalized and internationalized, and was brought to an end through battlefield victory, but the post-conflict peace was sustained through meaningful political and socioeconomic change.

Civil War in Somalia

Somalia has suffered from the ebbs and flows of civil war since the uprising against the regime of Siad Barre in 1991. The conflict has left around five hundred thousand dead and more than a million displaced. Armed groups have mobilized along tribal, regional, and ideological lines. International and regional attempts to end the conflict have borne some fruit in terms of establishing a recognized federal authority, but the weakness of national institutions has meant that recognized authorities have not been able to effectively extend their writ over a very decentralized and atomized territory. In addition, although external influence has been leveraged to back central authorities at times, competing regional and international influences have also fueled ongoing conflict and centripetal forces.

Somalia, like other countries in this overview, had a fault line from birth. In the nineteenth century the territory of modern Somalia was made up of British Somaliland in the north and Italian Somaliland in the east. British and Italian interventions seesawed back and forth, with the Italians taking over both territories in the late 1930s, followed by the British conquest of both in 1940–1. The two territories continued under separate British and UN–Italian trusteeship until 1960, at which point they united as the new sovereign Somali Republic. Like in other cases in this review, the boundaries of the modern unified state are very recent and paper over previous patterns and borders of political organization.

Also like in other cases (such as Libya, Yemen, Syria, Sudan, and Iraq), the country succumbed to a coup and takeover in 1969 in which the military put itself forward, under the leadership of a "strongman," as the avenue for unifying, modernizing, and developing the nascent nation. Similar to several other cases, a combination of excessive usurpation of power and repression by the military regime, as well as existing regional, tribal, and ideological pluralism and decentralized power in the country, led to a clash and an unraveling of the nascent nation-state.

Somalia has also suffered from more than its share of international and regional competition and intervention. We've seen how it was divided among British and Italian influence between the nineteenth century and 1960. After 1960 it joined the Non-Aligned Movement but had to manage relations not only between the Soviets and Americans, but also the rivalry between the Soviets and the Chinese. It has suffered spillover effects from the radicalization of Sunni Islamist thought and activism after 1979, as well as from chronic instability in the Horn of Africa and more than one intervention from Ethiopia. In recent years, Arab countries from Persian Gulf, most notably the UAE, Qatar, and Saudi Arabia, have increased their interest and influence in the Horn of Africa, as has Turkey. Somalia has also drawn the attention of international powers partly as a result of the effects of Somali pirate activity out of a general concern to maintain the security and free flow of trade through the strategic Bab al-Mandeb straits. Somalia has also been the scene of American military intervention—both direct and indirect—in the latter's ongoing war on terror.

The Somali civil war has not been definitively resolved or ended, but it has been considerably de-escalated. Much of this has been the result of negotiated agreement, achieved with international and regional diplomatic encouragement, which has established recognized national authorities. The challenge in Somalia—as is particularly the case in Libya at present and to some extent in Yemen as well—is that despite the achievement of some sort of negotiated agreement and the establishment of a recognized central government, this government suffers from a lack of state institutions that can translate its de jure authority into a de facto national reality. The continued opposition of groups that were either not part of the agreement or are not abiding by it, the continuation of regional and international contestation, and/or the persistence of transnational movements further enable a number of rebel groups to keep fighting.

Significant Civil Conflicts

Black September: The State–PLO Conflict in Jordan, 1970

The armed showdown in 1970 between the Jordanian state and the armed wing of the Palestinian movement in Jordan, often referred to as Black September, contained elements of what would unfold later in Lebanon. The PLO—including the Fatah, the Popular Front for the Liberation of Palestine (PFLP), and PFLP-General Command (PFLP-GC) militias—had effectively built a state-within-a-state in Jordan and compromised Jordanian sovereignty. It also threatened to tear apart the fabric of Jordanian political society, as almost half of the country's population was of Palestinian descent. The Jordanian state met the challenge head on, defeating and expelling the armed wing of the PLO, with significant loss of life. This may have enabled Jordan to avoid a fate similar to that of Lebanon, however—a drawn out civil war that would leave a collapsed state and broken society in its wake.

Like in Lebanon, there was external involvement in the Jordanian conflict. Syria supported the Palestinians and threatened to send its forces across the border. Israel and the United States stood with the Jordanian state and warned the Syrians against intervention. In the post-conflict period, Jordan received development assistance from Saudi Arabia and the Gulf states, as well as from the West.

The civil war in Jordan is also partly linked to decisions taken by colonial powers during and after the First World War, as the Palestinian presence in Jordan and the very existence of a Hashemite Kingdom in Jordan were the results of decisions taken decades before. The way a strong state in Jordan dealt with the armed Palestinian presence was markedly different from how a weak state in Lebanon tried to deal with the same presence. It is also important to note that Jordan accorded Palestinians' citizenship and full rights in Jordan, whereas the Lebanese state accepted them only as refugees and gave them none of those rights.

The Government–Islamist Conflict in Syria, 1979–82

The current civil war in Syria partially echoes the previous conflict of 1979–82. The Syrian Muslim Brotherhood opposed the Ba'ath Party's seizure of power in a coup in 1963. The conflict got more heated after the government outlawed the movement in 1964, leading to demonstrations in several Syrian cities, most notably Hama. The movement also opposed the consolidation of power by Hafez al-Assad in 1970, a minority Alawi leader in a majority Sunni country.

The conflict erupted in earnest in 1979 after Islamists killed dozens of army cadets in Aleppo, and organized attacks and assassinations in several Syrian cities. These events were accompanied by waves of anti-government demonstrations and a heavy government crackdown. The government sent tens of thousands of troops into Aleppo in 1980 to defeat the opposition and regain control. The rebellion peaked with the Muslim Brotherhood's takeover of Hama in February 1982. The government surrounded and bombarded the city, leading to thousands of deaths and the destruction of much of the city. That marked the defeat of the Brotherhood in Syria for a long while and the end of that round of insurgency. The Brotherhood would come back, of course, as one of the groups involved in the 2011 uprising and beyond.

Egypt's Armed Conflict with Islamists

Although the Muslim Brotherhood had been an initial ally in the Egyptian army's revolt against King Farouk in 1952, the two fell out as the army consolidated power in the post-monarchical period. Nasser accused the Brotherhood of an assassination attempt and a wave of arrests and repression followed. Part of the Brotherhood radicalized in prison, including its leader Sayyid Qutb, whose writings called for jihad against governments in Muslim countries that are not sufficiently Islamist. In 1981, radical Islamists assassinated President Sadat, although he had empowered the Muslim Brotherhood during his presidency—a move he used to weaken the Nasserists and consolidate his rule.

The Muslim Brotherhood mainstream presented a more political and moderate face in the 1990s and 2000s, eventually winning presidential and parliamentary elections after the fall of the Mubarak regime in 2011. After waves of protest against its rule in 2012–13, the army staged a coup against President Mohammed Morsi. Soon thereafter the army again moved in force against a Brotherhood sit-in in Rabaa Square, killing around a thousand people. The Egyptian state subsequently declared the Brotherhood a terrorist organization and has jailed thousands since.

The Egyptian government has also been battling an armed Islamist insurgency in northern Sinai since 2011, as well as intermittent terrorist attacks on government and civilian targets in the country. The insurgency in northern Sinai originates in discontent among Bedouins there who have traditionally felt neglected and repressed by the central state. After 2013, the insurgency took on a more radical Islamist turn, with the group Ansar Bayt al-Maqdis pledging allegiance to ISIS. Cairo has alleged that the insurgency has been supported from Gaza by Hamas and has received fighters and arms from radical Islamic groups in Libya and Syria. Despite repeated military offensives, and much loss of life and property, the government has not been able to fully put down the insurgency.

This conflict has three elements. First, it partly reflects the ideological chasm between Islamists and secular nationalists. Secondly, it is in part a symptom of the political impasse of authoritarian states, and the absence of a political pathway for Islamists that forswear violence. Finally, it is also a symptom of the wider militancy of Islamic jihadism that has taken root since 1979, and that has created networks of fighters and support systems that span the region and cross-national boundaries.

The Turkish–Kurdish Conflict

This long-standing conflict falls into that definitional gray zone described earlier in this chapter. It is not traditionally considered a civil war, in that it did not see clearly delineated lines of combat among parts of the country controlled by different armed groups, but rather a networked insurgency drawing a strong-armed response from the government. This conflict began in 1978 with the formation of the Kurdistan Workers' Party (PKK) and demands for independence or extensive autonomy for Turkey's mainly Kurdish southeast region. A full-scale insurgency was launched in 1984 and led to fierce clashes with Turkish security forces, tens of thousands dead, and extensive devastation in several cities and towns in the southeast. A unilateral cease-fire was declared by the PKK in 1999, but fighting began again in 2004. Peace talks between the government and jailed PKK leader Abdullah Ocalan led to another cease-fire and optimism about a more meaningful resolution. The process broke down, however, and fighting resumed in 2015 and continues to this day.

The Turkish–Kurdish conflict falls along the lines of conflicts over national identity that we have seen also in Iraq, Lebanon, and Palestine. In the Turkish case, it is not the result of colonial fiat, but rather of the contradiction between nationalist ideology that accorded every linguistic community the right to its own state and the multiethnic and polyglot nature of the Ottoman Empire, and what was left of it in post–First World War Turkey. The option of separatism and a "two-state solution" for the Kurds of Turkey has never seriously been on the table. The conflict instead has been over whether to either suppress Kurdish identity and community to impose the centralizing and integrating will of a central government or to accord Kurdish communities and regions increasing representation, autonomy, and sociocultural rights. Despite some progress in the recent past toward the latter goal, the situation has regressed in the past few years as President Erdoğan has faced political challenges at home, as well as increasingly empowered Kurdish communities next door in Syria and Iraq.

The Wars of Saudi Consolidation, 1902–32

Modern Saudi Arabia, or what is sometimes referred to as the Third Saudi State, is the result of a number of successful military campaigns led by the al-Saud army and the Ikhwan against rival emirates and regions. The al-Saud recaptured the erstwhile capital at Riyadh in 1902 and consolidated control over the surrounding Nejd region. They then moved against the Hejaz and captured the holy cities of Mecca and Medina by 1926, announcing the Kingdom of Nejd and Hejaz a year later in 1927. After the consolidation and inclusion of the regions of al-Hasa, al-Asir, and al-Qatif, it was dubbed the Kingdom of Saudi Arabia in 1932.

During this period there was an insurrection by the al-Saud's allies, the Ikhwan, a group of Islamically radicalized tribesmen that formed the main fighting force for the al-Saud during this period.[40] After the conquest of the Hejaz in 1924, the Ikhwan wanted to continue their military expansion, particularly to British controlled areas of Transjordan, while the al-Saud, who enjoyed support from the British, wanted to consolidate their holdings. A rebellion by the Ikhwan ensued and was put down by force in 1929 and 1930, leading to the defeat and dissolution of the Ikhwan.

One of the Ikhwan's descendants, Juhayman al-Otaibi, led an armed takeover of the Grand Mosque in Mecca in 1979 and called for the overthrow of the al-Saud government. The takeover was defeated by the Saudi military with help from French and Pakistani special forces, but it was one of the reasons why the al-Saud adopted a more Islamist domestic and foreign policy after 1979, in an attempt to fend off further challenges to their Islamist credentials.

Rebellions and Internal Struggles in Iran

Iran is an extremely ethnically diverse nation and has had its share of separatist or autonomist rebellions. In 1918 there was an Ottoman-backed Kurdish rebellion against Iran's Qajar dynasty. The fighting went on for several years, until Brigadier General Reza Khan deposed the dynasty in 1921, and restored order in the Kurdish regions by force. During the reign of Reza's son Mohammad from 1941 to 1979, the state faced many political challenges, as well as armed challenges from Marxist groups (such as the Tudeh party and the Fedaian guerillas), from the People's Mujahedin (Mujahedin e-Khalq), which combined Marxist and Islamist ideology, and from Islamist groups inspired or led by various clerics. Both Marxist and Islamist groups contributed to the overthrow of the shah in 1979.[41] This led to a period of disarray in which several groups and regions resisted the new Islamist authorities in Tehran, including rebel movements in Arab Khuzestan, Kurdistan, and Gonbad-e Qabus. It also included pitched battles with Marxist and federalist groups that opposed the new Islamist rule. The Islamic Republic finally consolidated its power over these groups in 1982–3. Iran has since experienced bouts of public political protest in 2009 and continuing up to the present day, as well as demonstrations and occasional insurrection in various ethnic minority provinces.

The Morocco–Polisario Front Conflict Over the Western Sahara

The conflict over the Western Sahara falls into a gray area in terms of civil conflict, as Saharan supporters of the Polisario Front consider it a war of national liberation while supporters of the Moroccan claim consider it an internal Moroccan dispute. In any case, the Western Sahara War took place between Morocco and the Polisario Front after the Spanish withdrawal from the region in 1975, until a cease-fire was agreed in 1991. Morocco claims sovereignty over the territory and controls its western portion. The Polisario and other indigenous Sahrawi groups seek independence and control the eastern desert portions of the region.[42] Morocco has enjoyed support from France and some Arab Gulf countries, while the Polisario has traditionally been backed by Algeria. The dispute has resisted numerous UN and other international attempts at resolution, continuing to generate protests—some leading to violent clashes—and in November 2020 the Polisario Front declared an end to the 29-year-long cease-fire with Morocco.

Conclusion

Any satisfactory examination of these cases of civil conflict in the modern Middle East would require several volumes of historical and analytical scholarship. Nonetheless, even a fairly cursory review of these sixteen case studies, as provided earlier, gives the reader of this volume some appreciation of the complexity and variety of civil wars and armed civil conflicts the region faced in the twentieth century, and offers plenty of food for thought as we proceed to examine the current civil wars, adding richness and comparative depth to our perceptions and discussions.

Even a brief review brings up a number of factors that led to the emergence of these conflicts. In some cases, the civil war is linked to the colonial makeup of the country after the First World War or the Second World War in which communities or national projects were thrown together in what amounted to a booby-trapped state. This applies in the case of Palestine, and to varying degrees to Iraq, Lebanon, Sudan, Jordan, and Somalia. In some cases, the civil war was in good measure the result of a weak state that was not able to contain or integrate the power structures of a strong society organized along tribal, regional, or sectarian lines. Such was the case to some degree in Yemen, Afghanistan, Somalia or again, Lebanon. Some civil conflicts were along primordial ethnic or sectarian lines, while others were along ideological—left-right or Islamist-secular—lines. Iraq, Sudan, Palestine, Afghanistan, Turkey, and Lebanon fall into the first category; Algeria, Syria, and Egypt are in the second.

What is of most concern to us, as we focus in this volume on how to end the current civil wars, is to look at how these sixteen conflicts ended, if at all. First, it is important to note that of the sixteen cases presented above, only six can be said to have ended: This includes the Omani conflict of the 1960s, the Jordanian civil war of 1970, the Lebanese civil war of 1975–90, and the Algerian-Islamist conflict of the 1990s; one would also add the Saudi wars of unification that ended in the 1930s, and the Iranian state's consolidation of power in 1979–82. Of these, five were settled by force with the government overcoming the rebels. In two of the cases— Oman and Jordan—the government's victory included some political and socioeconomic accommodation to the aggrieved communities. In Oman that included some of the groups and leaders that led the insurgency; in the Jordanian case it did not include the groups and leaders, but it did include the Palestinian communities in Jordan in whose name part of the conflict was fought. Lebanon presents the only case in which the war was ended not through victory by one side, but by a complex set of domestic and international negotiations. But even in the case of Lebanon, it is not certain whether 1990 really marks the end of civil war, or just a temporary lull in repeated rounds of conflict.[43]

This has been the case in ten of the other conflicts. In Syria, the government defeated the Muslim Brotherhood insurgency in 1982, but the insurgency came back, in a very different form, three decades later, as a popular uprising that included both Islamist and secular nationalist currents.[44] In Palestine also, there have been lulls between the rounds of conflict between Palestinians and Israelis. Some thought the Oslo Accords and the establishment of the PA spelled an end to conflict and a pathway to peace, but conflict has returned in the form of popular intifadas in the West Bank and repeated armed conflicts with Hamas in Gaza. In Yemen, there have been important stretches of peace between bouts of recurring civil war. Previous civil wars there have been settled partly by force but also partly through negotiation and power-sharing agreements of various sorts. But the peace has never held for long, and Yemen is once again engulfed in civil conflict. In Somalia, there has been some progress toward resolving elements of the conflict and marked movement toward de-escalation, but the civil war cannot be said to be over. In Turkey, the conflict with the Kurds continues to ebb and flow across the decades. The conflict over the Western Sahara continues to this day.

Iraq presents an interesting and perhaps hopeful example. Attempts by Saddam to put down demands for representation and inclusion by force took a heavy toll but did not prevail. Efforts by the government of Nouri al-Maliki after 2011 to sideline Kurdish and Arab Sunni representation also backfired. Iraq is now attempting to test whether an inclusive constitutional system can manage to contain the disparate communities and parties in the country, as well as help create stability and social peace where only recently there was brutal repression and devastating civil war.

Virtually all of the sixteen cases exhibit a deep involvement of external powers, both regional and international, either in the foundational contradictions that engendered the conflict, or in escalating and fueling conflict once it got under way. When we look at how the wars ended, if and when they did, we find that external players often had an influence over how long the conflict went on, and over when and how it ended. Of all the sixteen case studies, only perhaps in Algeria or Egypt was the external role fairly minor. What this means for us today is to underline the point that in addition to the complex domestic dynamics of the contemporary civil wars, there is a large role for external players in helping to bring an end to them.

I hope that through this chapter I've provided elements of a toolkit for understanding and defining various aspects of civil conflict, historical context for understanding the drivers and dynamics of civil war in the Middle East, and a rough sketch of case studies that provide comparative depth and perspective when looking at the contemporary map of conflict in the region. I trust that as the reader proceeds to the next chapters in this volume, she or he will find this historical and comparative perspective both relevant and useful.

Notes

1 I would like to thank the excellent interns that worked with me on researching elements of this chapter; they include Lori Younissess, Haneen Abu al-Neel, Kelly Baker, and Evan McKay.

2 Nathan Thrall, "How 1948 Still Influences the Israeli-Palestinian Conflict," *Time*, May 14, 2018. Available online: http://time.com/5273108/back-to-the-future-israeli-palestinian-conflict/ (accessed May 18, 2018).

3 "Total Casualties, Arab-Israeli Conflict," *Jewish Virtual Library*. Available online: https://www.jewishvirtuallibrary.org/total-casualties-arab-israeli-conflict (accessed May 7, 2019).

4 Ian Black, "Iran and Iraq Remember War That Cost More than a Million Lives," *The Guardian*, September 23, 2010. Available online: https://www.theguardian.com/world/2010/sep/23/iran-iraq-war-anniversary (accessed May 18, 2018).

5 Agnus McDowall, "Syrian Observatory Says War Has Killed More than Half a Million," *Reuters*, March 12, 2018. Available online: https://www.reuters.com/article/us-mideast-crisis-syria-idUSKCN1GO13M (accessed May 24, 2018).

6   David Armitage, *Civil Wars: A History in Ideas* (New Haven: Yale University Press, 2018), 5.

7   Ibid., emphasis in the original.

8   Kalevi J. Holsti, *The State, War, and The State of War* (Cambridge: Cambridge University Press, 2004), 14.

9   Florence Gaub, "Civil Wars: A Very Short Introduction," *European Union Institute for Security Studies*, Policy Brief no. 36 (2013): 1.

10 Brian Dodwell, Daniel Milton, and Don Rassler, *The Caliphate's Global Workforce: An Inside Look at the Islamic State's Foreign Fighter Paper Trail*, The Combating Terrorism Center at West Point (April 2016). Further readings: Mishali-Ram Meirav, "Foreign Fighters and Transnational Jihad in Syria," *Studies in Conflict & Terrorism* 41, no. 3 (March 2018): 22.

11 Armitage, *Civil Wars*, 13.

12 Ibid.

13 "About the Correlates of War Project," *The Correlates of War*. Available online: http://www.correlatesofwar.org (accessed June 17, 2019).

14 Carl von Clausewitz, *On War*, trans. Col. J. J. Graham, new and revised edition with introduction and notes by Col. F. N. Maude, in three volumes, vol. 1 (London: Kegan Paul, Trench, Trubner, 1918), 21.

15 Further reading: Markus Brückner, "Population Size, Per Capita Income, and the Risk of Civil War: Regional Heterogeneity in the Structural Relationship Matters," United Nations University, Working Paper no. 18 (2011).

16 Further reading: Christopher Blattman and Edward Miguel, "Civil War: A Review of Fifty Years of Research," Center for Global Development, Working Paper no. 166 (March 2009): 1–91.

17 Further reading: Tobias Hagmann and Markus V. Hoehne, "Failures of the State Failure Debate: Evidence from Somali Territories," *Journal of International Development* 21, no. 1 (October 2008): 42–57.

18 Further reading: Faten Ghosn and Amal Khoury, "Lebanon after the Civil War: Peace or the Illusion of Peace?" *Middle East Journal* 65, no. 3 (Summer 2011): 381–97.

19 Aaron Rock-Singer, "Religion and Secularism in the Middle East: A Primer," Foreign Policy Research Institute (November 2015): 1–6.

20 More on Sectarianism in the Levant: Nawfal, Ahmad Said, Atif Aljulani, Qasid Mahmoud, Abd Al Hamid Alkiali, and Jawad Al Ahmad, "Where Is the Trend of Sectarianism in the Arab World Headed?" *Middle East Studies Journal* 21, no. 81 (2017): 65–154.

21 More on state legitimacy in the MENA region: Karim Mezran and Arturo Varvelli, "The Arc of Crisis in the MENA Region," Italian Institute for International Political Studies (ISPI), Special Report (2018).

22 Further reading: James Barr, "A Line in the Sand: British-French Rivalry in the Middle East, 1915–1948," *Asian Affairs* 43, no. 2 (May 2002).

23 Further reading: Angela Stent, "Putin's Power Play in Syria: How to Respond to Russia's Intervention," *Foreign Affairs* (January/February 2016).

24 Bernard Haykel, "The Middle East's Cold War," Project Syndicate (January 8, 2016).

25 Hossein Sadeghi and Hassan Ahmadian, "Iran–Saudi Relations: Past Pattern, Future Outlook," *Iranian Review of Foreign Affairs* 1, no. 4 (2011): 117.

26 Baker Albdur, "Readings in the Development of the Crisis on the Relation between Saudi Arabia and Iran," *Middle East Studies Journal (MESJ)* 20, no. 75 (2016): 14–125, 118.

27 Further reading: Leila Fawaz, "The City and the Mountain: Beirut's Political Radius in the Nineteenth Century as Revealed in the Crisis of 1860," *International Journal of Middle East Studies* 16, no. 4 (November 1984): 489–95.

28 Further reading: Rajeshwar Dayal, "The 1958 Crisis in Lebanon—the Role of the U.N. and the Great Powers," *India Quarterly* 26 (April/June 1970): 123–33.

29 CNN Library, "Lebanon Fast Facts," *CNN*, August 31, 2018. Available online: https://www.cnn.com/2013/09/03/world/meast/leba non-fast-facts/index.html (accessed August 31, 2018).

30 I use the concept of "strong society" as used by Joel Migdal in his 1988 book *Strong Societies and Weak States*, Princeton University Press.

31 Asma al-Mohattwari, "Investigating Sa'ada's Six Wars," *National Yemen*, 2015.

32 "Wars since 1900," The Polynational War Memorial. Available online: https://www.war-memorial.net/wars_all.asp (accessed June 17, 2019).

33 Further reading: Kenneth Katzman, "The Kurds in Post-Saddam Iraq," RS22079, Congressional Research Service (October 1, 2010).

34 Further reading: James L. Gelvin, *The Israel–Palestine Conflict: One Hundred Years of War* (Cambridge: Cambridge University Press, 2014).

35 Jonathan Schanzer, *Hamas vs. Fatah: The Struggle for Palestine* (New York: St. Martin's Press, 2008).

36 Jonathan Schanzer, "The Challenge of Hamas to Fatah," *Middle East Quarterly* (Spring 2003): 32.

37 Stephen J. Kobrin, "Oil and Politics: Talisman Energy in Sudan," *New York University Journal of International Law and Politics* 36 (2004): 426.

38 M.S. Agwani, "The Saur Revolution and After," *International Studies* 19, no. 4 (1980): 557–73.

39 Further reading: Simon Chesterman, "Humanitarian Intervention and Afghanistan," in *Humanitarian Intervention and International Relations*, ed. Jennifer M. Welsh, 172 (Oxford: Oxford University Press, 2003).

40 Further reading: Godefroid de Callatay, *Ikhwan Al-Safa': A Brotherhood of Idealists on the Fringe of Orthodox Islam* (London: Oneworld, 2012).

41 Further reading: Theda Skocpol, "Rentier State and Shi'a Islam in the Iranian Revolution," *Theory and Society* 11, no. 3 (1982): 265–83.

42 Anthony G. Pazzanita, "Morocco versus Polisario: A Political Interpretation," *Journal of Modern African Studies* 32, no. 2 (1994): 265–78.

43 Ghosn and Khoury, "Lebanon after the Civil War," 381–97.

44 Ben Saul, "Syria Already Fought a Civil War between Islamists and Secularists in 1979–82," *Checkpoint Asia*, March 31, 2019.

2 WHAT WE KNOW ABOUT ENDING CIVIL WARS

Jessica Maves Braithwaite

The country chapters of this volume will examine several ongoing civil wars in the Middle East and North Africa, assessing previous and existing efforts to end these conflicts, as well as offering some thoughts on prospects for how to promote peace in the short and longer terms in each of these cases. The purpose of this chapter is to take a step back and consider what lessons academics have learned about terminating civil wars generally, and to use that knowledge to inform some possible lessons for ending the conflicts in this region.

A handful of these lessons are worth highlighting at the outset. With respect to terminating conflicts in the Middle East and North Africa, the near-ubiquitous state of international involvement, particularly by Russia and the United States, has a massive influence on what becomes advisable in terms of pursuing peace. Once military interventions have begun, it is difficult and risky (especially for local civilians) to subsequently pursue a disengagement strategy, so instead it is advisable to complement them with diplomatic efforts, namely mediation in pursuit of a negotiated outcome to the conflict.

In the event of termination, it is not particularly advisable for post-conflict states to rush democratization efforts, especially in places, like Syria, where political opposition was illegal and therefore rare. Instead, domestic, regional, and international actors should focus on encouraging a strengthening of political parties and civil society organizations, while nurturing trust in democratic processes locally and regionally before holding competitive national-level elections. Also, it is critical to ensure that peacekeepers, especially multidimensional missions, are present in order to secure respect for the rule of law and to promote local-level reconstruction, possibly while also helping to facilitate restorative transitional justice mechanisms. The implementation of power-sharing arrangements, especially those that are territorial and military in nature, as well as the adoption of distributive economic policies in places with natural resource wealth or resource scarcity, can help promote enduring peace as well. This should be encouraged by regional and international stakeholders, and become part of discussions about erecting a regional security and economic architecture.

How Civil Wars End

While the social, political, and economic landscape following a civil war varies considerably across conflicts, scholars tend to identify two general ways in which these wars end: either with a military victory for the government or the rebels, or through a negotiated outcome. It is worth examining these termination strategies and the conditions that make victories and settlements more and less likely, both generally and in the context of the Middle East.

Military victories for the government were, for a long time, an especially common way in which civil wars ended. This is changing with the rise of international actors being willing and able to help facilitate negotiated settlements after the end of the Cold War, though plenty of conflicts have resulted in government victory during this period as well.[1] Political scientists have offered some important insight into conditions that make various civil war outcomes more or less probable as compared to continued conflict.[2] With respect to military victory for the government, this outcome is most likely early on in conflicts, but the longer fighting drags on, the less likely the government is to win and rebel victory or negotiated settlements become more likely. Furthermore, victory for the incumbent regime has been found to be less likely when the rebels' fighting capacity is equal to or greater than that of the government.[3]

With respect to conditions that increase the likelihood of rebel military victory over the government, mountainous terrain—such as that characterizing the landscape of Afghanistan—can be advantageous to rebels as it affords them ample places to hide and establish safe bases to prolong their campaign. Conversely, conflicts are more likely to persist than to end in rebel victory when rebels are fighting civil wars over issues related to identity, as well as in situations where society is heavily divided along ethnic lines.[4] A greater prevalence of rebel alliances can lead to military defeat of the government; however, some scholarship emphasizes that rebel campaigns involving multiple factions have a more difficult time achieving victory or even a negotiated settlement in a timely manner, leading to protracted civil wars.[5] The ongoing conflict in Syria exemplifies this idea of a drawn-out, multiactor conflict to an extreme degree.

Negotiated settlements involve the combatants engaging in peace talks to reach an agreement that addresses the key issues motivating the civil war. Sometimes several rounds of talks are required before a settlement can be produced, and this process also often relies on cease-fires being established to get combatants to lay down their weapons, at least temporarily, in order to step away from the battlefield and toward the negotiating table. Negotiated settlements become possible when the warring parties doubt their ability to achieve an outright military victory, when both rebels and the government can agree to make compromises, and when they believe that the terms of the agreement will be respected by the other side once arms are laid down.[6] Conversely, when combatants cannot credibly demonstrate their willingness and ability to commit to implementation of a settlement or identify mutually acceptable terms, successful peace agreements are unlikely to result. Such conditions underlie (at least in part) key challenges to past negotiation efforts in Syria and Afghanistan, for example.

Comprehensive peace agreements intended to deal with the often myriad incompatibilities that compelled rebels to take up arms against the government are very difficult to come by, especially when civil wars feature multiple rebel groups with widely varying goals. Negotiated settlements are less likely (and conflicts last much longer) in "multiactor" conflicts where armed groups with adequate military resources have preferences and demands that do not overlap in a way that facilitates easily identified terms of an agreement.[7] In this regard, the extreme factionalization of the Syrian conflict immediately comes to mind, involving, among other groups, Kurdish and moderate Islamist rebels fighting alongside and against ISIS, which seeks to establish a transnational caliphate. Similarly, and for decades, groups in Afghanistan holding conflicting views of how the country should be governed, and by whom, have prevented lasting peace agreements from being feasible. In such contexts, one approach to pursuing a negotiated peace could involve reaching "piecemeal" agreements with one or a few compatible rebel groups that are willing to accept compromises and stop fighting against the government.[8]

However, such piecemeal approaches can be particularly vulnerable to the presence of "spoilers"—extreme organizations or factions of rebel groups that engage in attacks ahead of or during peace talks in hopes of preventing a compromise.[9] Spoilers use violence during efforts at pursuing peace in order to delegitimize moderate elements engaged in negotiations with the government, emphasizing the moderates' inability to control the more extreme wings of the broader anti-government campaign. For example, scholars of this region and peace processes generally have extensively explored terrorist attacks by radical Marxist and other "hardline" Palestinian groups objecting to the Palestine Liberation Organization's talks with the Israeli government.[10]

Scholarship has shown that negotiated settlements can be more likely in countries with natural resource endowments, perhaps because revenues from extraction and production can be used as bargaining chips to induce cooperation and bring the warring parties to the table.[11] Hydrocarbon resources—oil and natural gas—feature prominently in some conflicts in this region, especially in Iraq and Libya. Including economic provisions for resource revenue sharing, as well as addressing territorial authority over areas rich with hydrocarbons, can be a useful tool to facilitate cooperation should the opportunity to negotiate a settlement arise. Distributive policies are important components of peace agreements in these situations because combatants will likely fear being excluded from access to these economic resources in the future, which could also lead to security disparities for groups lacking access to resource revenues.[12] Iraq and Libya offer examples where such arrangements have been and likely will remain important components of conflict management and resolution.

Leadership change for both rebel groups and the government has also been found to be an important factor leading to resolution of civil wars by way of a negotiated settlement, as new leadership can help overcome immovable preferences and outdated beliefs among those responsible for starting the conflict.[13] Executives seen as being responsible for the onset of conflict are often reluctant to accept compromises that might lead to them being removed from office in the short to medium term; for example, Bashar al-Assad has been accused by many of hampering peace talks with Syrian rebels.[14]

Peace agreements are also significantly more likely in cases where there are security guarantees from other governments or international organizations involving the deployment of troops that are willing and able to oversee the transition from civil war to peace.[15] This helps to address concerns by combatants that their adversary will renege on terms of the peace deal once arms are laid down. Beyond security guarantees in the context of negotiated settlements, there are several additional ways that third-party actors can influence the termination of civil wars—a topic that is particularly important to consider in detail, given the extensive engagement by the international community during civil wars in this region.

The Role of International Actors in Ending Civil Wars

Intervention by foreign states and international organizations during civil wars can take a multitude of forms and have wildly varying consequences based on the form and timing of the engagement, as well as the characteristics of the relevant combatant group. Perhaps most common, and certainly prevalent in conflicts in the Middle East and North Africa, are military interventions. That said, we also see nonmilitary engagement in the form of diplomatic and economic interventions in plenty of conflicts as well. This section explores the general impacts that these various strategies of third-party engagement have had on civil wars around the world.

Military assistance to combatants fighting civil wars can be one-sided as well as balanced, where both the government and rebels receive some support from third parties. Scholars have shown that situations where both sides are beneficiaries of external sponsorship lead to prolonged civil wars, though some have shown these offsetting interventions can increase the likelihood of negotiations if both sides feel they cannot achieve military victory given the balanced nature of external sponsorship.[16] Such interventions have been found to introduce additional negative consequences such as higher combatant and civilian casualties.[17] These exacerbated costs of conflict were all too apparent in Syria, with Western and Gulf state support for anti-Assad forces poised against Iranian and Hezbollah support for the regime prior to 2015, when Russia put its thumb on the scale, tilting the advantage toward the Assad government. A similar dynamic has played out in Yemen, with Saudi Arabia intervening against the Iranian-assisted Houthi rebels.

It is important to note that in conflicts where one side attracts external support, the other side will typically receive subsequent counterbalancing sponsorship, unless the initial recipient side is able to achieve a swift military victory after support is given. Military interventions for one side only increase the likelihood of victory if the recipient previously struggled with conventional war-fighting capacity. This has been shown to be particularly true for rebel group beneficiaries of military support, but it only helps recipient governments when the rebels have equal or greater fighting strength (which is quite rare).[18]

Military intervention for rebels can be driven in large part by international rivalries, in the context of what has been sometimes dubbed a "proxy war." However, although this terminology might give the impression that rival external patrons use local combatants to fight their battles for them, it is important to note that these combatants often exhibit agency by actively seeking out this assistance on their own—for example, Ali Abdullah Saleh claimed to have pursued Iranian help for his efforts to return to power after he stepped down as president of Yemen. The tendency for regional powers like Saudi Arabia and Iran, as well as major power rivals in the international system, to be pulled into supporting opposing sides in conflicts is explored in much more detail in Ross Harrison's chapter in this volume on the global geopolitics of civil war in the Middle East.

Generally, though, rebel groups are more likely to receive external support if the regime they are fighting against has rivalries with other governments.[19] As mentioned earlier, this has been exemplified by counterbalancing sponsorship in the Syrian and Yemeni civil wars. At least in some cases, this general relationship between rivalries and external sponsorship may be attributed to rebels' willingness to use their campaign to help advance the preferences and goals of their adversary's rivals—the enemy of their enemy is a friend. There is some research to suggest that military assistance biased for rebels is more likely to lead to negotiations by forcing the government to come to the bargaining table when faced with increasing capabilities for the opposition, though we do not have conclusive evidence that this is sufficient to produce a final peace agreement.[20]

Nonmilitary interventions by third parties in civil wars can include humanitarian aid, economic assistance, and sanctions, as well as diplomatic engagement, particularly in the form of mediation. This lattermost form of third-party engagement has been found to be particularly effective at hastening the end of civil wars by facilitating negotiated settlements.[21] This is because mediators can provide information about combatants' war-fighting capabilities and resolve as well as help to overcome commitment problems that often serve to prolong civil wars.[22] The efficacy of third-party mediators has been seen to be influenced by the mediator's bias and leverage regarding the warring parties.[23] For example, mediators biased in favor of the government can help rebels overcome concerns about the regime's credibility in upholding terms of a settlement after the war ends.[24] Furthermore, as compared to neutral parties simply seeking a quick end to conflict, biased mediators are better able to produce high-quality negotiated settlements with extensive institutional arrangements that can lead to lasting peace.[25]

Economic sanctions tend to decrease conflict duration via a number of channels. When imposed by international organizations these sanctions tend to promote a negotiated outcome, whereas military victory becomes more likely when they are imposed by other states. Arms embargoes make military victory less likely, while economic embargoes make both negotiated settlements and military victory more probable than continued conflict.[26] However, it is important to note that economic sanctions that are imposed or even merely threatened can increase the severity of civil wars in terms of the number of fatalities—although the imposition of arms embargoes does seem to decrease casualties.[27]

These various forms of intervention by third parties need not be mutually exclusive; in fact, combinations of military and economic assistance can be more effective at ending civil wars than a policy involving just one of them. The potential fungibility of assistance being provided to rebels is what can drive the likelihood of conflict termination because assistance that can be used by rebels in many different ways (financial support, in particular) generates more uncertainty for the government and reduces the regime's willingness to agree to terms of a negotiated settlement.[28]

Ultimately, academics have found considerable evidence to suggest that interventions by third parties—particularly involving military assistance to warring parties—prolong civil wars and impose other negative consequences such as greater lethality of battles for both combatants and civilians. We have certainly seen this borne out in several conflicts across the region, including Iraq, Syria, and Yemen. However, once those third-party military interventions have taken place, it can be incredibly risky to reverse course and pull out—this can lead to even greater negative consequences for civilians, who are often subjected to increased abuses when a combatant side loses external support.[29]

As a result, combining ongoing military with diplomatic interventions might be an optimal strategy for many of the conflicts throughout the region. Diplomatic interventions, especially in the form of third-party mediation, have been found to hasten an end to the fighting by facilitating negotiated settlements. Although many of the region's civil wars feature rebel groups that do not seem at all interested in coming to the bargaining table, engaging in piecemeal agreements—and even temporary cease-fires to build initial trust and opportunities to negotiate—may prove beneficial in these multiactor conflicts. However, as the failed efforts at upholding negotiated settlements in Yemen make clear, following through and actually implementing terms of peace agreements is critical to ensuring a lasting peace. This is often not an easy task, and there are myriad factors that must be considered when designing and implementing terms of peace following a civil war. Political scientists offer some general insights into these and other factors that impact the risk of conflict recurrence. That is the focus of this final section.

Preventing a Return to the Battlefield

A growing amount of academic work on civil wars focuses on the conditions that fuel the breakdown of peace after a war has terminated. Conflict recurrence has been shown to be less likely given improved economic well-being and higher rates of political participation in the post-conflict environment.[30] Economic development following civil wars has been found to be more difficult when the country is also undergoing significant political transitions, particularly from autocracy to democracy.[31] Thus, it is worth being cautious when encouraging dramatic changes to the political environment after conflict termination, especially in previously closed societies where regime opposition was severely repressed and was not able to organize and participate meaningfully, as was the case in Libya post-Gaddafi or Iraq after the fall of Saddam Hussein. Lack of familiarity with and trust in democratic institutions can compel new groups seeking power to adopt more familiar methods of pursuing change through armed contestation, in the event that elections or other forms of legal political competition fail to go their way.

In addition to postwar economic development, the outcome of the initial conflict can have an important influence on the risk of renewed unrest. In particular, situations of "dual sovereignty"—where the former combatants continue to maintain separate armed forces and exercise territorial control—are most prone to civil war recurrence, namely cases of government victory as well as peace agreements without peacekeeping forces to oversee demobilization and disarmament procedures from an unbiased perspective.[32] This certainly seems like a possibility in Syria, and is a contributing factor to the persistent cycle of conflict in Afghanistan across recent decades as well.

Democratization in general is often viewed as a risky endeavor during the peacebuilding process, particularly in the context of post-conflict elections. Elections held too soon after a civil war ends can inflame tensions between political groups that do not yet trust opponents to respect unfavorable outcomes, leading to renewed unrest.[33] Thus, despite the temptation to immediately allow people from all walks of life to get involved in crafting their postwar government, setting up a transitional government and delaying the holding of national elections for a couple of years can be significantly beneficial for longer-term security. This also allows political parties to (re)develop organizations, build ties within and across communities, and work with third-party advisors to understand and believe in new systems of government. It has also been found that civil society organizations (CSOs) play a critical role in reducing conflict recurrence rates,[34] so nurturing the emergence of new CSOs and supporting existing groups to not only be involved in negotiations but also the peacebuilding process may prove beneficial in seeking lasting peace after many of the region's conflicts. Finally, though not well studied yet by academics, building trust in democratic processes by holding competitive elections at the local and regional levels prior to introducing meaningful democratic competition for national office, might help to generate greater levels of trust among various opposition groups and facilitate a willingness to forgo violence in the event of electoral disappointment in the immediate period.

Another option that can mitigate the risk of conflict recurrence in the presence of democratizing reforms is the construction *and implementation* of power-sharing arrangements.[35] These arrangements, most commonly observed in concert with negotiated settlements (though not exclusively by any means), come in a variety of forms, including political, economic, territorial, and military power sharing. Such provisions, particularly when used in combination with one another, are generally quite effective in preventing civil war recurrence when fully implemented.[36] In particular, power-sharing provisions lower the risk of renewed fighting, and the inclusion of such provisions in negotiated settlements reduces levels of fear among former combatants that their opponents will be able to renege on agreement terms.[37] Political power sharing, which encompasses a variety of strategies that distribute the authority of the central government among multiple groups, is a common element within efforts to promote postwar stability, but it is oftentimes not sufficient on its own to ensure peace in the longer term.[38]

The implementation of power-sharing provisions considered to be particularly costly—territorial and military in nature—are often seen as most effective at preventing renewed conflict, whereas implementation of political power sharing alone does not considerably improve the preservation of peace.[39] However, while some scholars do not find that rebel-military integration leads to improved prospects for long-term peace, this might be because such power-sharing arrangements are often poorly implemented.[40] When fully carried out, military power-sharing provisions, as well as territorial power-sharing arrangements, considerably increase the durability of peace.[41] Thus, overhauling the armed forces following the cessation of conflicts in the region may prove to be a beneficial strategy, as could the implementation and strengthening of territorial arrangements such as Kurdish autonomy in Iraq. As mentioned earlier in this chapter, if such territorial power sharing occurs in the context of natural resource-rich areas, considerations of economic power sharing would be advisable as well, where arrangements are clearly codified for how resources are extracted, and which groups get certain benefits. These are critical considerations for ending conflict in Iraq and Libya, for example. This could also extend to non-hydrocarbon resources, particularly water; if such resources are scarce, as they are in Iraq and Yemen, for example, designing and implementing provisions for sharing them could prove to be critical as well.

Another condition that can help prevent conflict recurrence generally, and perhaps even during democratization processes, is the presence of peacekeepers.[42] Peacekeeping is one of the most widely studied aspects of the post-conflict environment, and although the empirical evidence regarding the efficacy of such missions has been mixed, there is a good amount of compelling research to suggest that peacekeepers are beneficial in preventing a return to the battlefield despite often being sent to environments where conflicts are particularly difficult to prevent and resolve.[43] United Nations peacekeeping troops and police have also been shown to decrease violence against civilians, although deployments of United Nations observer missions correspond to more targeting of civilians.[44] Peacekeeping missions have been associated with conditions of post-conflict economic growth and recovery[45] as well as improved democratization outcomes,[46] though there is also evidence to suggest that these missions do not have a particularly discernable effect on the prospects for democracy.[47]

Providing some sort of third-party security guarantee after termination of civil wars in the Middle East seems to be quite an important consideration in pursuit of preventing conflict recurrence—especially if these conflicts end by way of a negotiated settlement. Multidimensional peacekeeping missions that are tasked not only with providing police and troops to help enforce the rule of law, but also involving civilian peacekeepers who can assist with political, bureaucratic, and security sector reforms and infrastructure redevelopment, could prove to be critical in helping so many of these countries in the region recover from years and even decades of heavily destructive warfare.

Finally, the destruction of these conflicts is not only material and physical but psychological and emotional as well. Such fighting, especially when intentional civilian victimization is widespread, as it has been across the conflicts in the region, has long-lasting consequences for individual health and for the social fabric of these countries—things that are not as readily addressed with foreign aid, election observers, and peacekeeping missions. Transitional justice mechanisms—including truth and reconciliation commissions, amnesties, trials, lustration, and so forth—are designed to help societies recover more deeply from the scars of civil war. However, these mechanisms have been found to have mixed success globally, and they have proven to be particularly ineffective and even problematic in the Middle East.[48] For example, the policy of de-Ba'athification in Iraq drove the excluded Sunnis to take up arms in an incredibly destructive manner. It has been argued that blanket amnesties for war crimes and a lack of meaningful reconciliation in Lebanon have contributed to fueling subsequent assassinations and other violent attacks long after that civil war terminated in 1990.[49]

While transitional justice mechanisms have a dubious success rate, they could be important in contexts of extreme civilian suffering. Domestic and international actors in Yemen, Syria, Iraq, and Afghanistan (though this seems unlikely under Taliban rule) may want to consider transitional justice mechanisms that are more restorative in nature, such as reparations or some sort of aid to those experiencing prolonged dire economic conditions and systematic exclusion from resources, or truth commissions that can engage in fact-finding efforts to shed light on particular crimes against humanity and lead to noncriminal sanctions and possibly even domestic or international trials for key perpetrators.[50] This combination of transitional justice mechanisms is important, as recent work has found that truth commissions conducted without subsequent trials and amnesties leads to diminished human rights practices in subsequent years.[51]

Conclusion

The extensive nature of international military interventions in conflicts across the region makes total withdrawal of this support quite risky, so these measures should (continue to) be supplemented with diplomatic engagement such as third-party mediation. Power-sharing arrangements on issues related to representation, territorial control, military integration, and natural resource distribution will be critical in ending many of these wars, and such provisions can be efficiently and effectively designed with the help of mediators. However, third-party engagement will likely not be able to end with the cessation of civil war, especially in the event of termination by a negotiated settlement, as third-party enforcement of agreement terms is often critical to ensuring lasting peace and adherence to the settlement by former adversaries. Finally, while democracy may be a desired goal for many rebels, civilians, and external actors, transitions from autocracy should not be rushed in the post-conflict period as democratization processes can be highly destabilizing. It is important to allow adequate time to ensure that opposition parties and CSOs can flourish alongside mechanisms that facilitate greater respect for the rule of law, and that trust in the legitimacy of competitive political institutions can be established among both elites and the masses.

Ultimately, preventing a return to the battlefield will be an incredibly complex and multifaceted challenge requiring a tremendous amount of local and international engagement to rebuild economies and infrastructure, overhaul previously repressive and closed political systems, and foster reconciliation at a communal level. There is no "one-size-fits-all" fix that will work to resolve and prevent recurrence of these conflicts across the region, but we can learn some lessons from these global patterns of strategies to try, and try again (and again), in the pursuit of peace in the Middle East.

Notes

1   Christine Bell and Catherine O'Rourke, "The People's Peace? Peace Agreements, Civil Society, and Participatory Democracy," *International Political Science Review* 28, no. 3 (2007): 293–324.
2   See, for example, Karl R. De Rouen Jr. and David Sobek, "The Dynamics of Civil War Duration and Outcome," *Journal of Peace Research* 41, no. 3 (2004): 303–20.
3   David E. Cunningham, Kristian Skrede Gleditsch, and Idean Salehyan, "It Takes Two: A Dyadic Analysis of Civil War Duration and Outcome," *Journal of Conflict Resolution* 53, no. 4 (2009): 570–97.
4   De Rouen and Sobek, "The Dynamics of Civil War."
5   Dylan Balch-Lindsay and Andrew J. Enterline, "Killing Time: The World Politics of Civil War Duration, 1820–1992," *International Studies Quarterly* 44, no. 4 (2000): 615–42; David E. Cunningham, "Veto Players and Civil War Duration," *American Journal of Political Science* 50, no. 4 (2006): 875–92.
6   David T. Mason, Joseph P. Weingarten Jr., and Patrick J. Fett, "Win, Lose, or Draw: Predicting the Outcome of Civil Wars," *Political Research Quarterly* 52, no. 2 (1999): 239–68; Barbara F. Walter, "The Critical Barrier to Civil War Settlement," *International Organization* 51, no. 3 (1997): 335–64.
7   Cunningham, "Veto Players."
8   David E. Cunningham, *Barriers to Peace in Civil War* (Cambridge: Cambridge University Press, 2011).
9   Wendy Pearlman and Kathleen Gallagher Cunningham, "Nonstate Actors, Fragmentation, and Conflict Processes," *Journal of Conflict Resolution* 56, no. 1 (2012): 3–15; Andrew Kydd and Barbara F. Walter, "Sabotaging the Peace: The Politics of Extremist Violence," *International Organization* 56, no. 2 (2002): 263–96; Stephen John Stedman, "Spoiler Problems in Peace Processes," *International Security* 22, no. 2 (1997): 5–53.

10 Wendy Pearlman, "Spoiling Inside and Out: Internal Political Contestation and the Middle East Peace Process," *International Security* 33, no. 3 (2009): 79–109; Alex Braithwaite, Dennis M. Foster, and David A. Sobek, "Ballots, Bargains, and Bombs: Terrorist Targeting of Spoiler Opportunities," *International Interactions* 36, no. 3 (2010): 294–305.

11 Michael L. Ross, "What Do We Know about Natural Resources and Civil War?" *Journal of Peace Research* 41, no. 3 (2004): 337–56; DeRouen and Sobek, "The Dynamics of Civil War."

12 Caroline A. Hartzell, "Explaining the Stability of Negotiated Settlements to Intrastate Wars," *Journal of Conflict Resolution* 43, no. 1 (1999): 3–22.

13 Alyssa K. Prorok, "Leader Incentives and Civil War Outcomes," *American Journal of Political Science* 60, no. 1 (2016): 70–84; Kirssa Cline Ryckman and Jessica Maves Braithwaite, "Changing Horses in Midstream: Leadership Changes and the Civil War Peace Process," *Conflict Management and Peace Science* (2020): 83–105; Michael Tiernay, "Killing Kony: Leadership Change and Civil War Termination," *Journal of Conflict Resolution* 59, no. 2 (2015): 175–206.

14 "The Lessons of Geneva," *The Economist*, February 22, 2014. Available online: http://www.economist.com/news/middle-east-andafrica/21596 983-long-bashar-assad-thinks-he-winningdiplomacy-will-fail-lessons (accessed May 1, 2018).

15 Walter, "The Critical Barrier," 335–64.

16 Patrick M. Regan, "Third-Party Interventions and the Duration of Intrastate Conflicts," *Journal of Conflict Resolution* 46, no. 1 (2002): 55–73; Dylan Balch-Lindsay, Andrew J. Enterline, and Kyle A. Joyce, "Third-Party Intervention and the Civil War Process," *Journal of Peace Research* 45, no. 3 (2008): 345–63.

17 Bethany Lacina, "Explaining the Severity of Civil Wars," *Journal of Conflict Resolution* 50, no. 2 (2006): 276–89; Matthew Krain, "International Interventions and the Severity of Genocides and Politicides," *International Studies Quarterly* 49, no. 3 (2005): 363–88; Reed M. Wood, Jacob D. Kathman, and Stephen E. Gent, "Armed Intervention and Civilian Victimization in Intrastate Conflicts," *Journal of Peace Research* 49, no. 5 (2012): 647–60.

18 Patricia L. Sullivan and Johannes Karreth, "The Conditional Impact of Military Intervention on Internal Armed Conflict Outcomes," *Conflict Management and Peace Science* 32, no. 3 (2015): 269–88.

19 Seden Akcinaroglu and Elizabeth Radziszewski, "Expectations, Rivalries, and Civil War Duration," *International Interactions* 31 (2005): 349–74.

20 Rupen Cetinyan, "Ethnic Bargaining in the Shadow of Third Party Intervention," *International Organization* 56, no. 3 (2002): 645–77; Lindsay Dylan Balch, Andrew Enterline, and Kyle Joyce, "Third Party Intervention and Civil War Process," *Journal of Peace Research* 45, no. 3 (2008): 345–63; Stephen Gent, "Going in When it Counts," *International Studies Quarterly* 52, no. 4 (2008): 713–35.

21 Patrick M. Regan and Aysegul Aydin, "Diplomacy and Other Forms of Intervention," *Journal of Conflict Resolution* 50, no. 5 (2006): 736–56.

22 J. Michael Greig and Patrick M. Regan, "When Do They Say Yes? An Analysis of the Willingness to Offer and Accept Mediation in Civil Wars," *International Studies Quarterly* 52, no. 4 (2008): 759–81; Shanna A. Kirschner, "Knowing Your Enemy: Information and Commitment Problems in Civil Wars," *Journal of Conflict Resolution* 54, no. 5 (2010): 745–70.

23 Burcu Savun, "Information, Bias, and Mediation Success," *International Studies Quarterly* 52, no. 1 (2008): 25–47.

24 Isak Svensson, "Bargaining, Bias and Peace Brokers: How Rebels Commit to Peace," *Journal of Peace Research* 44, no. 2 (2007): 177–94.

25 Isak Svensson, "Who Brings Which Peace? Neutral Versus Biased Mediation and Institutional Peace Arrangements in Civil Wars," *Journal of Conflict Resolution* 53, no. 3 (2009): 446–69.

26 Abel Escribà-Folch, "Economic Sanctions and the Duration of Civil Conflicts," *Journal of Peace Research* 47, no. 2 (2010): 129–41.

27 Lisa Hultman and Dursun Peksen, "Successful or Counterproductive Coercion? The Effect of International Sanctions on Conflict Intensity," *Journal of Conflict Resolution* 61, no. 6 (2017): 1315–39.

28 Katherine Sawyer, Kathleen Gallagher Cunningham, and William Reed, "The Role of External Support in Civil War Termination," *Journal of Conflict Resolution* 61, no. 6 (2017): 1174–202.

29 Reed M. Wood, "From Loss to Looting? Battlefield Costs and Rebel Incentives for Violence," *International Organization* 68, no. 4 (2014): 979–99.

30 Barbara F. Walter, "Does Conflict Beget Conflict? Explaining Recurring Civil War," *Journal of Peace Research* 41, no. 3 (2004): 371–88.

31 Thomas Edward Flores and Irfan Nooruddin, "Democracy under the Gun Understanding Postconflict Economic Recovery," *Journal of Conflict Resolution* 53, no. 1 (2009): 3–29.

32 J. Michael Quinn, T. David Mason, and Mehmet Gurses, "Sustaining the Peace: Determinants of Civil War Recurrence," *International Interactions* 33, no. 2 (2007): 167–93.

33 Thomas Edward Flores and Irfan Nooruddin, "The Effect of Elections on Postconflict Peace and Reconstruction," *Journal of Politics* 74, no. 2 (2012): 558–70.

34 Desirée Nilsson, "Anchoring the Peace: Civil Society Actors in Peace Accords and Durable Peace," *International Interactions* 38, no. 2 (2012): 243–66.

35 Dawn Brancati and Jack L. Snyder, "Time to Kill: The Impact of Election Timing on Postconflict Stability," *Journal of Conflict Resolution* 57, no. 5 (2013): 822–53.

36 Caroline Hartzell and Matthew Hoddie, "Institutionalizing Peace: Power Sharing and Post-Civil War Conflict Management," *American Journal of Political Science* 47, no. 2 (2003): 318–32; Caroline A. Hartzell and Matthew

Hoddie, *Crafting Peace: Power-Sharing Institutions and the Negotiated Settlement of Civil Wars* (Pennsylvania, PA: Penn State Press, 2007).

37 Michaela Mattes and Burcu Savun, "Fostering Peace after Civil War: Commitment Problems and Agreement Design," *International Studies Quarterly* 53, no. 3 (2009): 737–59.

38 This is discussed with respect to the Syrian conflict in Amal Khoury and Faten Ghosn, "Bridging Elite and Grassroots Initiatives: The Road to Sustainable Peace in Syria," in *Post-Conflict Power-Sharing Agreements* (London: Palgrave Macmillan, 2018), 43–61.

39 Anna K. Desirée Nilsson, "From Words to Deeds: The Implementation of Power-Sharing Pacts in Peace Accords," *Conflict Management and Peace Science* 25, no. 3 (2008): 206–23.

40 Katherine Glassmyer and Nicholas Sambanis, "Rebel-Military Integration and Civil War Termination," *Journal of Peace Research* 45, no. 3 (2008): 365–84.

41 Matthew Hoddie and Caroline Hartzell, "Civil War Settlements and the Implementation of Military Power-sharing Arrangements," *Journal of Peace Research* 40, no. 3 (2003): 303–20; Jarstad and Nilsson, "From Words to Deeds."

42 Admittedly, peacekeeping has not been used in the context of civil wars in this region—the closest example would perhaps be third-party engagement in the Lebanese conflict in 1976 by the Arab Deterrent Force (ADF), arranged by the Arab League. However, most Arab states pulled out of the ADF shortly thereafter and only Syria was left as the intervening party, and the mission transformed into something beyond conventional conceptions of peacekeeping. The historical and normative implications of interventions by Western parties and organizations in the Middle East, among other factors, present challenges for composing a viable and acceptable peacekeeping missions for civil wars; "ideal" facilitating organizations and participating countries would necessarily be different for each civil war environment. For example, perhaps the African Union could take a lead role in a peacekeeping mission for Libya, but they would not be able to engage in such efforts outside the African continent.

43 Virginia Page Fortna, "Does Peacekeeping Keep Peace? International Intervention and the Duration of Peace After Civil War," *International Studies Quarterly* 48, no. 2 (2004): 269–92; Walter, "The Critical Barrier."

44 Lisa Hultman, Jacob Kathman, and Megan Shannon, "United Nations Peacekeeping and Civilian Protection in Civil War," *American Journal of Political Science* 57, no. 4 (2013): 875–91; Reed M. Wood and Jacob D. Kathman, "Too Much of a Bad Thing? Civilian Victimization and Bargaining in Civil War," *British Journal of Political Science* 44, no. 3 (2014): 685–706.

45 Michael Carnahan, Scott Gilmore, and William Durch, "New Data on the Economic Impact of UN Peacekeeping," *International Peacekeeping* 14, no. 3 (2007): 384–402.

46 Michael W. Doyle and Nicholas Sambanis, *Making War and Building Peace: United Nations Peace Operations* (Princeton, NJ: Princeton University Press, 2006); Mark Peceny and Jeffrey Pickering, "Can Liberal Intervention Build Liberal Democracy," *Conflict Prevention and Peacebuilding in Post-War Societies: Sustaining the Peace* (2006): 130–48.

47 Virginia Page Fortna, "Peacekeeping and Democratization," *From War to Democracy: Dilemmas of Peacebuilding* (2008): 39–79; Mehmet Gurses and T. David Mason, "Democracy Out of Anarchy: The Prospects for Post-Civil-War Democracy," *Social Science Quarterly* 89, no. 2 (2008): 315–36.

48 See, for example, James D. Meernik, Angela Nichols, and Kimi L. King, "The Impact of International Tribunals and Domestic Trials on Peace and Human Rights after Civil War," *International Studies Perspectives* 11, no. 4 (2010): 309–34; Tricia D. Olsen, Leigh A. Payne, and Andrew G. Reiter, "The Justice Balance: When Transitional Justice Improves Human Rights and Democracy," *Human Rights Quarterly* 32 (2010): 980; Kathryn Sikkink and Carrie Booth Walling, "The Impact of Human Rights Trials in Latin America," *Journal of Peace Research* 44, no. 4 (2007): 427–45.

49 Faten Ghosn and Amal Khoury, "Lebanon After the Civil War: Peace or the Illusion of Peace?" *Middle East Journal* 65, no. 3 (2011): 381–97; Khoury and Ghosn, "Bridging Elite and Grassroots Initiatives."

50 Admittedly, truth commissions have not been extensively developed or implemented in the aftermath of civil wars in the Middle East. For example, such initiatives have failed to take hold in Iraq for a variety of reasons discussed in Ibrahim Al-Marashi and Aysegul Keskin, "Reconciliation Dilemmas in Post-Ba'athist Iraq: Truth Commissions, Media and Ethno-Sectarian Conflicts," *Mediterranean Politics* 13, no. 2 (2008): 243–59: "A post-war reconciliation process was neglected due to logistical, security and administrative constraints. Both the Coalition Provisional Authority (CPA) and the Iraqi government were too overwhelmed by insurgency and reconstruction matters to invest in TRCs. Realizing that this process was a necessity, the governments in Iraq since 2003 have been unsuccessful in initiating a state-orchestrated truth and reconciliation process as have external regional actors, such as the Arab League. Their efforts in the past have wavered as some parties questioned the neutrality of their role as mediator and facilitator" (247). However, these authors also highlight compelling efforts from civil society groups like the Iraq Memory Foundation to engage in "truth-telling" exercises beyond the official efforts of the state, so if official channels struggle to facilitate truth commissions, more private or community-level efforts could be promising alternatives. Furthermore, the Truth and Dignity Commission (*Instance Vérité et Dignité*) in the aftermath of dictatorial rule in Tunisia could be another model for future truth commissions to follow in contexts of civil war in the region.

51 Tricia D. Olsen, Leigh A. Payne, Andrew G. Reiter, and Eric Wiebelhaus-Brahm, "When Truth Commissions Improve Human Rights," *International Journal of Transitional Justice* 4, no. 3 (2010): 457–76.

3 THE GLOBAL AND REGIONAL GEOPOLITICS OF CIVIL WAR IN THE MIDDLE EAST

Ross Harrison

A large proportion of the post-World War II civil wars have been "internationalized" in the sense that one or more nations intervened in the conflict on the side of the government or rebels.[1]

Introduction

The Middle East has been one of the regions of the world most deeply impacted by outside powers. For centuries great powers like Great Britain and France, and later the United States and the Soviet Union, intervened in the domestic politics of individual states, as well as conflicts between states in this troubled region.

There is a wide range of thinking of how these global power interventions have impacted conflicts within states. Egyptian academic Samir Amin argued in the 1970s that the countries in the Middle East had for decades been in a chokehold of dependence on the global, Western-dominated economic system. According to this line of thinking, the exploitive nature of that system kept countries in a chronic state of underdevelopment and poverty, a condition which could eventually percolate to the surface in the form of civil conflict or even revolution.[2]

Other analysts have focused less on the disruptive economic effects of interventions by global powers but more on how civil conflict is a byproduct of state fragility engendered by the arbitrary drawing of the region's political map by European powers after the First World War. Writers of this ilk also tend to assign blame to the superpowers for pursuing their ambitions vis-à-vis one another during the Cold War in a region replete with fragile and tentative states. Extending this logic out, both European and superpower interventions came at the expense of the political and economic health of the region, leading to societal discontent and ultimately insurrection.[3]

Today, intervention doesn't just come from global powers. Major regional powers have also played a role in the dynamics of domestic politics and, in many cases, *civil war*, beyond their immediate borders. The roles of Iran, Turkey, Saudi Arabia, the UAE, and Qatar in current conflicts—or Egypt, Israel, and Libya in previous ones—come to mind.

This chapter will explore the role that both global and regional geopolitics have played in the civil conflicts currently plaguing the region. The focus will be less on the specifics of the interventions in Iraq, Syria, Libya, Yemen, and Afghanistan, as these are analyzed in the country chapters of this volume. Instead, we will step back and look more at how the power dynamics between the major global and regional powers have indirectly influenced how civil wars in the Middle East have played out.

The Arguments: The Violent Civil War Vortex

It will be argued that while local grievances and the regional dynamics of the Arab Spring were the underlying causes that sparked the civil wars in the Middle East, it is also important to consider how the disbandment of the Soviet Union and the resultant collapse of the Cold War power structure put all the states in the region, but particularly the erstwhile Soviet allies, under stress.

We will chronicle how the loss of the Soviet Union as a benefactor compelled Syria, Iraq, Libya, and Yemen to scramble in the face of new political and economic realities, some of which translated into stresses that came to the surface decades later during the Arab Spring. We will also examine how the reality of American unipolarity at the end of the Cold War was a prelude to US invasions of Afghanistan and Iraq after the events of September 11, 2001. Moreover, we will show how this ultimately strengthened an "axis of resistance," consisting of Iran, Syria, and Hezbollah, against what these countries saw as efforts by the United States and its allies (Saudi Arabia, the UAE, and Israel) to impose their will on the region. It was these two opposing poles which later competed for regional primacy in the civil wars of Iraq, Syria, and Yemen. Later Turkey and Israel were added to the mix of regional powers competing for influence in the civil war zones of the region. It is this still ongoing struggle for power in the civil war zones by regional powers that is helping shape the political order of the Middle East.

While this regional power competition has played out on the backs of the civil wars, it is misleading to simplify these as merely proxy wars. Yes, it is true that Iran, Saudi Arabia, and Turkey have in fact treated the civil wars as proxy venues for competition with one another. But this chapter will argue that the regional powers don't just "push" themselves into these conflicts, as a proxy war dynamic would suggest, but also get "pulled" in based on threats (and in some cases opportunities) created by the civil wars. This phenomenon will be described as "vertical contagion," where beyond just exploiting the civil wars top-down, regional, and international actors get drawn into the vortex of a "conflict trap."[4]

These distinctions in how we define the relationships between regional and international powers and the civil wars are not trivial. How we look at this relationship has real implications for the challenges of forging the cooperation necessary globally (and regionally) to advance the cause of peace in the countries racked by civil war.

Cold War Global Dimensions of Civil Wars

To properly assess the global context of the civil wars today, it is essential that we look at what has changed over time, starting with the early days of the Cold War.

The onset of the Cold War was the "big bang" moment of the modern Middle East. At the same time the United States and Soviet Union were ramping up their global competition, almost all Arab states were making the transition from being under the thumb of European colonialism to becoming independent sovereign states. At this critical juncture in Middle East history, supply and demand dynamics worked to create a region defined by the Cold War. In terms of supply, the superpowers were eager to create alliances with these newly independent states as a way of competing with one another, and in terms of demand the Middle East states themselves needed foreign economic and military aid from the rival superpowers. In other words, there was a collision between two profound historical forces: the emerging Cold War global conflict between the two superpowers, and Arab states becoming independent and entering the headiest, but also most vulnerable, period of their histories.

The clearest evidence of the influence the US–Soviet rivalry exerted on the political order of the Middle East is that the region started to mirror the bipolar structure of the international system. The major manifestation of this "mimicking effect" was the emergence of an Arab Cold War, which pitted Egypt's populist Arab nationalist leader, Gamal Abdel Nasser (backed by the Soviet Union), against more conservative Arab states such as Jordan and Saudi Arabia (allies of the United States).[5]

The different sides of this Arab Cold War competed for influence in the civil wars in Lebanon in the 1950s and Yemen in the 1960s; they also backed rival political factions intermittently in Syria, Jordan, Iraq, Sudan, and Libya. This rivalry was also a theme in Iraq's 1958 revolution, and the United States and Soviet Union both intervened indirectly in the Lebanese civil war which started in 1975.[6]

The Role the Superpowers Played in the Domestic Politics of Arab Regimes

To fully understand why several of the Arab states descended into civil war after 2010, we must unpack how the superpower competition during the Cold War influenced the domestic politics of these states.

Each of the fledgling independent states that emerged from colonialism at the onset of the Cold War struggled with stability and legitimacy due to rising expectations and limited state capacity to meet societal demands. Because of this, most newly independent states ultimately felt compelled to accept support from either the United States or the Soviet Union.

Countries which aligned themselves with the United States, like Saudi Arabia, Jordan, and Iran, gained regime security from this alliance, but at the expense of regime legitimacy. Given the US support for Israel, the Arab regimes (and Iran) paid a domestic legitimacy price for being on the receiving end of American largesse. But the gains in regime security helped offset the legitimacy liability, signaling to opposition groups that the United States would shore up the regime against domestic challenges.

The Soviet Union, on the other hand, didn't have this drag on the legitimacy of its Arab allies given that its revolutionary brand overlapped with the Arab nationalist agendas of Egypt, Syria, Iraq, and Libya.[7] Moscow tended to back countries (e.g., Nasser's Egypt) which built their legitimizing formulas on a stance of resistance against the United States and its regional allies, Israel in particular.[8] Arab countries aligned with the Soviet Union presented themselves as part of a worldwide struggle against what was viewed as Western hegemonic designs over the Middle East, a view which enjoyed considerable popular legitimacy among their publics. While these states still had legitimacy issues, their relationship with Moscow wasn't the source of them.

Syria and Egypt: Case Studies in Cold War Politics

Syrian Domestic Policy

The alliance with the Soviet Union helped Syria patch over some of the legitimacy deficiencies that had plagued it since independence. Soviet aid packages helped shore up the country's political economy by spurring the growth of the public sector, from which flowed benefits to the regime's social base.[9] Despite the fractious nature of the Syrian political system, evidenced by the series of coups that took place after independence and before the ascension of Hafez al-Assad to the presidency in 1971, the support from Moscow was a considerable buttress to state capacity.[10] One could argue that the alliance with the Soviet Union had a "disciplining effect" on the Syrian political system, sidelining potential challengers to the regime.[11] While there was a formidable challenge from the Muslim Brotherhood from 1976 to 1982, which was brutally quashed, the social contract enabled by the state's relationship with Moscow kept Syria reasonably stable, particularly starting in the 1970s under President Hafez al-Assad. Through the transfer of security-related equipment and weaponry, Moscow facilitated the transformation of the Assad regime into a powerful authoritarian police state.

There was also an ideological component to the relationship between Moscow and Damascus. The expansion of the public sector at the expense of private enterprise, the emergence of a vibrant communist party in Syria, and the socialist tenets of the Ba'ath party, signaled at least a modicum of ideological alignment between Syria and the Soviet Union.

While the state continued to struggle with overcoming divisions and settling on a legitimacy formula in its formative years, exacerbated by the failure to defeat the fledgling Israeli state in 1948 and the short-lived merger with Egypt a decade later, the alliance with the Soviet Union provided an ideological, financial, and military support system.

Syrian Foreign Policy: Intervening in the Lebanese Civil War

One could make an argument that the Cold War prolonged the civil war in Lebanon, which started in 1975. With the United States supporting Israel's involvement and the Soviet Union backing Syrian involvement, the conflict quickly internationalized such that resolution proved to be almost impossible.

Syria was caught on the horns of a vexing dilemma when it came to Lebanon, evidenced by the fact that it switched sides during the war, first coming on the side of the Christian-led Lebanese Front and then later turning against them and backing the Leftist-Muslim–Palestine Liberation Organization (PLO) coalition.[12] Because of its historical ties to the Arab nationalist movement, the legitimacy of the Syrian state depended on a strident foreign policy which included at least appearing to support the PLO and opposing Israeli interests in Lebanon. But the weakness of the Syrian state made pursuing a directly aggressive foreign policy perilous to the regime's legitimacy and stability, particularly in the wake of having lost the Golan Heights to the Israelis in the still fresh devastating defeat of the 1967 war.[13]

Soviet military and economic aid enabled Syria to at least take indirect moves against Israel, particularly in Lebanon. But Hafez al-Assad still followed a circumspect path in Lebanon, which both reinforced the Syrian state and eschewed policies that threatened its stability. He sought to preserve a Palestinian resistance for later bargaining with Israel on the Golan Heights, while balancing this against the risk that a PLO victory in Lebanon might lead to a total collapse of the Lebanese state, and draw direct Israeli military action—both developments which could blow back to Syria, or drag it into an unwanted war with Israel.[14] To reduce this risk Hafez al-Assad fielded his own Palestinian force, al-Sai'qa, as a hedge against more independent PLO groups, such as Fatah and the even more radical Popular Front for the Liberation of Palestine (PFLP).

The Soviet Union also had a direct effect on the civil war in Lebanon, by acting as a spoiler in efforts to end the fighting. In the zero-sum-game mentality of the Cold War, Moscow had an interest in pushing back against any Lebanese initiative to end the war that might redound to the advantage of the United States or its regional allies.[15]

Egypt's Involvement in the Yemen Civil War

While Egypt had stronger political fundamentals than Syria, its domestic and foreign policy options were also heavily shaped by its alliance with the Soviet Union, which was forged after a failed attempt by Washington to strike an arms deal with Nasser. Moscow gave Egypt the military wherewithal to intervene in the 1960s civil war in Yemen on the side of the republicans, against the US-backed Saudi and Jordanian support for the monarchists. While Egypt's involvement was inspired by and became part of Nasser's pan-Arab agenda, the relationship with Moscow was instrumental. The Soviets were involved directly in activities like financing the building of the strategically important port of Hodeida (which today is seen as a fulcrum of the current Yemen civil war).[16]

While it would be an oversimplification to paint the civil war in Yemen in the 1960s as simply a proxy war, as local actors willingly exploited and drew resources from the superpowers to prosecute their own agendas, the United States and the Soviet Union certainly played a role by helping regional actors like Saudi Arabia and Egypt, respectively, play out their ambitions vis-à-vis one another on the backs of a Yemeni civil conflict.[17]

Regional Dynamics During the Cold War

Enlightened thinkers like Fénelon who believed in Europe's cultural unity feared that all wars between Europeans would become civil wars, because they were fought within the bounds of a community of fellow citizens who recognized one another as such.[18]

During much of the Cold War the Middle East was an Arab-centric region. One reason for this is that the Arab world quickly became contested by the United States and the Soviet Union, each staking out allies as part of the global power struggle. In contrast, non-Arab states Israel, Turkey, and Iran (until 1979) all leaned hard toward the West.

This competition between the superpowers split the Arab world into two ideological camps. Allies of the Soviet Union adopted a socialist, anti-imperialist attitude. This aligned with and reinforced the fiery revolutionary rhetoric of Egypt's President Nasser, who built his country's legitimizing formula on a stance of state-led socialism in domestic policies, and resistance against the West in foreign policy.[19] In contrast, allies of the United States, which were more ideologically conservative regimes, such as the monarchies of Jordan and Saudi Arabia, as well as Israel, adopted an anti-communist and sometimes even an anti-nationalist agenda.

This ideological framing had real consequences in Lebanon's first civil war in 1958, where leftist and Sunni Muslim groups inspired by Nasser's pan-Arabism were pitted against the more Western-leaning, state-centric, and conservative Maronite Christian dominated state. The brief civil war was fought over competing visions of Lebanon and its role in the region. These divisions were widened by the revolution in Iraq during the same year, and the resultant weakening of the Western-led Baghdad Pact, as well as Nasser's formation of the United Arab Republic, which unified Syria and Egypt under a single Arab nationalist banner. This split drew the Americans into both Lebanon and Jordan in 1958, while the Soviet Union consolidated its influence over Egypt, Syria, and Iraq.

Asher Orkaby summarized eloquently how the Cold War, and particularly involvement by the United States, framed out regional struggles that played out in the first Lebanese civil war as well as in other developments in the region:

President Dwight Eisenhower's Middle East policy, known as the Eisenhower Doctrine, supported and united the conservative Arab regimes of Iraq, Jordan, Kuwait, Lebanon, and Saudi Arabia, placing them as an ideological counter to "Nasserism." By June 1957, Eisenhower succeeded in polarizing the Arab world and creating a "royalist axis" of conservative regimes that were willing to counter and criticize Egypt and Syria. The 1958 coup in Iraq and the U.S. military intervention in Lebanon conversely discredited U.S. intentions in the Middle East and strengthened Nasser as the anti-imperialist power.[20]

Global Geopolitics and Civil Wars in the Post–Cold War Era

An intrastate war may be interrupted by an external power or become internationalized.[21]

Any power equilibrium that existed between Soviet and American allies in the Middle East fell away with the end of the Cold War and the collapse of the Soviet Union. The asymmetry became apparent very quickly, with US allies Israel, Saudi Arabia, Egypt, and Turkey emerging from the Cold War period still having their US benefactor, while former Soviet allies Syria, Iraq, Yemen (south), and Libya were handed tougher cards to play.

While the end of the Cold War wasn't a direct causal factor in these latter four countries succumbing to the Arab Spring and sliding into civil war two decades later, the loss of the Soviet patron put pressure on each of them that affected their capacity to cope with the social, economic, and political pressures that later came their way.

The End of the Cold War and the Effect on the Domestic Politics of Former Soviet Allies

All countries in the region, including American allies, took a strategic "haircut" when the superpower competition came to an end. The US alliances in the Middle East had been largely forged as instruments for containing the Soviet Union, and when the Cold War struggle ended, a core strategic underpinning of those alliances dropped away. But despite the disappearance of the containment imperative at the end of the Cold War, commitments to Israel, oil interests, and challenges from Iran, kept the United States tethered to its allies in the region.

But former Soviet allies were disproportionally and negatively affected by the end of the Cold War and were left holding the bag. The effect the end of the Cold War had on the political economy of these countries was almost immediate. With the loss of their Soviet benefactor, weak states became even weaker economically and politically, as they saw their external support and internal legitimizing principles dissipate.[22]

When the Soviet Union collapsed, it was clear that to avoid a legitimacy crisis the Syrian regime had to develop new internal sources of financial investment as a substitute for the loss of Soviet era transfers.[23] This required a revision of the old social contract that had been maintained for decades by a sprawling public sector kept afloat with the help of the Soviet Union, and a private sector that had been gutted by the state in the 1960s with the concomitant rise of crony capitalism.

But there were difficult obstacles to overcome in transitioning to a new social contract, as the Syrian political economy couldn't easily be shifted toward the private sector. There were significant attempts, such as the passage of Investment Law 10 in the 1990s, which was an initiative to spur investment in key areas of the private sector, such as tourism and telecoms. But there were problems, such as economic drags associated with attempts to retire Soviet-era debt, an effort that began before the end of the Cold War.[24] Another problem was that the compact by which the state provided subsidies for food to the lower and middle classes made escape from the old public-sector model very difficult, at least not without risking serious instability. More specifically, the regime was unable to widen its base of support and cling to its traditional constituencies of the lower and middle classes, and at the same time tilt the economy toward the private sector.

Moreover, the reality of a crony capitalist class beholden to the state and the Assad family itself made a transition to a private sector system difficult. Instead, the government of Bashar al-Assad tried to forge a middle path, a "social market" approach to economic and political governance. But the sprawling public sector that had been created over the decades made successful adjustment to the new approach difficult. Instead of privatizing public sector holdings to stimulate growth, the government merely tried to reform them, mostly unsuccessfully. There was also the reality of regime distrust of an independent private sector, perhaps a hangover from the years of Soviet influence.

In sum, the rigid, praetorian nature of the Syrian state militated against successful adjustment to the shock of the Soviet collapse, particularly given its inability to access significant sources of foreign direct investment. And a full transition from the old Ba'athist political-economy toward a hybrid social market approach risked unleashing unrest in the country.[25] Moreover, the inability to strike a balance between the private and public sectors and the lingering effects of decisions made during the Soviet era hobbled the regime's capacity to respond effectively to the drought that affected Syria from 2006 to 2010, a factor that contributed to the slide into civil war in 2011.[26] Climate refugees who had migrated to the major cities in response to the drought acted as kindling for the firestorm of the Arab Spring protests that beset Syria. The sclerotic state structure, that was a legacy of the Cold War era, proved incapable of responding effectively to the catastrophic water shortages that occurred.

Shifting our gaze to the macro level, it seems clear that in the post–Cold War era, Syria was forced to choose between state security and economic reform. To meet its security needs and cope with the isolation it felt at the end of the Cold War, Syria felt compelled to strengthen its already strong ties with Iran.[27] But this left it facing the impossibility of trying to square the circle of allying with Iran for security reasons, yet at the same time needing capital investments from Western sources as part of an economic reform program. One way to think about this is that the loss of its superpower patron put the Syrian regime in the unenviable position of having to forego its economic interests vis-à-vis the west in favor of its security interests served by moving closer to Iran. While there was investment from the Gulf Arab states in a few projects, it wasn't enough to compensate for the shortfalls of the Syrian government's dire economic condition.

It would be foolhardy to suggest that the Syrian civil war which started in 2011 was the exclusive or direct result of these earlier post-Cold War adjustments. Indeed, Syria's descent into conflict was largely a result of the contagion effect of the Arab Spring moment, the brutality of the regime, and the accumulated impact of increasingly skewed socioeconomic realities, as well as the onset of drought. But it wouldn't be reckless to say that the decisions the Assad regime confronted at the end of the Cold War limited the options it had as stresses accumulated in the late 2010s, and after the 2011 crisis erupted.

American Unipolarity in the Middle East

The United States started to flex its muscles even before the formal collapse of the Soviet Union. In the last gasps of the Cold War, Moscow did not make a move when the United States assembled an army in the Gulf in 1990 to liberate Kuwait from Iraq, and barely objected when the United States crossed the Kuwaiti border into Iraq in 1991 to chase down Saddam Hussein's much vaunted Republican Guard Corps, and pummeled Baghdad from the air.[28] This earlier invasion of Iraq created a precedent for the later US-led invasion of 2003, which ultimately contributed to the outbreak of civil war in that country.

It is useful to look at the overall strategic patterns of a US running unopposed in the Middle East during this period. There were two phases to this unipolar moment. The first is "soft unipolarity," when the United States imposed a sort of Pax Americana on the region. This took the form of the Clinton administration's strategy of dual containment of both Iran and Iraq in the 1990s a policy, which emerged in response to the continued perceived threat from revolutionary Iran—even after the end of the Iraq–Iran War in 1988—and the perceived need to contain an aggressive Saddam Hussein in the wake of his attempt to annex Kuwait in 1990. This approach of indirectly trying to shape the power dynamics of the Middle East gave way to a more aggressive "hard unipolarity" in the wake of 9/11, when the United States saw an opportunity to use military power to reorder the region in its own image. The invasion of Afghanistan in 2001, the invasion and occupation of Iraq in 2003, and the ultimatum issued to Damascus to withdraw Syrian forces from Lebanon in 2005, were all part of this new "sharp-elbowed" approach.

These manifestations of unipolarity had a profound effect on the foreign policy calculations of former Soviet allies. Just as the end of the Cold War had a shock effect on their domestic politics, the reality of American unipolarity during this period altered their foreign policy calculus as well.[29] As fleeting of a moment as it might have been, US dominance posed foreign policy challenges for Syria, Iraq, Libya, Yemen, and Afghanistan.

A Resistance Front Forms

In the realist tradition of international relations theory, imbalances of power within a system will lead to an adjustive response, such as the formation of new alliances.[30] In this vein, once the Soviet Union collapsed, its former Middle Eastern allies had to contend with the resultant regional imbalances largely on their own.

Syria had already started hedging its bet on the Soviet Union before the formal end of the Cold War. To compensate for the poor hand Syria believed it was being dealt with an obviously weakening Soviet Union, Damascus forged closer ties with Washington, evidenced by its inclusion in the US-led coalition that went to war against Iraq in 1990, participation in the Madrid peace conference in 1991, and subsequent negotiations with Israel.

But after the US invasion of Iraq in 2003, Damascus feared it might be next. To preclude an attack the Syrians tried to weaken the United States position by allowing Sunni Iraqi insurgents to cross over from Syria into Iraq to bog down the American military. The Iraqi invasion and Syria's later forced expulsion from Lebanon by the United States after the assassination of Rafik Hariri in 2005 pushed Damascus into a further defensive crouch.[31] The loss of its Soviet patron, and the "hard" edge of American unipolarity, gave Syria the incentive to move even closer to Iran's axis of resistance.

It is important to note that the close relationship between Iran and Syria predated the end of the Cold War. It was in fact cemented shortly after the Iranian Revolution of 1979 and was forged into a strategic partnership after Iraq invaded Iran in 1980, when Syria broke ranks with all its Arab brethren to back Tehran, in a bid to weaken Iraq's Saddam Hussein.[32]

But that partnership was fortified and took on a new meaning at the end of the Cold War, particularly after the 2003 US invasion of Iraq. For Syria it was a need to break out of an isolation that could make it susceptible to an American attack in a post-9/11 environment, and a desire to better position itself as a strategic counterweight to Israel now that Soviet patronage had disappeared.

For Iran, Syria represented a toehold in the Arab world, and a conduit through which to offer material and logistic support for Hezbollah in Lebanon. The Iranian-led resistance front, which included Syria, was also a defensive shield against efforts by the United States and Saudi Arabia to contain it, particularly after George W. Bush's 2002 "axis-of-evil" speech, and it was motivated by a need to develop a deterrence and retaliatory capability against an Israeli or US attack.[33] After the United States became mired in Iraq, and after the Arab Spring started, Iran saw not just threat but also opportunity to use the alliance to further its broader interests in the region.

Unipolarity and the Rise of Jihadi International Terrorism

Using Islam to target the perceived injustices of colonialism and other forms of international intervention has a precedent in the Middle East. In the Arab and Iranian experience mosques have long been the center of resistance against outsiders, going back to the late nineteenth century.

The Salafist-jihadi international terror organizations that have arisen over previous decades grew out of some of the same ideological traditions as more mainstream, non-jihadi groups like the Muslim Brotherhood.[34] But these new organizations used more violent means and sowed sectarian conflict as a way to challenge the identity boundaries of the region.[35]

In a way, al-Qaeda and ISIS can be thought of as another embodiment of a "resistance front" targeting the asymmetry of power in the region that favors the United States. The belief is that the United States should be targeted, as it is an oppressor of the Muslim masses that props up Arab authoritarian regimes in the Middle East. Some groups like ISIS also attack the colonial legacy, trying to erase the boundaries that were established after the First World War. While it is a different kind of resistance front than the Iran-Syria–Hezbollah axis, nonetheless these groups emerged to fight what they saw as the excesses of American unipolarity.

The Collapse of the Arab Regional Order

Countries located in "bad neighborhoods" … are increasingly likely to experience armed conflict themselves, compared to a country located in a region that is predominately at peace.[36]

The emergence of a resistance axis in the Middle East after the Cold War as a counterweight to US dominance created the contours of a new regional order. It wasn't an Arab-dominated regional order, as had been the case in the 1960s, but rather a broader system pitting US-backed Israel and Saudi Arabia against Iran, Syria, Islamic Jihad, Hamas, and Hezbollah, with Turkey at various points acting as a bridge between the two camps.[37]

Until the Arab Spring broke out, this emerging regional order could be described as a bloodless rivalry between two opposing camps. The rivalry consisted of activities like Saudi Arabia and Israel lobbying Washington during the George W. Bush administration to take a hardened stance against Iran. Iran responded by using Hezbollah to undermine Saudi interests in Lebanon and the broader region. But for the most part the competition between these two camps was a jostling for regional power, not the intense, destructive rivalry between two enemies it would later become. Eventually, the resistance front led by Iran and the US-backed Saudi Arabia would be on opposing sides of a regional battle as the civil wars in Syria, Yemen, and Iraq turned into broader and much bloodier proxy conflicts.

The Vertical Contagion Civil War Vortex

There are two ways to think about the relationship between the post–Cold War regional order and the civil wars in Syria, Iraq, Yemen, and Libya. One is that the regional powers, namely Iran, Saudi Arabia, and Turkey, jockeyed for position by backing different sides in the civil wars. While this dynamic was certainly at play, regional power involvement in the civil wars was (and still is) more complex than this one-dimensional proxy war view. In addition to the regional powers pushing themselves into the civil wars, they were pulled into these conflicts by local actors.[38]

Much of the work on how civil wars spread describe "horizontal contagion" where violence crosses state borders through rebel groups and terrorist organizations, refugees crossing state borders, and arms transfers.[39] The spread of mass protest movements across borders is also contagion of the horizontal type. The Arab Spring phenomenon, where protests in Tunisia had a contagion effect on Egypt, Yemen, Bahrain, and Libya, and the sequence of civil war outbreaks across the Arab world are examples of this phenomenon. And should the civil wars in Syria and Iraq spread to Jordan or Lebanon, this too would be a form of horizontal contagion.

But "vertical contagion" involves conflict spreading, not just laterally to neighboring fragile countries but also upward to stronger regional powers. When we talk about contagion in this light, we aren't suggesting that civil war violence itself spreads to the major regional powers, but rather that the conflicts change the strategic calculus of these powers vis-à-vis one another. Factors like the compression of time, security threats, the "fog of war," and "bad neighborhood" effects have drawn in all of the regional actors as part of a regional competition. But being drawn into civil wars isn't exactly cost free for the regional powers. The effects of the violence of the civil wars are in fact imported into the major regional powers in the form of refugees (to Turkey and Israel), the strengthening of hardliners (in Turkey, Iran, and Saudi Arabia), and terrorist attacks (Iran and Turkey).

But the most interesting feature of vertical contagion is that the individual civil wars in Yemen, Libya, Syria, and Iraq have spawned a conflict at the regional level that is connected to, but also distinct from, the individual country-level wars. The dynamic is that the individual country-level civil wars morph into a broader regional civil war among the major regional powers, where common interests in a stable and prosperous Middle East give way to a more dangerous competition for regional dominance.[40]

Let's unpack this notion of vertical contagion a bit further. As stated previously, a new regional order started to emerge at the end of the Cold War. It started out as a bipolar structure pitting a resistance front led by Iran against US-supported regional allies such as Saudi Arabia and Israel. Since that time, other regional actors, such as Turkey and the UAE, have asserted themselves into this new regional order.

Vertical contagion means that the country-level civil wars have turned this struggle for power within the emerging regional order from constructive competition between regional powers in the pre–Arab Spring era to a destructive competition in the Arab Spring and civil war era, something which has lethal implications for the entire Middle East.

We witnessed how regional competition could manifest itself militarily with the attacks on the Saudi Aramco facilities in Abqaiq, presumably by the Iran-sponsored Houthis in Yemen, in 2019. While this was most likely a response to the "maximum pressure" campaign against Iran by the Trump administration, it shows how Saudi and Iranian involvement in the civil war in Yemen could bring the two regional actors to blows and only inches from war. Unlike the country-level civil wars, where the battles are about who governs territory, the regional civil war is about which country asserts dominance over the region. In other words, the civil wars aren't just fueled by the regional order; they are in the process of shaping that order.

This analysis of vertical contagion, where the civil wars spread to engulf the region, has significance for the prospects of ending the current violence. It points to the reality that ending the country-level civil wars isn't possible without disentangling what Wallensteen and Sollenberg have described as a "regional conflict complex."[41] In other words, without some form of cooperation between the regional actors, there is little likelihood of any kind of sustainable peace in the countries now embroiled in civil war, and any reconstruction efforts will likely prove to be elusive and futile.

Another layer of this vertical contagion phenomenon is the rivalry in the region between the United States and Russia, global powers which were drawn into Syria, the former to fight ISIS in the eastern part of the country, and the latter to buttress the Assad government. While great power competition between the United States and Russia (as well as China) predated the war in Syria, civil war dynamics made that competition more intense and adversarial.

Unipolarity and the Country-Level Civil Wars

Here we will look individually at the countries now in civil war, focusing on the role global and regional powers played in each.

Iraq: The Original Sin

In many ways Iraq was the first shot across the bow of resistance against the rise of American power. As the Cold War was waning, Iraq's Saddam Hussein challenged the Western-backed political order in the region by invading Kuwait in the summer of 1990. Given that he had alienated almost all other regional and international powers in the lead up to the invasion, the Iraqi leader was isolated and this early attempt at resistance failed.

After the attacks on the US homeland on 9/11, Washington showed it had developed zero tolerance for Saddam Hussein's posture of resistance, and it invaded Iraq in 2003, toppling the dictator and his Ba'athist regime.

The connection between the invasion of Iraq in 2003 and the civil war between Sunni and Shi'i that emerged in 2006 is clear. Not only was the regime of Saddam Hussein toppled, but also the entire Iraqi state was collapsed. De-Ba'athification and the dismantlement of the military essentially removed the pillars that had held the country together, sending disenfranchised Sunnis into the opposition, and plunging the country into civil war. Had the United States worked to prevent disenfranchisement on the part of the Sunnis, the worst of the violence that broke out in Ramadi, Fallujah, and Mosul might have been forestalled.[42] While a different approach to the invasion and subsequent occupation of Iraq might have prevented this crisis, once unleashed the forces of disunity took on an inexorable life of their own.

Part of this momentum toward disunity involved a violent Sunni response, from which al-Qaeda benefited and ISIS emerged. While ISIS came late to the game in Iraq (and Syria), it certainly added to the complexity of the conflict, drawing in the United States and Turkey. Once ISIS turned back toward Iraq from Syria in 2014, capturing Mosul and large swaths of Anbar Province, the civil wars in Syria and Iraq became in many ways a single battlefield.

The vertical contagion phenomenon introduced in the previous section was evident in the civil war in Iraq as well. After the US invasion, Iran was drawn into Iraq, taking advantage of an opportunity to extend its influence into the Arab world. It would be drawn in again and deeper after the surge of ISIS in Iraq in 2014 which was threatening to overrun both Baghdad and Erbil. Turkey, too, was pulled into the civil war vortex, intervening to attack the Kurdistan Workers' Party (PKK) in the north of the country, and coddling the Kurds friendly to Ankara in the Kurdistan Regional Government. It was also to have the Shi'i-led government in Baghdad take account of Turkey's regional interests and ambitions. Saudi Arabia also recently reengaged with Iraq as part of its struggle to counterbalance Iran where it can. The results of Iraq's May 2018 and October 2021 elections, and efforts by Iraqi Prime Minister Mustafa al-Kadhimi to mediate talks between Iran and Saudi Arabia, indicate a desire on the part of Iraqis to remain as neutral as possible in these struggles.

Syria: Ground Zero

The rising star of the Shi'i majority in Iraq after the US invasion, and the disenfranchisement of the country's Sunni minority, wasn't lost on the Sunni majority in Syria, which since 1970 has been dominated by leaders from the Alawite Shi'i sect. And it also wasn't lost on majority Sunni Saudi Arabia and Turkey, which initially saw the Syrian Civil War as an opportunity to try to reclaim leadership of the Muslim world from Shi'i Iran.

The US invasion of Iraq in 2003 had a demonstration effect on Syria. Even though it was widely thought that Syria's inclusion in the resistance front against a US-dominated regional order made it immune to the fate that had beset many other Arab states, Syria showed that the civil wars hit Arab countries, irrespective of which side of the new regional order they were on.

The moment of American unipolarity in the Middle East had an impact on the Syrian civil war in other ways too. The departure of Syrian troops from Lebanon in 2005 under pressure from the United States put added stress on the Syrian system. Its corrupt intelligence service, which had been exploiting Lebanon for decades, now turned its sights on towns in rural areas of Syria, sparking discontent and eroding the base of support for the regime. It was the rural areas where the first demonstrations broke out in 2011 that would ultimately lead to civil war.

Moreover, a line can be drawn between the Syrian civil war in 2011 and the 2005 release of the Damascus Declaration, a joint statement by members of the Syrian opposition pushing for reform in Syria and disengagement from Lebanon.[43] Many of the signatories of the Damascus Declaration ended up forming the Syrian National Council in 2011, which became a focal point of the opposition in the early days of the war.[44]

In terms of vertical contagion, Syria has drawn in all major regional and international actors, including Turkey, Iran, Israel, and Saudi Arabia, as well as the United States and Russia. In many ways Syria has become ground zero for the regional civil war described earlier. While it appears the Syrian government and its Iranian patrons have the upper hand due to the disintegration of a viable opposition to the Assad regime, parts of the country, Idlib in particular, are likely to remain contested for some time. Turkey is still playing a role, but one of the biggest wildcards for Syria is the relationship between Iran and Israel. The fact that these two countries are battling on the back of the Syrian civil war underscores the degree of uncertainty about Syria's future.

Libya: Hermit State

Other Arab states had their own strategic imperatives and responses to US unipolarity. Libya, which had alienated most of its regional neighbors, found itself isolated at the end of the Cold War. This contrasts with Syria, which amplified its power through an alliance with Iran and Hezbollah. Tripoli's response was to essentially switch sides from the resistance front to the United States and relinquish all remnants of its fledgling nuclear program.

In Libya, the connection between the end of the Cold War and the change in the country's foreign policy is clear, though a direct link to the civil war is more difficult to establish. Muammar Gaddafi's agreement to relinquish his weapons of mass destruction after the US invasion of Iraq in 2003 certainly was connected to the rise of American "hard unipolarity." This, in turn, made possible the NATO military action that was taken against the regime nearly a decade later. But it was the broader themes of the Arab Spring and a desire for Gaddafi's removal that sparked the uprisings in Libya.

Yemen: Shotgun Wedding

In Yemen, the end of the Cold War coincided with the unification of north and south. While the Soviets began winding down their support for South Yemen (the People's Democratic Republic of Yemen, or PDRY), Salim al-Beidh from South Yemen and Ali Abdullah Saleh from the north (the Yemen Arab Republic) began discussing unification, which was consummated in 1990. According to Charles Dunbar, who was the US ambassador to Sana'a at the time, because of Moscow's changed attitudes toward Eastern Europe and elsewhere, the leadership in the south felt compelled to strike the best deal with the north possible.[45]

But it is important not to make too deterministic an argument about the causal link between the end of the Cold War and Yemen's unification in 1990. First, the unity ultimately collapsed into civil war in 1994. Second, local actors had considerable agency. Despite the Treaty of Friendship and Cooperation between the PDRY and the Soviet Union, Ali Nasser Mohammed, who presided over South Yemen from 1980 to 1986, showed an interest in rebuilding relations with the United States, which had been broken since the 1967 war. In other words, even before the end of the Cold War, South Yemen was becoming less ideologically rigid.

Today, Yemen is playing into the vertical contagion vortex through Saudi Arabia's belief that this conflict represents an existential battle between itself and Iran. The logic is that while Iran may have won the strategic advantage through the civil wars in Syria, Iraq, and Lebanon, that pattern needs to be broken on the Arabian Peninsula. Even though Saudi Arabia and the UAE may be shadowboxing against Iran in Yemen, the regional civil war is evident in this battle. The idea of a regional conflict complex identified previously also pertains here, where the regional and local civil wars are intertwined.

Afghanistan: Genesis

At the end of the Cold War, the United States, which had used Pakistan as a conduit for arming the anti-Soviet *mujahedeen* in Afghanistan, essentially downgraded its relationship with Islamabad and turned its sights away from Afghanistan. Steve Coll argues that former Afghan President Mohammad Najibullah, who served at the end of the Soviet occupation and until the Taliban took over in 1992, saw the handwriting on the wall that the Americans had moved on.

> He could see the future, but there was no one to listen. He had lost his Soviet patrons, and he was discredited and desperate ... and Washington had just announced a new policy: hands off.[46]

Moreover, by walking away from Pakistan, the United States enabled Islamabad to get more involved in Afghanistan, backing different factions of the mujahedeen. These different factions ultimately went to war against one another. By 1992, it was clear for all to see that Kabul would fall to the Taliban. And the series of events after the Taliban took over, including the attacks of 9/11 hatched in the Afghan mountains by al-Qaeda, drew the United States in to rout the terror organization and topple the Taliban, consequently plunging the country into a new phase of civil war. With the US withdrawal in 2021 and the return of the Taliban to control of the country, whether Afghanistan can avoid a new civil war is unclear at the time of this writing.

Multipolarity and Conflict in the Middle East

> *As is now clear, the end of the Cold War produced a unipolar moment, not a unipolar era.*[47]

In this chapter we have tried to demonstrate how the Middle East adjusted to the reality of American unipolarity, and to explore how this adds some context to our understanding of civil wars. We have also looked at how this unipolar moment led to a reordering of the region at the end of the Cold War, and how this set up a struggle for power that is playing out now in the civil wars in Yemen, Syria, Iraq, and Libya.

The historical period when the United States was ascendant in the region was but a fleeting moment. The international system and the Middle East have already made the transition from unipolarity to multipolarity.

This happened for a couple of reasons. First, the United States became mired in Afghanistan and Iraq, breaking the ideological certainty that Washington could fashion the Middle East in its own image. This led to at least a perception among regional actors that the United States was retrenching from the Middle East, a view that was reinforced by President Barack Obama's stated intention to "pivot to Asia," the lack of a US response to the attacks on Saudi oil facilities in 2019, and the messy US withdrawal from Afghanistan in 2021.[48]

Second, the entrance of Russia into Syria in 2015 turned what had been a unipolar moment into a new geopolitical reality of multipolarity, with Russia aligning itself with the resistance front of Iran, Syria, and Hezbollah, while maintaining civil relations with Israel. Moscow saw Syria as an opportunity to push back against a pattern of hapless US-led efforts to topple regimes, from Afghanistan and Iraq to Libya, correcting for the imbalance that had been created by the end of the Cold War.[49]

And when the United States withdrew in 2018 from the Joint Comprehensive Plan of Action (JCPOA), as the Iran nuclear deal is officially known, Russia assumed a capability previously monopolized by the United States, which is the power to convene. Even though Moscow has thrown its weight behind Iran and Syria, it has some sway with Israel and Saudi Arabia as well. Because of these relationships it has been working to manage tensions between Israel and Iran, Turkey and Iran, and possibly even Iran and Saudi Arabia, tensions that need to be mitigated if the civil wars besetting the Arab world are to be wound down. Whether Moscow can maintain its posture in the Middle East given the 2022 invasion of Ukraine is uncertain at this time.

In addition to Russia, this multipolar environment also includes other influencers in the Middle East. China and the European Union, while less involved in the region than the United States and Russia on security matters, do nevertheless play a role as well. Europe sees the Middle East as strategically important because of issues related to energy, refugees, and terrorism. And

China sees the Middle East as a critical part of its Belt and Road Initiative and a solution to its massive energy needs. India is also starting to play a role in the region, something that is likely to grow in the future.

Toward Ending the Civil Wars

How is this discussion about the role the global order has played in conflicts in the Middle East relevant for ending the civil wars today? The global powers will need to play a role in quieting these conflicts and moving toward the early phases of reconstruction. While there may be a reluctance by the United States, Europe, and Russia to commit to expensive reconstruction efforts in the Middle East when there are pressing priorities at home and a war in Ukraine, there has been a strategic shift in that the global powers can no longer take a cavalier attitude toward the security and economic issues of the Middle East. During the Cold War, the United States and Soviet Union could meddle in the region and even sow civil conflict, with little concern that these actions could redound to their own lack of security. Today that has changed, as the Middle East is both a recipient of and contributor to international politics. What starts in the Middle East quickly globalizes, meaning that instability in the region affects the security interests of all states in the international system, in the form of refugees, terrorism, and oil prices.

The fact that the security and economic interests of the great powers are linked to what happens in the Middle East should be a positive development, creating an alignment between what is best for the region and what is good for the global powers. It should open pathways for the settlement of conflicts and reconstruction, in contrast to the negative externalities of vertical contagion.[50]

There are two possible approaches to how international powers, like the United States, Russia, China, and the European Union, might involve themselves in trying to help end the civil wars. One is a model of directly intervening. This is the approach currently being pursued by Russia, which has tipped the scales in the Syrian civil war toward the government of Bashar al-Assad. The United States also has followed this approach in the northeast part of Syria, where it battled ISIS through its support for the Kurdish fighting force, the People's Defense Units (YPG).

But another model is to get involved indirectly, working with regional powers on behalf of settling the conflicts. Moscow has augmented its direct approach in Syria with this kind of indirect initiative, where it is worked with regional stakeholders, namely Iran and Turkey through the Astana process, to quiet the civil war and bring it to an end. It claimed it was trying to break the destructive vortex of violence by doubling down on the side of Bashar al-Assad, and publicly defended this tilt by touting the principles of state sovereignty, counterterrorism and stability.

Given that the regional powers, Iran, Saudi Arabia, Turkey, and Israel, hold significant sway over the civil wars in the Middle East, the model of working to forge compromise among them is sound and should be expanded beyond Syria. One approach for the future would be for the international community to work with the regional powers on some type of security architecture.[51] While it is unlikely to gain traction with civil wars still raging, such an arrangement could become viable after the violence ends to prevent a relapse, which occurs in about 50 percent of the countries that experience civil war. Such a regional architecture could also work to break the cycle of major regional players working counterproductively and at cross-purposes with each other in the countries in civil war.[52]

The Trump administration's approach contrasted with a regional cooperation model. Instead of working to quiet the region, Donald Trump took sides, using Israel and Saudi Arabia as cudgels against Iran. The problem with this kind of approach was that it stoked rather than quieted the civil wars in the region.[53] It gave Iran an incentive to spread its tentacles further into the Arab heartland to create deterrence against a possible U.S. or Israeli attack, and presumably to give it a retaliatory capability should such an attack occur. Another problem with the Trump approach was that its attempts to counter Iran led to a ratcheting up of the conflict among regional powers in the Middle East, giving neither Iran nor Saudi Arabia an incentive to move toward diplomacy.[54] In fact it was during the Trump era that we saw attacks on Saudi oil facilities and the growing tensions between Iran and Turkey.

Rather than pushing Iran to play a constructive regional role, this approach forced it into a threat-induced aggressive crouch, something that strengthened the hardliners in Tehran, culminating with the election of President Ebrahim Raisi in 2021. The danger now is that instead of Iran working cooperatively with other regional powers, its leadership will have an incentive to further sow regional discord.

The Biden administration seems to be taking a more balanced approach with the actors in the region, which while promising, could unravel if talks to return the United States to the nuclear deal (JCPOA) and Iran back into compliance fail to produce an agreement.

Conclusion

The end of the Cold War didn't just create a global imbalance, it led to a concomitant shift in the distribution of power in the Middle East, where US allies were emboldened, and erstwhile Soviet allies saw their domestic and foreign power challenged. Countries like Syria and Iraq had their political and economic legitimacy tested and were forced to face the consequences of losing their superpower benefactor. This fragility was one factor that made these already tenuous states vulnerable to domestic unrest, particularly given the momentum of the Arab Spring.

But another way in which this period contributed to the civil wars was in the alliances that formed in response to a moment of American unipolarity. The rebalancing that took place in the region, with the emergence of a resistance front consisting of Iran, Syria, Hezbollah, and even terrorist organizations like al-Qaeda and ISIS, against a US-dominated political order, changed the balance of power in the region and created opposing camps, which ultimately competed in and perpetuated the Arab civil wars. And as the wars at the country level unfolded, conflict spread to the regional level increasing tensions between Saudi Arabia, Iran, Turkey, and Israel.[55]

The period of American unipolarity is long over, and we are now in an era of multipolarity. The question going forward will be can Russia and the United States, along with Europe and China, coalesce to help the regional actors bring the civil wars to an end and help the region transition from chaos to stability. While the Trump administration played a divisive role in this regard, all eyes will be on whether the Biden administration can and will send the proper signals to the regional powers that Washington, despite the withdrawal from Afghanistan, can play a constructive role to help create a better future for this most tumultuous of regions.

Notes

1   T. David Mason, Sara McLaughlin Mitchell, and Alyssa K. Prorok, "What Do We Know about Civil Wars? Introduction and Overview," in *What Do We Know about Civil Wars?* ed. T. David Mason and Sara McLaughlin

Mitchell (New York: Rowman & Littlefield, 2016), Kindle Version Location 313.

2 Samir Amin takes the Latin American-originated "dependencia" or dependence theory of international political-economy and applies it to the Arab world in *Les Effets Structurels De L'intégration Internationale Des Économies Précapitalistes. Une Étude Théorique Du Mécanisme Qui a Engendré Les Économies Dites Sous Développées* (Paris: Université de Paris, 1957), and in *The Law of Value and Historical Materialism* (London: Harvester, 1977).

3 For an example of this logic, see Robin Wright, "How the Curse of Sykes-Picot Still Haunts the Middle East," *New Yorker*, April 30, 2016.

4 Erika Forsberg, "Transnational Dimensions of Civil Wars: Clustering, Contagion, and Connectedness," in *What Do We Know about Civil Wars?* ed. T. David Mason and Sara McLaughlin Mitchell (New York: Rowman & Littlefield, 2016), Kindle Version location 1913. She claims that conflict issues become complex, drawing in a number of external actors.

5 Malcolm H. Kerr, *The Arab Cold War: Gamal 'Abd al-Nasir and His Rivals, 1958–1970*, 3rd ed. (Oxford: Oxford University Press, 1971).

6 See Efraim Karsh, "Influence through Arms Supplies: The Soviet Experience in the Middle East," *Conflict Quarterly* (1986): 45–54.

7 See Yevgeny Primakov, *Russia and the Arabs: Behind the Scenes in the Middle East from the Cold War to the Present* (New York: Basic Books, 2009), 10. He argues that there was a significant deviation between Soviet-style communism and Nasser's Arab socialism: where the former was built on class, the latter was not. But is hard to deny the ideological ripple effect of the Russian revolution and the Soviet Union on socialist movements, from Nasser's Arab nationalism to the Syrian and Iraq Ba'ath parties.

8 Raymond Hinnebusch, "Syria: From Authoritarian Upgrading to Revolution?" *International Affairs* 88, no. 1 (2012): 95–113.

9 John F. Devlin, *Syria: Modern State in an Ancient Land* (Boulder: Westview Press, 1983), 81–2.

10 Hinnebusch, "Syria."

11 Stathis N. Kalyvas and Laia Balcells, "International System and Technologies of Rebellion: How the End of the Cold War Shaped Internal Conflict," *American Political Science Review* 104, no. 3 (2010): 416.

12 Itamar Rabinovich, *The War for Lebanon: 1970–1985*, revised edition (Ithaca: Cornell University Press, 1985), 44–59.

13 See Michael C. Hudson, *Arab Politics: The Search for Legitimacy* (New Haven: Yale University Press, 1977) for the most in-depth analysis of the legitimacy problems that have plagued Arab countries since independence.

14 See Fred H. Lawson, "Syria's Intervention in the Lebanese Civil War, 1976: A Domestic Conflict Explanation," in *International Organization* 38, no. 3 (Summer 1984): 451–80 and Itamar Rabinovich, *The War for Lebanon*

for Syria's motivation for entering the Lebanese civil war. Also, Guy Laron, *The Six Day War: The Breaking of the Middle East* (New Haven: Yale University Press, 2017).

15 For the story about how the Soviets acted as a spoiler in Lebanon, see Elie A. Salem, *Violence and Diplomacy in Lebanon* (London: I.B. Tauris, 1995), who was foreign minister in Lebanon from 1982 to 1984.

16 Asher Orkaby, *Beyond the Arab Cold War: The International History of the Yemen Civil War, 1962–68* (Oxford: Oxford University Press, 2017), 1.

17 William Harris, *Quicksilver War: Syria, Iraq and the Spiral of Conflict* (New York: Oxford University Press, 2018), Kindle Location 271.

18 David Armitage, *Civil Wars: A History of Ideas* (New York: Alfred A. Knopf, 2017).

19 Hinnebusch, "Syria," 95–113.

20 Orkaby, *Beyond the Arab Cold War*, 20–1.

21 Joseph K. Young, "Antecedents of Civil War Onset: Greed, Grievance, and State Repression," in *What Do We Know about Civil Wars?* ed. T. David Mason and Sara McLaughlin Mitchell (New York: Rowman & Littlefield, 2016), Kindle Version Location 799.

22 Stathis N. Kalyvas and Laia Balcells, "International System and Technologies of Rebellion: How the End of the Cold War Shaped Internal Conflict," *American Political Science Review* 104, no. 3 (2010): 421.

23 Hinnebusch, "Syria," 97.

24 I want to thank Abdallah Dardari, former deputy prime minister of Syria from 2005 to 2011, who provided insights about the attempts to retire the Soviet-era debt, as well as Sami Moubayed, a Damascus-based academic who has written extensively on the political-economy of Syria.

25 Hinnebusch, "Syria," 98.

26 I want to thank Robert Ford, US ambassador to Syria from 2010 to 2014 (and a contributor to this book), for his insights about the refugees from the drought, who set up shantytowns outside Damascus and became a factor in the uprisings of 2011.

27 David Wallsh, "Syrian Alliance Strategy in the Post-Cold-War Era: The Impact of Unipolarity," *Fletcher Forum of World Affairs* 37, no. 2 (2013): 108.

28 Roger E. Kanet, "The Superpower Quest for Empire: The Cold War and Soviet Support for Wars of National Liberation," *Cold War History* 6, no. 3 (2006): 343; Graham E. Fuller, "Moscow and the Gulf War," *Foreign Affairs* (1991): 55–76.

29 Stathis N. Kalyvas and Laia Balcells, "International System and Technologies of Rebellion: How the End of the Cold War Shaped Internal Conflict," *American Political Science Review* 104, no. 3 (2010): 427.

30 Hans J. Morganthau, *Politics Among Nations: The Struggle for Power and Peace* (New York: McGraw Hill, 1993).

31 I want to thank former US Ambassador to Syria Robert Ford for his invaluable insights into how Syria changed its foreign policy calculus after

2005 and details on how Syria secreted Iraqi insurgents across the border to Iraq.

32 For a discussion of this partnership and how it was forged, see Jubin M. Goodarzi, *Syria and Iran: Diplomatic Alliance and Power Politics in the Middle East* (London: I.B. Tauris, 2009), 11–58.

33 Goodarzi, *Syria and Iran*, 292.

34 See Richard P. Mitchell, *The Society of Muslim Brothers* (Oxford: Oxford University Press, 1993) for an excellent analysis of the evolution of the Brotherhood.

35 Michael W. S. Ryan, *Decoding Al-Qaeda's Strategy: The Deep Battle against America* (New York: Columbia University Press, 2013), Chapter 1.

36 Forsberg, "Transnational Dimensions of Civil Wars," Kindle Location 1760.

37 Goodarzi, *Syria and Iran*, Chapter 4.

38 Ross Harrison, "Regionalism in the Middle East," *German Journal for Politics, Economics, and Culture of the Middle East* 59 (2018): 10–11.

39 Forsberg, "Transnational Dimensions of Civil Wars," Kindle Location 1805.

40 For a portrayal of this "regional war," see Marc Lynch, *The New Arab Wars: Uprisings and Anarchy in the Middle East* (New York: Public Affairs, 2017).

41 Forsberg, "Transnational Dimensions of Civil Wars," Kindle Location 1901. She has described and analyzed this "regional conflict complex," which she draws from Peter Wallenstein and Margareta Sollenberg, "Armed Conflict and Regional Conflict Complexes: 1989–97," *Journal of Peace Research* 35, no. 5 (1998): 621–34.

42 Discussion with Robert Ford, former US ambassador to Syria, and also Political Counselor to the US Embassy, Baghdad, Iraq, 2004–6.

43 Hinnebusch, "Syria," 100.

44 Carnegie Middle East Center, "The Damascus Declaration," *Diwan*, March 1, 2012.

45 Charles Dunbar, "The Unification of Yemen: Process, Politics, and Prospects," *Middle East Journal* 46, no. 3 (1992): 463.

46 Steve Coll, *Ghost Wars: The Secret History of the CIA, Afghanistan, and Bin Laden, from the Soviet Invasion to September 10th, 2001* (New York: Penguin Books, 2005), Chapter 12.

47 Graham Allison, "The Myth of the Liberal Order: From Historical Accident to Conventional Wisdom," *Foreign Affairs*, July/August 2018.

48 Stephen P. Cohen and Robert Ward, "Asia Pivot: Obama's Ticket Out of the Middle East?" *Brookings*, August 21, 2013.

49 Stathis N. Kalyvas and Laia Balcells, "International System and Technologies of Rebellion: How the End of the Cold War Shaped Internal Conflict," *American Political Science Review* 104, no. 3 (2010): 415–29.

50 Forsberg, "Transnational Dimensions of Civil Wars," Kindle Location 2040.

51 See Ross Harrison, "Toward a Regional Framework for the Middle East: Takeaways from other Regions," in *From Chaos to Cooperation: Towards Regional Order in the Middle East*, ed. Ross Harrison and Paul Salem (Washington, DC: Middle East Institute, 2017).

52 Forsberg, "Transnational Dimensions of Civil Wars."
53 Ibid.
54 Hal Brands, *The Limits of Offshore Balancing* (Pennsylvania, PA: Strategic Studies Institute, US Army War College, September 2015).
55 Forsberg, "Transnational Dimensions of Civil Wars."

4 YEMEN

The Sixty-Year War

Gerald M. Feierstein

Introduction

Yemen's political transition, which began with much hope and optimism in 2011, collapsed by the fall of 2014 when Houthi insurgents occupied Sana'a, the capital, with the support of forces loyal to former President Ali Abdullah Saleh. Intervention by a Saudi-led coalition of primarily Gulf Cooperation Council (GCC) member states in March 2015 turned the civil conflict into a broader war, attracting regional and international attention, although at its core this remained a civil war, not a proxy fight. As the conflict enters its eighth year, Yemen has become more fractured. Persistent efforts by the United Nations, now with renewed support from the US administration of Joe Biden, have been unsuccessful in brokering a sustained return to negotiations and a resumption of the political process. Despite the international community's reiterated commitment to support the sovereignty, unity, and territorial integrity of Yemen, the future of the country itself is in doubt.

Most analyses of the Yemen conflict since 2014–15 have focused on the issues and circumstances that led to the current round of fighting in isolation from the larger problems that have long confronted Yemen. But the current conflict is more accurately seen as a continuation of over sixty years of failed state formation leading to a cycle of violence, coups, assassinations, and open warfare. The shotgun unification of North and South Yemen in 1990 only served to add a new layer of complexity to the already fraught political, social, and economic environment. If this perspective is correct, a resolution of the current conflict will only be a prelude to the next outbreak of violence. To avoid that outcome, Yemenis not only must agree on steps needed to build sustainable solutions to the country's problems but must also demand that their leaders implement them.

Historic Antecedents

Yemen bears all the hallmarks of a failed state as described by Daron Acemoglu and James Robinson in their landmark book, *Why Nations Fail*.[1] The country suffers from an extractive political and economic system. By definition, such systems are characterized by the concentration of power in the hands of a narrow elite and place few constraints on its exercise of power. As a general principle, Acemoglu and Robinson assert, extractive systems like Yemen's are vulnerable to violence, anarchy, and political upheaval and are unlikely to achieve growth or make major changes toward more inclusive institutions successfully.

But the origins of the current conflict in Yemen go beyond even the consequences of the rentier state described by Acemoglu and Robinson. In fact, the political crisis that emerged in mid-2014 and metastasized into the current war is only the latest eruption in a cycle of violence that has shaken Yemen repeatedly for nearly sixty years. Nor is it unique among these conflicts in the level of violence or its duration.[2] There is no ten-year period in Yemen's history since the 1960s that has not witnessed violent conflict, coups, or civil insurrection. Beginning with the 1962 uprising against the Zaydi Shi'a theocracy, or Imamate, Yemenis have yet to find a means to build institutions of state and society that can address successfully the grievances of political disenfranchisement, economic marginalization, and the alienation of populations disadvantaged by governing institutions and ethnic and sectarian discrimination. The unification of North and South Yemen in 1990 only added an extra layer of complexity to the country's problems.

The failure to build the institutional structures of a modern, cohesive state, however, does not reflect an inability to understand the nature of the problems or devise reasonable solutions. Yemenis have come together repeatedly in efforts to resolve their recurring challenges.

Moreover, the efforts to find solutions have generally advocated similar reforms: decentralization and enhanced local autonomy, equal geographic representation in national government, federalism, and an equitable distribution of the country's natural resources. The most comprehensive effort followed the Arab Spring uprising against President Saleh's government in 2011. For over a year, more than five hundred delegates labored to produce proposals to resolve persistent regional divisions within Yemen and the grievances of the Zaydi majority population of the northwestern highlands. But, beyond that, the delegates to the most representative body of Yemenis ever assembled provided recommendations on a broad array of critical issues facing the country, including economics, governance, and the structure of military and security forces.

The failure of state formation in Yemen, then, is not a result of the inability of Yemenis to understand the challenges, devise solutions, or create a road map for a unified state at peace with itself. The failure, instead, rests with the inability or unwillingness of Yemeni elites to implement the agreements reached. In at least two instances, in 1994 and in 2014, signed agreements were followed within weeks by a new outbreak of conflict.

Yemen will not succeed in breaking this decades-long cycle of violence until there is a national consensus on the need to put in place the structures that enable implementation of agreed reforms: capable local governing institutions, equal access to basic social services including health and education, and an end to the extractive political and economic systems that allowed a small, largely northern tribal elite to dominate the country, exploit its resources for their own narrow interests, and block access to the political and economic arena to the vast majority of Yemeni citizens.

A Tale of Failed Transitions, 1962–90

Rebellions in the 1960s against theocratic rule in the north and British occupation in the south ushered in decades of political and economic turmoil throughout Yemen. By the end of the twentieth century, the modern Yemeni state emerged but was unsuccessful in addressing the failure of state formation that has plagued Yemen since the revolt against the Imamate.

The Imamate Defeated: Triumph of Sheikhs

Northern Yemen was ruled for a millennium by a theocracy, the Imamate, which drew its social and political support from the Zaydi Shi'a tribes of the northwestern highlands. But the Imamate's economic survival rested on the exploitation of the relatively richer, predominantly Shafi'i Sunni midlands, including Taiz, Ibb, al-Baida, and the Red Sea coastal region, or Tihama.

By the early 1960s, an Arab nationalist movement, the self-styled "Free Yemenis," emerged in the midlands region and, in 1962, launched a full-scale rebellion against the Imamate, with the support of Egypt under President Gamal Abdel Nasser. That struggle persisted until the end of the decade, when the republican forces triumphed.[3] The demise of the Imamate and rise of the republic did not substantially change the political balance in the country, however, as the traditional northern highlands tribal leaders retained positions of power and influence in the new political order.

But, in challenging the rule by the *sadah* or *sayyids*, a Shi'a religious leadership that claimed its legitimacy based on its direct descent from the Prophet Muhammad, the Free Yemenis developed an Arab nationalist counter-narrative that would have long-term implications for Yemen's internal cohesion. While it made political sense to paper over sectarian differences between Zaydi Shi'a and Shafi'i Sunni populations, the Free Yemenis introduced a new concept: "Real" Yemenis were the descendants of the *Qahtanis*—southern Arabian tribes that were the original inhabitants of Yemen. By contrast, they asserted that the sayyids ruling Yemen were *Adnanis*—descendants of northern tribes that immigrated to southern Arabia following the arrival of Islam and became the rulers of Yemen. Over the course of the eight-year rebellion against the Imamate, this distinction (which Stephen Day notes is likely mythical[4]) became an important factor in building the broad, pro-republican consensus that won the war and established the Yemen Arab Republic (YAR).

The midlands population prospered in the first decade of republican rule. The Shafi'i business community developed local cooperative organizations and began managing its own affairs. Keeping their tax revenue available for local improvements, the region's political leaders invested in the infrastructure that allowed the economy to grow. By the end of the civil war and the reintegration of the highland elites into the national consensus, Stephen Day writes, an informal balance of power emerged between highland elites and the lowlands merchant class. "In effect," Day notes, "informal power-sharing allowed highland elites to maintain political hegemony, while business elites from the western midland and coastal regions ran the economy."[5] This extended to the government as well, with an informal power-sharing arrangement that the president of the republic would represent the highland elites while the prime minister would be a midlands figure.[6]

When Ali Abdullah Saleh became president in 1978 following the assassination of Ahmad al-Ghashmi, the rough balance between highlands and lowlands interests began to unravel. Saleh reintroduced the exploitative taxation system not seen since the rule of the Imamate. Citizens in the midlands region were once again taxed at a rate approximately double that paid by the highlands population.[7] At the same time, Saleh's policies favored the rise of highland tribal sheikhs, challenging the formerly dominant sayyids and their allies. The sheikhs, especially Abdullah al-Ahmar, the paramount sheikh of the Hashid tribal confederation, assumed leading roles in the republic's political circles. Building on their political dominance, the sheikhs, especially those of the Hashid and Bakil tribal confederations, next entered into competition with the traditional midlands merchant class for economic control. Under Saleh, therefore, northwestern highlands tribal sheikhs were the principal beneficiaries of the extractive political and economic system that has plagued Yemen's development ever since. The discovery of oil in Marib Governorate in 1984 provided new opportunities for corrupt exploitation by the highlands elites and became a new source of grievance for the marginalized populations of the north and the midlands.

A Unity Accord in 1990 Leads Quickly to Disunity

North and South Yemen enjoyed a roller-coaster relationship from independence until their unity agreement in 1990. At various times, both Sana'a and Aden promoted unification as interest waxed and waned depending on the personalities of the leaders in the two states. The charter of the Yemeni Socialist Party (YSP), the ruling party in South Yemen after its formation in 1978, for instance, employs Marxist terminology, declaring that the revolutionary struggle in Yemen is "dialectically correlated in its unity"[8] to argue that unity between the north and south is an essential component of Yemen's evolution. But the leaders of the People's Democratic Republic of Yemen (PDRY) were responsible for the June 1978 assassination of YAR President al-Ghashmi, and the two states fought a brief border war between January and March 1979. Despite the persistent tensions, the two sides managed to develop a dialogue. PDRY President Ali Nasser Mohammed visited Sana'a in November 1981 and, after the two presidents met in Kuwait, Saleh traveled to Aden.

The discovery of oil in the border regions between the two states provided both sides with a financial incentive to strengthen their relations. In April 1990, Saleh and Ali Salem al-Beidh, secretary general of the YSP, signed a unity agreement to merge the PDRY and YAR into a new, single entity, the Republic of Yemen (RoY). Aside from organizing the basic elements of a new governing structure, the two-page deal was remarkably short on detail. Under the terms of the agreement, over the course of a thirty-month interim period a five-member Presidential Council would draft a constitution. Until then, the council would rule by decree.

In addition to the financial motivation from the discovery of oil, two other factors drove the south's agreement to the "shotgun marriage" with the north in 1990. First, the collapse of the former Soviet Union deprived the PDRY of its most significant political and economic partner. Second, the brutal 1986 intra-YSP conflict significantly weakened the PDRY government.[9]

Populations on both sides of the border greeted the announcement of unity with enthusiasm. But southern satisfaction with the new RoY quickly waned. Southern political leaders, who initially enjoyed a 50:50 power-sharing arrangement with the much more populous north based on the unity agreement, had envisioned that they would dominate the political structure of the newly unified state. In particular, they expected to do well in parliamentary elections scheduled for 1992 (eventually conducted in 1993), and perhaps win a majority of seats based on their anticipated support among northern voters. But they were disappointed when they finished a poor third after Saleh's General People's Congress (GPC) and the newly former northern Islamist party, Islah. Rather than dominating the new political arrangement, the southerners saw their political influence rapidly dissipating.

Economically, conditions in the PDRY were far poorer than in the north at the time of unification, a product not only of state control of the economy but also because of the declining revenue stream from the Aden port. The PDRY leadership had counted on the port as the main economic engine that would finance southern development programs, but the closure of the Suez Canal from 1967 to 1975 forced international shipping to develop new trade routes and left Aden uncompetitive. Nevertheless, PDRY citizens did enjoy benefits unmatched in the north, including subsidized basic commodities as well as guaranteed employment in state enterprises. The south also compared well to the north on provision of basic services, particularly in health care and education.[10] Those advantages began to erode as the north introduced its crony capitalist economic system and the highland tribal elites started to extend their economic domination to the south.

Thus, by the end of 1993, frustrated southerners were openly rejecting unity and advocating a return to an independent state. After a last attempt at a political resolution to the growing north–south confrontation failed (see below for a discussion of the negotiations that produced the "Document of Pledge and Accord"), southern leaders declared independence and the north launched military operations to retake the south.

The brief civil war in 1994 that followed the collapse of political negotiations failed to resolve the basic issues that led to the conflict. Although Saleh maintained power-sharing arrangements with the south, appointing Abed Rabbo Mansour Hadi as vice president in place of the exiled Ali Salim al-Beidh, Stephen Day observes that Saleh was "mainly interested in the appearance of power sharing, not genuine representation of southern interests in government."[11] The number of southerners in the Yemen cabinet dropped significantly as Saleh formed a coalition government with the Islah party and appointed Abdul Aziz Abdul Ghani, an experienced, midlands GPC technocrat, as prime minister.

Those same core issues continue to plague north–south relations until the present time and form the basis of southern challenges not only to the Hadi government but more broadly to the idea of Yemeni unity. The social and economic consequences of the civil conflict were harsh for southern citizens. The Saleh government accelerated the expansion of the north's rentier political and economic system in the south. Aden itself was ransacked by victorious highland tribes, southern civil servants and military personnel were dismissed, and southerners charged that northerners plundered the south's energy, mineral, and fish resources. In sum, notes April Longley Alley, "two profoundly different narratives took shape" about the outcome of the conflict. "Under one version, the war laid to rest the notion of separation and solidified national unity. According to the other, the war laid to rest the notion of unity and ushered in a period of northern occupation of the South."[12]

By the middle of the following decade, southern anger over their treatment at northern hands began to boil over. The outcome of the civil war, in particular the forced retirement of southern civilian and military officials, contributed to the rise of an organized opposition movement in the south.[13] Beginning in a series of peaceful protests in 2006, the movement, initially cast as a "local association for military retirees," evolved into a large-scale, generally peaceful but occasionally violent protest movement, *al-Hirak*. Pursuing his well-worn strategy of divide and conquer ("dancing on the heads of snakes"), Saleh struggled to dilute the southern movement, offering some concessions to military retirees and advocating resolution of land disputes while continuing efforts to marginalize or eliminate political opposition.

The government's inability to defeat the Houthis, an armed Zaydi insurgency, in the northwest (see below) encouraged the al-Hirak movement to intensify its own campaign, and it clashed more aggressively with government forces. The demands of the al-Hirak movement focused on access to government jobs and benefits and more equitable resource sharing, especially in the energy sector, according to April Longley Alley. She cites the late mayor of Sana'a and advocate of decentralization, Abdul Qadir al-Hilal, stating "even within a single governorate, one district will complain of marginalization or discrimination when compared to another. However, in the south, this feeling of marginalization has taken on a political dimension because of the absence of political opportunities and because it used to be an independent state."[14] By the time of the Arab Spring in 2011, southern support for al-Hirak and new calls for separation from the north were again on the rise.[15]

Populism in the North Reflected in Six Sa'dah Wars

Many of the unresolved issues from the republican revolt of the 1960s and its aftermath, particularly in the years of Saleh's rule, helped to trigger the Houthi rebellion in six Sa'dah wars between June 2004 and February 2010. Like the post-unity south, northern Zaydi populations grew increasingly militant over the growth of extractive political and economic systems during the Saleh era and the failure of republican Yemen to provide equitable sharing of resources. Zaydi revivalism began to grow as a counter to this marginalization in the 1980s, predating the rise of the Houthi movement. Marieke Brandt noted in her comprehensive history of the Houthi movement that "the economic and political marginalization of the Sa'dah region, the uneven distribution of economic resources and political participation, and the religious discrimination against its Zaydi population provided fertile soil in which the Houthi movement could take root and blossom."[16] Indeed, the scion of the Houthi clan, Badr al-Din al-Houthi, and his son Husayn, enjoyed strong reputations in Sa'dah as much for their deep commitment to community service as for their position as sayyids. It was that role in the community that made them natural leaders of the "Believing Youth" movement in the 1990s. By the early 2000s, Husayn had developed a broad platform articulated in a series of lectures encompassing anti-Americanism, anti-Zionism, Zaydi revivalism, and intense criticism of the Saleh regime for its economic neglect and underdevelopment of the north.

Brandt notes that, despite Husayn al-Houthi's complaint that the government was supporting Sunni and Salafist communities at the expense of the Zaydis, his appeal was not restricted to the Zaydi community, but was pan-Islamic in content.[17] Thus, the image of the al-Houthi family as the face of Zaydi Shi'ism confronting the threat of "Sunnization" in the Zaydi heartland, thereby embodying sectarian conflict, is at best an incomplete narrative of the Houthi movement even if it is not an entirely inaccurate one. "In the local context," Brandt writes, "the Zaydi revival was far more than a sectarian movement: Under Husayn's direction, it also embraced powerful social-revolutionary and political components."[18]

Nevertheless, the Saleh regime focused its attack on the Houthi rebellion by exploiting the Houthis' support for the reintroduction of several predominantly Shi'a religious observances, including Ashura, maintaining that the Houthis were not only advocates of Zaydi Shi'ism but in fact represented the quest for a return of the Imamate and the introduction of Iranian style Twelver Shi'ism.

This angle of attack on the Houthis reopened a second, unresolved wound from the anti-Imamate rebellion of the 1960s. As noted previously, pro-republican forces in the 1960s created a narrative of Yemen's earliest history that distinguished between so-called real Yemenis—the Qahtani or original South Yemen tribes—versus later arrivals—the Adnani tribes from northern Arabia and especially the non-tribal sayyids, the "strangers in the house"[19] who established themselves in the northwestern highlands as religious scholars and tribal mediators. The distinction marginalized the sayyids, traditional rulers of Yemen's Imamate theocracy. Within the Zaydi population, where the Houthis did not enjoy universal support, criticism of their movement often reflected this anti-sayyid, Qahtani viewpoint that interpreted the Houthi movement as anti-democratic and backward looking.

The principal beneficiaries of this marginalization of the sayyids were the tribal sheikhs of the northwestern highlands and especially the newly minted "revolution sheikhs"[20] who had fought on behalf of republican forces in the eight-year civil conflict and profited from the rise of Yemen's rentier political and economic system. "The sheikhs benefited disproportionately from the republican system," Brandt notes, "at [the] local level, in many respects they were the republic."[21] But the elevation of the sheikhs was not synonymous with the rise of the tribes. Once again, Brandt notes that "the politics of patronage was a double-edged sword: Rather than 'nurturing' the tribal system governmental patronage has driven a wedge between some influential sheikhs and their tribal home constituencies and has generated discontent and alienation among many ordinary tribal members."[22] In the conflict between sheikhs and sayyids, many of the tribes were pulled toward the Houthi movement by the failure of the sheikhs to use their new-found power and influence in the republican government to support the tribes.

Despite its enormous military advantage, Sana'a was unable to defeat the Houthi rebellion, and the fighting divided the northern population. "Instead of putting down the rebellion," Brandt writes,

the government's military campaigns triggered destructive cycles of violence and counter-violence in Sa'dah's tribal environment, which, step-by-step, engulfed Yemen's North. During these battles, Sa'dah's citizenry became increasingly polarized along government-Houthi lines. From the second war, it became evident that a significant number of people joining the Houthis' ranks were no longer religiously or ideologically motivated but were drawn into the conflict for other reasons. (Brandt 2017, p. 349)

By the outbreak of the Arab Spring in February 2011, the Houthis had built the most effective military force in the country and had taken control of all of Sa'dah Governorate as well as large portions of neighboring Amran and al-Jawf. Although the so-called North of the North was momentarily at peace, the popular anger and frustration directed toward the Saleh government had by no means decreased.

The Arab Spring and a New Push for National Unity

By the end of 2010 and the beginning of 2011, President Saleh was basking in a vision of overwhelming political mastery. He portrayed his successful hosting of the GCC Cup soccer tournament in Aden in December 2010, as evidence that his control of the south was uncontested. In the far north, Saleh had convinced himself that he had mastered the Houthi threat and that the lull in fighting would be sustained. His domination of the National Assembly allowed him to push through legislation guaranteeing that he and his son Ahmed Ali would keep their grip on power for the foreseeable future. He ignored earlier commitments to the political opposition that he would negotiate new rules for planned parliamentary elections deferred from 2009 and rescheduled for mid-2011.

But Saleh's sense of confidence proved misplaced. When the streets erupted in February 2011, the government was caught by surprise. Inspired by youth revolutions in Tunisia and Egypt, young, urbanized Yemenis took to the streets to demand that Saleh step down. The protesters focused not only on the corruption and cronyism of the Saleh government but also on the political, economic, and social stagnation that beset the country and threatened to deprive young people, including educated youth, of any prospect for a secure future.

Marginalized populations, including southerners, the Houthis, tribal youth, and the Shafi'i population in the midlands, joined in the protest demonstrations and demanded, beyond Saleh's ouster, that the transition seek to address the underlying conditions that had prevented Yemen's development as a modern state. An International Crisis Group analysis suggested that the popular protests promoted cooperation between northern and southern protesters and "broke through the barriers of fear."[23]

Meanwhile, Saleh's too clever by half political maneuvering had deeply angered the opposition. General Ali Mohsen, Saleh's heir apparent for decades until he promoted his son, Ahmed Ali, as his successor, no longer stood firmly behind his old comrade-in-arms. Thus, Saleh was left without friends or negotiating partners as he scrambled to parry the street demonstrations and quell the uprising. Running out of options, he tabled a proposal to step down, triggering a negotiating process that would stretch out over many months, punctuated by sporadic street battles in Sana'a and other major cities as well as an assassination attempt that spared Saleh (albeit seriously wounding him) but killed and injured a number of his senior advisors, including Prime Minister Abdul Aziz Abdul Ghani.

In desperation, Saleh turned to the international community to help him retain his grip on power. Having frozen cooperation with the United States on counterterrorism initiatives earlier in 2010, Saleh suddenly expressed a new willingness to work closely with US counterparts in an effort to garner continued support. He similarly sought help from the GCC states, the other P-5 members of the UN Security Council, and even from the African Union. In response, the diplomatic corps in Sana'a, particularly embassies of the Security Council P-5, the GCC, and the EU representative, joined together in a coordinated effort to help mediate among the Yemeni parties.[24] The UN subsequently joined the effort, appointing a special envoy, Jamal Benomar.

Saleh had initially agreed to step down but then maneuvered to reverse his commitment to leave office. Saudi King Abdullah eventually forced Saleh's hand when the Saudis became frustrated with his constant twisting (as well as his personal attacks on GCC Secretary-General Abdul Latif al-Zayani, who the Saudis had designated to help negotiate the transition agreement). When King Abdullah called Saleh and told him that his time was up, Saleh was left with little choice but to comply. The signing ceremony took place in Riyadh in November.

Yemenis saw the protest movement and the end of the Saleh regime as a new opportunity to resolve the deeper political and economic crisis confronting the country. Not only the political opposition but also Saleh's own GPC supported the demand for a broad-based initiative to address Yemen's deep-seated problems. Thus, among its other elements, the transition document, the GCC Initiative and Implementing Mechanism, included a requirement to conduct within its two-year timeframe a National Dialogue Conference (NDC) to address the full range of political, economic, and social problems, including specifically southern and Houthi grievances. Launched in 2013, the NDC quickly organized itself into working groups and began addressing a broad agenda of issues. (See below for a discussion of the NDC recommendations.)

But despite the serious negotiations taking place within the NDC, the external environment was increasingly fraught. The government, evenly divided between Saleh's GPC and the opposition Joint Meeting Parties (JMP), proved incapable of fulfilling its responsibilities, reassuring Yemenis that the political transition could succeed, or establishing control of the government and the military and security forces. As the transitional government slid more deeply into dysfunction, the economic and security conditions around the country, including Sana'a, steadily deteriorated.

Forces in opposition to the GCC Initiative, including Saleh loyalists (who were determined to regain power), the Houthis (who simultaneously participated in the process and impeded its work), and determined southern secessionists, undertook concerted efforts to undermine popular confidence in the transition. Saboteurs attacked critical infrastructure, especially electrical generation facilities in Marib, leaving the capital without power for days or weeks at a time. Roads were blocked and water supplies were cut off. Southerners remained deeply divided about the benefit of participating in the transition process versus boycotting it and demanding independence. The Houthis reignited their conflict with Salafists in the north.[25]

The Interregnum Ends and the Seventh Sa'dah War Begins

Against this backdrop, implementation of the political transition agreement through the summer of 2014 increasingly took a back seat to the rising tensions. Most concerning, the Houthis resumed their siege of the Salafist Dar al-Hadith madrassa in the town of Dammaj, forcing its evacuation and breaking a two-year-old cease-fire. Emboldened by their success at Dammaj, the Houthis continued their advance into Amran Governorate, defeating forces loyal to archenemies Ali Mohsen and the Hashid tribal federation. Saleh, despite his earlier antagonistic relationship with the Houthis, joined his forces with theirs, seizing the opportunity to confront their common enemies: President Hadi, Ali Mohsen, the al-Ahmars,[26] and the Islah party.

By late summer, the Houthi/Saleh forces were able to take advantage of the weakness of the transitional government and the collapse of Yemen's security forces—fueled by the defection of pro-Saleh troops—to move aggressively into Sana'a. On entry into the capital, the Houthis built on a strong base of support, including not only pro-Houthi elements among the majority Zaydi Shi'a population but also the many citizens who were simply exhausted by the political stalemate and angered by the failure of the transitional government to address the central issues confronting Yemen, including deteriorating economic and security conditions.[27]

The Houthis claimed that they aimed to strike a blow against a corrupt political elite. Repeating their tactics from earlier conflicts with the Saleh government, they capitalized on populist sentiments to gain support, this time opposition to the government's decision to end oil subsidies. For his part, Saleh, who was responsible for many of the attacks on infrastructure and the general undermining of security in Sana'a, claimed that he could restore order and security if he were returned to power.

After a new round of negotiations under UN auspices produced a road map for resolving the conflict (see below for a discussion of the Peace and National Partnership Agreement, or PNPA), the plan was quickly discarded by the Houthis and tensions in the capital rose again. In early 2015, Hadi angered the Houthis by promulgating the new constitution that had been prepared by the drafting committee and unveiling a new political map of Yemen that created six federal regions that the Houthis viewed as discriminatory.[28] Amid fresh fighting between their units and government security forces, the Houthis moved to dissolve parliament and the government and forced President Hadi to resign, appointing a revolutionary committee to replace the government. Hadi, who had been placed under "house arrest" by the Houthis, fled to Aden in February 2015 and ultimately to Saudi Arabia a month later.

From there, Hadi sent a letter to the UN Security Council requesting a Chapter VII resolution to block the Houthi advance into southern Yemen. The Council soon complied and issued UN Security Council Resolution (UNSCR) 2216, which remains the operative expression of international community views on the conflict until now. (UNSCR 2451, passed in December 2018, maintains in place the key provisions of 2216, but adds support for the agreements worked out in UN Special Envoy Martin Griffiths' negotiations with the parties in Stockholm.) Among other things, the resolution recognizes the Hadi government as the legitimate government of Yemen and demands a return to the political transition. The Saudi-led coalition launched operations shortly before the resolution in response to a request for support from Hadi.

The Houthi-Saleh forces, now united primarily by their opposition to the Saudi-led coalition's intervention, quickly moved south, claiming that they intended to confront al-Qaeda, but more likely in an effort to consolidate political control over the entire country. Their movement into the more heavily Shafi'i midlands and south sparked a new civil conflict that metastasized into the broader conflict that has persisted and is now in its eighth year.[29]

Despite their initial success in seizing control of the capital and most of northwestern Yemen, home to the vast majority of Yemenis, the alliance between former President Saleh and the Houthis was never more than a marriage of convenience. Expectations from the very beginning were that the two sides would eventually confront one another over mutually exclusive goals and objectives. The balance of power between the two sides shifted in the Houthis' favor over the course of the conflict. The Houthis increased their military capability vis-à-vis the pro-Saleh forces, including establishing control over the remnants of the Republican Guard, the most potent military organization formerly under the command of Ahmed Ali Saleh. Infighting over the formation of a National Salvation Government in August 2016 further deepened the internal divisions within the alliance. A series of violent confrontations between the Saleh and Houthi forces peaked with Saleh's abrupt announcement in December 2017 that he was abandoning the alliance with the Houthis and would join his greatly diminished force with the Saudi-led coalition. His uprising was short-lived, however, and Saleh was murdered by the Houthis on December 4.

Although southerners largely viewed the conflict as primarily a northern internal fight, many in the south resisted the Houthi incursions and joined forces with the coalition and the Hadi government to expel them. At the same time, frustration over the collapse of the transition process sparked a new round of support for southern secession and the emergence of a new alliance, the Southern Transitional Council (STC), that advocated separation from the north. The UAE supported the STC, providing arms and training to build up their military capability and partnering with them on military operations, although not openly embracing their secessionist agenda. An STC move in January 2018 to expel Hadi government officials from Aden appeared to enjoy preliminary support from the UAE until Saudi Arabia forced a stand-down.[30] Despite continued Saudi efforts to pressure the parties into political and security cooperation, most recently through the Riyadh Agreement forged in

November 2019, tensions persist between the two sides, undermining resistance to the Houthis and sustaining political friction in Aden.

The collapse of the Houthi–Saleh alliance gave fresh impetus to the Saudi-led coalition and revived hopes for a potentially decisive defeat of the Houthi forces in the stalemated military conflict. Coalition forces expanded control of the strategically important and relatively resource-rich Marib Governorate east of Sana'a, and a mix of militias, pro-government forces, mercenaries, and Emirati military units began moving slowly north along the Tihama, the Red Sea coast, toward Hodeida, the main port supplying the 75 percent of Yemenis who live in the north. Successful capture of the port, some believed, would compel the Houthis to return to the negotiating table and participate in the UN-led political process under the guidance of the new UN special representative, Martin Griffiths. In December 2018, Griffiths successfully brought the parties together in Stockholm for their first face-to-face meetings since the failed Kuwait talks in 2016. This round of talks resulted in a preliminary agreement to withdraw forces from Hodeida and allow for third-party management of the port, along with a prisoner exchange and a humanitarian corridor to relieve Taiz. Despite some optimism that the agreement would open a new window of opportunity for comprehensive negotiations to end the conflict, efforts to promote its implementation failed as the coalition accused the Houthis of serial violations. Thus, the situation around Hodeida has remained largely stalemated, although the surprise withdrawal of government-aligned Joint Forces from large parts of the governorate in November 2021 allowed the Houthis to take control of the vacated territory.

Repeated Attempts to Address Yemen's Systemic Divisions

As noted previously, Yemen's deep internal divisions have repeatedly led to eruptions of violence. At the same time, Yemenis have also repeatedly come together in an effort to find peaceful solutions to their differences. Common themes have linked all of the initiatives: recognizing the legitimate grievances of marginalized populations, promoting structural changes through constitutional reforms, ensuring regional political balances of power and the equitable distribution of resources, and emphasizing the need for decentralization and greater local autonomy.

Document of Pledge and Accord

In 1994, as relations between the GPC and YSP leadership deteriorated, civil society activists from North and South Yemen formed an independent commission, the Yemeni National Dialogue of Popular Forces, to address perceived shortcomings in the original unity agreement. They succeeded in drafting an eighteen-point "Document of Pledge and Accord." The agreement called for a new constitutional arrangement with a bicameral legislature and equal representation for the north and the south in the upper chamber. The proposal also recommended significant decentralization.[31] The plan would create local government bodies with direct election of provincial governors and district managers.[32] Both Ali Abdullah Saleh and Ali Salem al-Beidh signed the document in Amman, Jordan, but fighting soon broke out and the agreement was never implemented following the south's defeat in the short civil conflict.

Sa'dah War Mediation

There were also repeated efforts, both from within Yemen and by external actors, throughout the course of the six Sa'dah wars to mediate an end to the conflict. In the most serious effort, anxious to resolve the conflict before scheduled elections in September 2006, President Saleh initiated a mediation at the end of the third Sa'dah war, led by a committee composed nearly entirely of sayyids. The committee negotiated a number of agreements with Abdul-Malek al-Houthi, providing amnesty and compensation for war victims in exchange for a Houthi declaration of adherence to the constitution. The government also announced that it would restore damaged public facilities in Sa'dah and invest in new infrastructure projects.

Nevertheless, another round of fighting followed shortly thereafter. Shortly after the sixth war was launched in 2009, the government issued a six-point list of demands for a cease-fire: (1) withdraw from all mountains, fortifications, and districts of Sa'dah; (2) remove all checkpoints; (3) cease all acts of banditry and destruction; (4) return all seized military and civilian equipment; (5) clarify the situation of six kidnapped foreigners believed to have been taken by the Houthis; and (6) refrain from intervening in the affairs of the local authorities. After initially rejecting the government's demands, the Houthis agreed to accept all but the fifth (later replaced by a requirement to end cross-border attacks into Saudi

Arabia), but the two sides were unable to reach an agreement for a cease-fire until early 2010 when the promise of foreign assistance from the "Friends of Yemen" (FoY) group meeting in London triggered a unilateral cease-fire declaration by the government.[33] There matters stood until February 2011 and the onset of the Arab Spring anti-Saleh uprising.

National Dialogue Conference

Although the immediate trigger for the Arab Spring protests was the demand for President Saleh to resign, both the protesters and the political elites saw the uprising as an opportunity to seek again to resolve Yemen's more intractable challenges. Given the history of these efforts, there appeared to be a window of opportunity to do so. Not only had most of the core issues long been identified and accepted by the majority of political actors, a number of the solutions had been agreed in previous negotiations as well. But there were also important differences between the process launched under the terms of the GCC Initiative and Implementing Mechanism and its predecessors. For the first time, not only civil society but also women and youth were to be guaranteed a voice in the negotiations. Moreover, unlike the 1994 talks, which addressed only the issues between north and south, or the mediation efforts during the six Sa'dah wars that sought only to end the fighting in the north, the NDC organized under the GCC Initiative was charged with providing comprehensive solutions to a broad range of issues.

In addition to addressing the southern and Sa'dah issues, the NDC organized working groups to provide recommendations on governance, development, military and security reorganization, reconciliation and transitional justice, and social and environmental issues, among others. After a year of debate, the 500+ delegates to the NDC provided some 1,800 recommendations and formed a committee to revise the constitution in accordance with them. Most controversially, the NDC proposed the establishment of a federal state divided into six regions. While the delegates to the NDC favored the federation proposal in principle, the government's proposed map identifying the boundaries of the new federal units provoked a strongly negative reaction from the Houthis, and became one of the casus belli of the current conflict. Following the conclusion of the NDC, the government mounted a significant campaign in the country to advertise and explain its recommendations and to build popular support. At the same time, the constitutional drafting committee commenced work on revisions to the constitution. These were completed by late summer and referred back to the NDC.

Peace and National Partnership Agreement

The last effort by the Yemeni parties to negotiate a peaceful resolution of the growing conflict followed the Houthi's successful military campaign and entry into Sana'a in September 2014. In response to their demands, UN Special Representative Jamal Benomar negotiated an agreement among the various parties, the PNPA. The agreement was a victory for Yemen's marginalized populations; it stipulated that Hadi, in consultation with Ansarullah (the Houthis) and al-Hirak (the southern movement), should appoint a new prime minister, Khaled al-Bahah, and set out criteria for new cabinet appointments. It also established a number of committees to supervise elements of the political transition and implementation of the NDC recommendations. Despite the fact that their representatives had signed the agreement, the Houthis refused to fulfill its terms and the initiative collapsed by the end of the year.

External Factors in the Conflict

Although it is often characterized by outside observers as a proxy war between Saudi Arabia and Iran, the critical drivers of the Yemen civil conflict rest entirely within the country's own history. Undoubtedly, Yemen has drawn external actors into its conflicts through the years. Earlier in the nineteenth and twentieth centuries, Britain and the Ottoman Empire competed for influence in Yemen and, together, drew the first boundary between North and South Yemen. In the 1960s, Egypt and Saudi Arabia backed competing forces in the conflict between the Imamate and republican elements. Since 2014, the Saudi–Iranian regional rivalry has exacerbated the current conflict and complicated efforts to find a solution. While there are some who maintain that Iranian intervention in the Yemen conflict was provoked by Saudi involvement, the reverse is the more likely explanation: Saudi intervention in March 2015 was a direct result of the perceived threat to Saudi security posed by the growing Houthi–Iranian alliance in Yemen. The UAE was also a significant player in the conflict, initially in support of the Saudis but it increasingly pursued objectives independent of Saudi policy as its engagement deepened until its decision to withdraw its military forces (except for continued counter-terrorism operations, primarily in the southeast) in 2019. Most recently, questions have emerged over the possible influence that the UAE and Saudi Arabia might have exerted on government-aligned forces in the Hodeida Governorate to evacuate positions in a surprise move, possibly as a means of reducing regional tension with Iran but also as a prelude to the successful operations against Houthi forces in Shabwa and Marib governorates.

Saudi Arabia

Saudi Arabia's involvement in Yemen is long standing and extensive. It dates to the earliest period in modern Saudi history. The kingdom fought a war with the Yemeni Imamate in the 1930s that led to the transfer of three provinces—Jizan, Najran, and Asir (sometimes referred to by Yemenis as the three "lost" provinces)—to Saudi Arabia and established a border between the two countries. (The border was not finally demarcated until the Treaty of Jeddah was signed in 2000.)

Saudi Arabia's focus has generally been on ensuring the security of its southern border and preventing instability in Yemen from undermining Saudi interests. The Saudis supported the Zaydi Shi'a Imamate in the 1960s primarily because they saw the republican revolution backed by Egypt as a potential threat to their domestic interests. Despite their support for the Imamate, the Saudis reconciled with the YAR once the civil war ended in 1970. They collaborated with the Yemeni authorities and built their own patronage system, particularly for northern tribes under the leadership of the paramount sheikh of the Hashid tribal confederation, Sheikh Abdullah al-Ahmar, which largely supported the Saleh regime. Historically, millions of Yemeni workers have crossed the border to find jobs in Saudi Arabia, providing remittances to their families that were critical to their economic survival. Most controversially, the Saudis supported southern secessionists in the 1994 civil war, presumably because they saw a united Yemen as a threat to Saudi security and, in part, due to President Saleh's brief alliance with Saddam Hussein, which was a direct threat to the security of all of the Gulf monarchies. The Saudis were also briefly involved in the sixth Sa'dah war provoked by a Houthi cross-border raid that killed a Saudi border guard in 2009.

During the Arab Spring uprising, the Saudis were constructively engaged in helping to mediate among the Yemeni parties and assisting in the drafting of the GCC Initiative and Implementing Mechanism. King Abdullah's personal intervention was key to convincing President Saleh to sign the agreement in November 2011. Afterwards, direct Saudi engagement in Yemen's political transition was reduced until the second half of 2014 when the Houthis, with Iranian encouragement, again threatened Saudi security along its southern border.

Despite their concerns about the shortcomings of the Yemeni Transitional Government, the Saudi decision to intervene in the Yemen conflict militarily reflected worries about Iranian intervention and the possibility that a Houthi-dominated Yemen would become a platform for Iranian destabilizing activities. Although their coalition campaign quickly blunted Houthi advances in the South and stabilized the situation around Aden, their efforts to push the Houthis back and force a negotiated resolution to the conflict soon bogged down. Moreover, the Saudi intervention triggered a hostile response in much of the world, including the United States, inflicting reputational damage on the Saudi regime both for its failure to secure a military victory and for what were broadly perceived to be excessive civilian casualties as a result of its air campaign. Confronting its challenging political and diplomatic situation, Saudi Arabia has been in search of a peaceful way out of the conflict since 2016. Since the arrival of the Biden administration in Washington in January 2021, the Saudis have aligned their negotiating position more closely with the UN effort now spearheaded by the new special envoy, Hans Grundberg, at least in part to address pressure from the United States to do more to bring an end to the conflict. Most recently, as the security situation in Yemen has continued to deteriorate, and Saudi Arabia itself has confronted increased Houthi cross-border attacks utilizing drones, Scud missiles, and other Iranian-provided weapons, Saudi military engagement has been a crucial element in preventing broader Houthi military advances that would further undermine possibilities of a peaceful political resolution to the conflict.

The United Arab Emirates

Like Saudi Arabia, the UAE played an important role in helping to facilitate the GCC Initiative and Implementing Mechanism, but its active participation diminished after Saleh stepped down from power. In 2015, the UAE joined the Saudi-led coalition largely as a symbol of its support for the Saudis and in recognition of the threat that Saudi Arabia faced from a hostile Houthi presence on its border associated with Iranian provocations. Over the course of the conflict, however, the UAE's role in Yemen, especially in support of the STC, grew more controversial. Emirati support for the STC as well as for members of the Saleh family, its hostile stance toward the Hadi government, and its military deployment to the island of Socotra raised questions about Emirati intentions and whether UAE policy remained consistent with Saudi goals and objectives as well as with UNSCR 2216.[34] Concerns over the increasingly confrontational posture with Iran eventually triggered a UAE decision to withdraw from its military engagement in Yemen in 2019. Official Emirati pronouncements explained that the decision was meant as a signal to Tehran that it was seeking to lower the regional temperature. Following the end of its active participation in the Saudi-led coalition, UAE engagement in Yemen is largely limited to its counter-terrorism operations in the eastern part of the country. Nevertheless, it has continued to provide support for militia elements it has trained, including in the South and the Tihama, and has supported the Saudi effort, the Riyadh Agreement, to paper over differences within the anti-Houthi coalition between the Hadi government and the southern secessionists. In fact, Yemeni militia units trained and equipped by the UAE were instrumental in efforts in early 2022 to blunt Houthi military operations in Shabwa and Marib governorates and roll-back some Houthi gains. In retaliation for the Emirati role, the Houthis targeted Abu Dhabi with drone and missile strikes.

Iran

Unlike Saudi Arabia, there is no history of substantial Iranian involvement in Yemen in the modern era. Although President Saleh routinely alleged during the six Sa'dah wars that Iran was actively supporting the Houthis, there was little evidence to support his claims. (Indeed, Saudi frustration over Saleh's exaggeration of the Iranian role in the Sa'dah wars was likely one of the factors that influenced their decision to support the political transition in 2011.[35]) Nor did Iran participate in the international community's effort to facilitate the political negotiations leading to

Saleh's departure in 2011. But, belying claims that Iran's support to the Houthis was a reaction to Saudi intervention, Iranian training and assistance began to expand in 2012, when the majority of Yemenis were fully committed to the implementation of the GCC Initiative.[36] Later on, Saleh also actively sought Iranian support in his efforts to regain control, dispatching trusted emissaries to Tehran to meet with the Iranians during this time period.[37]

In the fall of 2014, when the Houthis had established de facto control of Sana'a, Iranian support expanded along with an increase in specific threats by the Houthis to attack Saudi Arabia. Iran's support for the Houthis became more overt following the Saudi-led coalition's intervention in March 2015 as Iran claimed that its intentions were to support the Yemeni people resisting outside aggression. Indeed, support for the Houthis has become an increasingly significant element of Iranian regional policies and the Houthis have more vocally aligned their policies with Iran. In exchange for Iran providing more sophisticated weapons, extended-range Scuds, drones, and anti-ship missiles, the Houthis have declared their support for Iran and its regional affiliates, notably Lebanese Hezbollah. The Houthis have also claimed that their cross-border targeting of Saudi infrastructure is in support of Iran. While recent talks between Saudi Arabia and Iran, and the United States and Iran have raised hopes that the Iranians might play a constructive role in bringing an end to the Yemeni conflict, there is no evidence that they have encouraged the Houthis to return to negotiations and may, in fact, see the Yemen conflict as potential leverage in their negotiations in Vienna with the United States on a return to the Joint Comprehensive Plan of Action (JCPOA).

Russia and the United States

The Soviet Union historically tried to balance its relations between North and South Yemen. The closer relationship, of course, was with the south. The actual level of assistance to the PDRY is unclear. One assessment suggested it was about thirty million dollars a year, so not a massive amount of aid, and it was part in loans and part in grants. Military assistance started in 1968 and the two sides signed an Economic and Technical Assistance Agreement in 1969. At its peak, there appeared to be about 2,500 Russian military advisers in the PDRY. East Germans and

Cubans also provided support: The East Germans aided the development of PDRY security services and the Cubans provided medical assistance as well as subsidized sugar. The Soviets also did a lot on the education side and even at the time the author was ambassador, some twenty years after the end of the Soviet Union and the PDRY, there were a number of Russian-speaking Yemenis scattered around (and Russian spouses as well).[38]

The Soviet military used Aden, particularly operating out of the airbase at Khormakser and conducting ship visits to the port. PDRY-Soviet relations reached their peak in 1978–80, when a pro-Moscow president, Abd al-Fattah Ismail, ruled in Aden. The Russians signed a Treaty of Friendship and Cooperation in November 1979. In 1980, Ismail was overthrown by the more moderate Ali Nasser Mohammed, who was reportedly more interested in rebuilding relations with the West, although he wanted to preserve ties with Moscow as well.

At the same time, the Soviets were also interested in maintaining their ties with North Yemen, especially as an entree to relations with Saudi Arabia. The Soviets aided the development of Hodeida port and provided military assistance as well, delivering MiG-21 aircraft to the YAR when the Saudis and United States balked at building Yemeni military capabilities.

Despite their long history of engagement in Yemen, the Russians were initially reluctant to become involved in the international mediation effort in 2011, preferring to observe from a distance. But their position changed when President Saleh opened the door for their engagement. To Saleh's surprise, rather than presenting a counter-balance to the United States and the West, which were pressing for a political transition, the Russians joined the larger international effort and were full partners in the transition. Since the outbreak of the conflict, however, the Russians have once again avoided playing an active role in efforts to bring it to an end and have used their position in the UN Security Council to stymie criticism of the Houthis and their Iranian patrons.

In contrast to the Russians, the US involvement in Yemen was generally a subset of US relations with Saudi Arabia until 2001, when concerns about the rise of al-Qaeda in the Arabian Peninsula became the driving force in US–Yemeni relations. In the 1960s, President John F. Kennedy directed that the US support Saudi backing of the Imamate in its resistance to the Egyptian-backed republican forces. Subsequently, the United States viewed North Yemen as a bulwark preventing Communist expansion from the PDRY into the Arabian Peninsula and threatening

Saudi stability. The PDRY broke relations with the United States in October 1969 and did not reestablish them until April 1990, just weeks before the announcement of the YAR-PDRY unification agreement. The United States and Saudi Arabia jointly formed a military assistance mission for North Yemen, including the eventual sale of F-5 fighter aircraft. But the Saudi-Yemeni military relationship was never an easy one, and it ended when the YAR supported the Iraqi invasion of Kuwait in 1990. Shortly before 9/11, the USS Cole was the target of a terror attack in Aden, presaging the rise of al-Qaeda in the Arabian Peninsula as the most capable of the al-Qaeda affiliates. At that point, the US focus on Yemen (with Saudi assistance) shifted to the global counter-terrorism campaign. Despite the urgency of US demands for support from the Saleh government, the Yemenis were difficult partners and remained so until the Arab Spring uprising.

Yemen's Economic Collapse and the Growth of a War Economy

War profiteering has been a persistent factor in Yemen's cyclical conflicts. Smuggling, corruption from bloated military budgets, and arms trafficking were common features throughout the six Sa'dah wars. Marieke Brandt noted the impact of the rise of the war economy in the early 2000s: "Many stakeholders profited from the war and, over time, the conflict became a permanent tool for generating personal wealth. By perpetuating the war and artificially controlling its intensity, they could provide themselves with an almost infinite source of income."

The significance of the war economy over the course of the current conflict has grown exponentially. The legitimate Yemen economy ground to a near halt. Yemen's GDP declined by nearly 42 percent between 2015 and 2017 while the 25 percent of Yemenis who received government payments—both civil service employees and those dependent on social welfare payments—went unpaid for more than a year and private sector unemployment reached 50 percent.[39]

More recently, Yemenis have been hit by an even more dramatic economic downturn as the impact of the Covid-19 pandemic has added to the war-induced collapse. According to a report by the World Bank in 2021, Yemen's sharp economic contraction in 2020 was exacerbated by low global oil prices, exceptionally heavy rainfall and flooding, the winding down of Saudi Arabia's basic import finance facility, as well as reduced humanitarian funding. Based on a phone survey it conducted in 2020, the World Bank reported that some 80 percent of respondents said they had difficulty accessing food or basic services. While improving prices in the energy sector will help reduce the strain on public finances, at least in the government-held areas, the World Bank report concludes that "a cessation of hostilities and eventual political reconciliation remain prerequisites for the reconstruction of the economy."[40] In his most recent report to the UN Security Council, Special Envoy Grundberg emphasized the implications for a peaceful resolution of the conflict posed by the country's economic collapse, advising the Council that "there is an urgent need for economic de-escalation, and wider reforms to improve livelihoods, lower the cost of goods, and protect the currency."[41]

Further compounding Yemen's economic woes is the rise of essentially two monetary and economic zones. As R. Joseph Huddleston and David Wood observe in their recent research paper on Yemen's war economy,

> The conflict in Yemen has undone several pillars of the formal economy: public sector employment has plummeted, to be replaced by more informal work; public service infrastructure like roads and water have been severely damaged; many have been displaced; and still more have sold off valuable assets and parts of their livelihoods. Perhaps most troubling, the bare provision of food for the family has come to consume an enormous portion of most Yemenis' income. In this environment of severe economic uncertainty, away from the regulatory arm of the internationally recognized government, they have come to rely on the alternatively regulated economic spaces that have emerged to fill the void, which we call the "functional economy."[42]

They concluded that, "Our analysis implies that close attention should be paid to these factors by international agencies committing resources to using economic means to improve the situation in Yemen and incentivize peaceful change."[43]

Can Yemen's Problems Be Solved?

Yemen has suffered from violent conflict repeatedly over the past decades driven in large part by fundamental divisions and identity issues within

Yemeni society, a sense of marginalization, and deep-rooted inequality engendered by an extractive, rentier political and economic system. At the same time, as we have seen, there have been repeated attempts to define the root causes of the conflict and resolve them.

Undoubtedly, the most comprehensive attempt to end the cycle of violent conflict grew out of the Arab Spring revolt against the Saleh government and the resultant GCC Initiative–mandated NDC. While there has been criticism of the conference and it has been cast as a failure by many observers, the fact is that the NDC itself did not fail. The conferees, the most representative body to ever come together in Yemen, agreed on hundreds of recommendations meant to resolve many of the most pressing political, economic, and social issues challenging the country. In its broadest sweep, the NDC reiterated recommendations drawn from previous dialogues that promoted decentralization and greater local autonomy, a federalized state structure, and greater representation in parliament for the disaffected south.

While the NDC's recommendations may be faulted for their ambition, many, if not most, of them were fundamentally sound. Yet, despite the well-intentioned efforts of hundreds of Yemeni political figures, civil society activists, and women and youth representatives, the conclusions reached through this process of negotiation did not succeed in resolving differences or ending conflict. Instead, Yemen repeated the historic pattern. Despite intense efforts to "sell" the NDC results to the Yemeni people and follow through on the remaining elements of an agreed political transition, from the end of the NDC in April 2014 until the Houthi–Saleh coup in the fall of 2014 and the outbreak of a new round of fighting in March 2015, the political consensus behind the conference results continued to fray and the impetus toward a new round of fighting continued to build. Once again, Yemeni leaders—the country's political and economic elites—were unwilling to make the concessions required or sacrifice their advantaged positions to implement the agreement, while the population at large remained disengaged and disinterested in pressing for it. Negotiations were dismissed and force of arms became the preferred tactic.

In a conflict now in its eighth year with no real prospect of an end in sight, the initial promise of the NDC and political transition has long been forgotten. What started as a binary struggle between the transitional government under President Hadi and a Houthi–Saleh alliance has now metastasized into a Hobbesian war of all against all. UN Special Envoy

Grundberg, the fourth to lead the UN effort in Yemen, has been given the task of attempting to resurrect a negotiating process that has been stalemated since 2016 and has not produced even transitory results since the flawed Stockholm Agreement of 2018. But even achieving limited success in the UN-led process would produce little prospect of a return to stability or reopening a political process. Instead, the Yemen Civil War is at an inflection point as Yemenis themselves have come to question the future of the country, whether it can survive as a unified nation, and whether they can once again find a basis for addressing the fundamental challenges that have crippled national development for sixty years. The outcome of that effort is important not only for Yemen, but for the region and the broader international community as the country's collapse into two or more statelets would pose a threat to global peace and security.

Recommendations

As noted at the beginning of this chapter and in subsequent sections related to the history of political negotiations, the main reason that Yemenis have not been able to break out of the cycle of violence for over six decades is not because of an inability to identify solutions to their problems but because the political and economic leadership has lacked the resolve to actually follow through on the agreements they have reached. Their failure is in implementation not in vision. The recommendations listed below are suggestions for how the Yemenis, their Gulf neighbors, and the international community can reverse that history and help move Yemen on to a sustainable course of state-building. It should be clear that real change in Yemen is a decades-long challenge. But another failure to begin will mean that Yemenis will be doomed to repeat the current conflict again, with all of the attendant humanitarian consequences as well as the regional and international problems that will arise.

For Yemenis:
As the conflict continues:

- Where possible, continue to build networks of civil society, women's activists, and tribes to address local issues and negotiate local cease-fires and prisoner exchanges, as well as build institutions of self-government.

- Re-examine the recommendations of the NDC and earlier political initiatives and develop a consensus strategy for implementing agreed recommendations.

- Promote discussions at a regional and sub-regional level to prepare for re-engagement in a post-conflict situation.

- Seek to inform and influence the UN-led international negotiating process to ensure that local voices and initiatives are factored into the UN effort.

In a post-conflict situation:

- Focus on institutional capacity building, especially in support of existing projects at the local and governorate levels.

- To end crony capitalism, promote transparency and accountability in government contracting and allocation of resources. Develop bottom-up democratic institutions including the direct election of local and governorate-level councils to encourage more broad-based participation in politics.

- To break the war economy, remove all import restrictions and ensure that no market shortages exist to be exploited by war profiteers.

- Redraw the federalist map to ensure that the federating units provide an equitable geographic distribution of resources.

- Develop a national infrastructure plan that provides a timeline for extending access for all Yemenis to essential water, power, and transportation utilities.

- Extend job creation and economic diversification programs to all regions of the country. Guarantee access to health care and education for all Yemenis. Promote programs, including the social fund for development and small business loans, to expand citizens' participation in the economy.

For Yemen's Neighbors:

- The GCC should take the lead in addressing Yemen's economic crisis, especially by integrating Yemen into full membership in the organization. The two dominant Gulf economies—Saudi Arabia and the UAE—should take the lead in promoting regional support for Yemen's recovery.

- GCC states should declare their support for Yemen's unity and respect for its sovereignty and territorial integrity.

- Provide rapidly disbursing regional development assistance to repair war-damaged infrastructure as well as undertake new infrastructure projects, including development of Aden port, to promote broad-based economic development.

- Extend preferential access for Yemeni workers to find employment in regional economies, generating a near-term capital injection into Yemen's economy.

- Eliminate tariff and nontariff barriers to trade between Yemen and regional economies to help Yemen attract foreign direct investment and generate labor-intensive industrial development, providing jobs and business development opportunities at home.

For the Broader International Community:
As the conflict continues:

- Recognize that achievement of a sustainable political resolution must take into account current realities on the ground in an increasingly fractured Yemen. A binary negotiating process between the legitimate government of Yemen and the Houthis is no longer a viable strategy for ending the fighting.

- Make clear that an end to the fighting will require clearly establishing that the Houthis cannot achieve a military victory and the international community will support efforts to resist continued Houthi military aggression.

- Make economic issues a central element of the negotiating process. In the absence of a political resolution to the conflict, focus on addressing pressing economic issues in both North and South Yemen, expanding legitimate economic activities and restoring job opportunities for Yemenis.

- As part of its UN-led negotiating strategy, the international community should do more to incorporate the efforts and the recommendations of civil society, women's and youth groups, and tribes operating on the ground into the process. These groups should be included in future negotiations.

In a post-conflict situation:

- Through the FoY, the international community should make clear that it is making a long-term, sustained commitment to assist Yemen's political and economic development and that it continues to support Yemen's unity, sovereignty, and territorial integrity.

- The UN should provide continued expert assistance to the reappraisal of NDC recommendations and to the completion of the remaining steps in the GCC Initiative and Implementing Mechanism.

- The International Foundation for Electoral Systems should assist in updating voter registration lists and preparing for new elections as a final step in completing Yemen's political transition.

- The World Bank and the International Monetary Fund should develop programs to promote broad-based economic development, infrastructure planning, and the establishment of reliable institutions to promote transparency, accountability, and the fight against corruption.

- The FoY, through bilateral development assistance programs, should focus on institutional capacity building as well as ensuring that all Yemenis have access to effective health care and educational facilities.

Conclusion: The Consequences of Failure

The future of Yemen as a unified state has never been in greater jeopardy since the unification agreement of 1990. The potential exists that the state may devolve not into two parts, as the pre-1990 arrangement existed, but into multiple statelets, weak and unable to provide basic services for their population while offering an inviting environment for the rise of extremist groups. Yet this current threat should not come as a surprise to Yemen watchers. I've tried to demonstrate in this chapter that an understanding of the current civil conflict in Yemen requires looking at the basic elements of Yemeni history going back to at least the upheavals of the 1960s—the uprising against the Imamate in the

North and the revolt against the British in the south. The same elements appear as factors in each of the violent eruptions: political, social, and economic marginalization, sectional discrimination, denial of equal access to health care and education, corruption, and cronyism. Yet time and again, Yemenis have sat at the negotiating table in an effort to agree on the means to address and resolve these issues. In the Document of Pledge and Accord, the NDC recommendations, and even in the PNPA, the parties agreed on basic principles: decentralization of government, equitable sharing of resources, more representative government, as well as fundamental social and economic reforms. But the agreements were never implemented and the parties soon returned to a new round of struggle and conflict.

Today, there is, once again, a proposed road map out of the sixty-year-old Yemeni Civil War. Once again, any serious effort to end six decades of state failure must be based on an honest reckoning of the sources of past failures and a new commitment by the nation's leaders to ensure that the political process succeeds. The Yemeni people, as well, need to demand as much from their leaders. Moreover, it requires that the international community, both in the region and more broadly, commit to long-term engagement to support Yemen's transition. Success will not come easily. The institutions that could be expected to help guide the process are weak and increasingly fragmented. In fairness, Acemoglu and Robinson argue that attempts at such radical transformations rarely succeed. But the price of failure is reflected clearly in Yemen's history since the early 1960s: a continuation of the cycles of violent conflict and deepening fissures in Yemen's society that threaten to become irreparable. Once again, failure will ensure that the current civil conflict will merely serve as a prelude to the next round of fighting and the round after that. But we have also seen, since 2015, the potential that new rounds of internal conflict in Yemen can spill over and destabilize the entire region, even provoking an interstate conflict. Thus, more than ever, the international community has a vested interest, along with the Yemeni people themselves, to ensure that this time the outcome is different.

Notes

1   Daron Acemoglu and James Robinson, *Why Nations Fail: The Origins of Power, Prosperity and Poverty* (London: Crown Publishing Group, 2012).

2 The republican rebellion against the Imamate in North Yemen lasted from 1962 to 1970. The internal Yemeni Socialist Party dispute in the People's Democratic Republic of Yemen inflicted an estimated ten thousand casualties among the civilian population of Aden in approximately two weeks of street battles.

3 Despite their support for the winning side, involvement in the Yemen civil war had real consequences for Nasser's Egypt. Analysts have long considered that Egypt's extensive deployments in Yemen weakened its military capabilities, enabling Israel's complete destruction of the Egyptian army and air force in the 1967 war.

4 Stephen Day, *Regionalism and Rebellion in Yemen: A Troubled National Union* (Cambridge: Cambridge University Press, 2012), 65–70.

5 Ibid., 66.

6 Ibid.

7 Ibid., Table 2.3: Regional Government Revenues (per capita) in the Northern YAR, 1985 and 1989, 71.

8 Paul Dresch, *A History of Modern Yemen* (Cambridge: Cambridge University Press, 2000), 149.

9 Echoes of the 1986 conflict continue to infect Yemeni politics and were a factor in undermining southern participation in the National Dialogue Conference. The intra-YSP conflict, which pitted Ali Nasser Mohammed and his allies against Ali Salim al-Beidh and his allies, had both geographic as well as ideological foundations. The Ali Nasser group, or "Zumra," which included Abed Rabbo Mansour Hadi, came mostly from Abyan and Shabwa governorates, while the Ali Salim group, or "Tughma," were primarily from Dhahle, Lahij, and Hadramawt. As president, Hadi tried desperately to bring his former colleagues, including Ali Nasser Mohammed, on board in support of the political transition, but only Mohammed Ali Ahmed, former governor of Abyan, joined the process and, at that, only half-heartedly. Ali Nasser stayed away despite Hadi's efforts. Meanwhile, Ali Salim al-Beidh attacked Hadi and the GCC Initiative from his safe haven in Beirut and broadcast pro-secessionist propaganda on the Hezbollah station, al-Manar.

10 April Longley Alley, "Breaking Point? Yemen's Southern Question," International Crisis Group (October 2011), 2.

11 Day, *Regionalism and Rebellion*, 134.

12 Alley, "Breaking Point?" 1.

13 Day, *Regionalism and Rebellion*, 230.

14 Alley, "Breaking Point?" 6.

15 Ibid., 9.

16 Marieke Brandt, *Tribes and Politics in Yemen: A History of the Houthi Conflict* (Oxford: Oxford University Press, 2017), 135.

17 Ibid., 134.

18 Ibid., 348.

19 Ibid., 54.

20 Ibid., 55.

21 Ibid., 345.

22 Ibid., 346.

23 Alley, "Breaking Point?" 1.

24 Saleh tried to exploit divisions within the international community, attempting in particular to gain support from Russia and China in opposition to the West. But the diplomatic corps joined together, organizing a Group of Ten—United States, UK, France, Russia, China, Saudi Arabia, UAE, Oman, Kuwait, and the EU—to maintain unity and present a solid front. Despite the subsequent collapse of the transition process, the cooperative approach taken by the diplomatic community in Sana'a remains a model for international engagement in support of peaceful resolutions of internal disputes.

25 Ginny Hill, *Yemen Endures: Civil War, Saudi Adventurism and the Future of Arabia* (Oxford: Oxford University Press, 2017), 261.

26 During his lifetime, Sheikh Abdullah al-Ahmar had been both a major beneficiary and a prominent benefactor of Ali Abdullah Saleh's regime. Although he was one of the founders of the Islah party, Sheikh Abdullah maintained his support for Saleh through the 2006 presidential election. Following Sheikh Abdullah's death in late 2007, however, support for Saleh among the al-Ahmar sons declined. In particular, Hamid al-Ahmar, a prominent businessman and Islah party activist, became one of Saleh's most vocal critics and was widely assumed to harbor his own presidential ambitions. During the Arab Spring protests, Hamid was one of the main financiers of the protest movement. Pro-Saleh loyalists asserted that Hamid was a coconspirator in the June 2011 assassination attempt that gravely wounded Saleh and many of his closest lieutenants, although this was never established. In the subsequent fighting, Saleh's forces targeted al-Ahmar properties in Sana'a, destroying Hamid's home as well as that of his eldest brother and heir to the family position as paramount sheikhs of the Hashid tribal federation, Sheikh Sadiq al-Ahmar. Hamid currently lives in exile in Istanbul, Turkey.

27 Brandt, *Tribes and Politics in Yemen*, 338.

28 Despite Hadi's pledge that the map would divide Yemen's natural resources equitably, the Houthis maintained that the Azal region, which included the Houthi's Sa'dah Governorate, lacked either natural resources or access to the sea.

29 April Longley Alley, "Collapse of the Houthi-Saleh Alliance and the Future of Yemen's War," Project on Middle East Political Science (January 11, 2018).

30 Kelly F. Thornberry, "The UAE's Divisive Strategy in Yemen," *RealClear Defense* 16, no. 8 (April 2018).

31 Alley, "Breaking Point?" 4.

32 Day, *Regionalism and Rebellion in Yemen*, 127.

33 Ibid., 318.

34 Abdulwahab Al-Qassab, "Strategic Considerations of the UAE Role in Yemen," The Arab Center (March 9, 2018), 2.

35 Hill, *Yemen Endures*, 238.

36 Author's information. Note the capture of the Iranian dhow, *Jihan I*, in December 2012 carrying 40 tons of arms and ammunition intended for the Houthis.

37 Author discussions with President Abed Rabbo Mansour Hadi.

38 For example, the author took piano lessons from a Russian woman married to a Yemeni doctor who had trained in the Soviet Union. She was a much better teacher than the author was a music student.

39 *Humanitarian Needs Overview* (New York: United Nations Office for Coordination of Humanitarian Affairs, UNOCHA, December 2017).

40 "Middle East and North Africa: Macro Poverty Outlook," The World Bank (April 2021), 180.

41 Briefing to United Nations Security Council by the Special Envoy for Yemen-Hans Grundberg, December 14, 2021.

42 R. J. Huddleston and D. Wood, "Functional Markets in Yemen's War Economy," *Journal of Illicit Economies and Development* 2, no. 2 (2021): 204–21

43 R. Joseph Huddleston and David Wood, "Functional Markets in Yemen's War Economy," *Journal of Illicit Economies and Development* 2, no. 2 (2021): 204–21.

5 THE SYRIAN CIVIL WAR

Bringing the Conflict to a Close

Robert S. Ford

Introduction

The Syrian civil war is winding down, and President Bashar al-Assad has a new seven-year term in office, as he won 95 percent of the vote in the May 2021 election that Western governments said was neither free nor fair. Assad's government will remain in power on his terms for the foreseeable future. And its staying power has drawn some regional states to begin normalizing relations with Damascus despite its many economic and governance weaknesses. On the ground, the patchwork of control that predominated for the first part of the conflict now has consolidated to three zones. In the first, Assad's government, bolstered by vital aid from Iran and Russia, controls most of the country and its key population centers in western Syria. In the second zone, Syrian opposition fighters and Turkish soldiers are deployed inside Syria near the Turkish border. These Turkish troops in northwestern Syria oversee uneasy cease-fires between the opposition forces and the Syrian government in the northern parts of Idlib and Aleppo provinces. Farther east along the border the Turkish troops aim to contain Syrian Kurdish fighters. The Turkish position is exposed as Syrian forces with Russian help occasionally attack parts of the opposition-held pocket of northern Idlib and Aleppo provinces, causing yet more civilian suffering. In northeastern Syria, a reduced

American ground force, backed by an American no-fly zone, enables a mixed Kurdish–Arab armed force to administer territories captured from ISIS. The Trump and Biden administrations have not wanted to contest Turkish incursions and strikes along the northeastern Syrian border with Turkey as Washington focuses on fighting ISIS. Faced with unremitting Turkish hostility and an American unwillingness to contest Kurdish towns along the border with Turkey, the Kurdish leadership of this mixed armed force has sought help from Russia and even the Syrian government to deter and restrain Turkey.

The Syrian government and its allies will not accept partition of the country and will continue pushing to reassert central government control over the Turkish and American zones. Final resolution of the Syrian conflict will require negotiations over the future of those zones. Eventual negotiations will cover the terms under which the Syrian government reasserts its authority and will involve Russia, Turkey, the Syrian government, and Syrian armed opposition groups; the Americans will have a role in the talks about eastern Syria. Turkey will prioritize stability for Syrian civilian populations in areas it now controls and seek dismantling of the Autonomous Administration of North and East Syria (AANES) now under the leadership of a Syrian Kurdish faction backed by the Americans. The American focus in negotiations will be on a sustained fight against ISIS remnants in eastern Syria after their departure.

The negotiations to end Turkish and American occupation of northern and eastern Syria likely will take years. In the meantime, there will be sporadic outbreaks of fighting and violence, albeit at a far more limited scale and scope than what Syria experienced in the first years of the war. While the Damascus government is slowly getting closer to recapturing all preuprising Syrian territories, it lacks resources to rebuild the shattered economy. For many years ahead the country will be an economic basket case, hobbled by Western sanctions and a scarcity of funding for reconstruction, as well as corruption and occasional extremist attacks. As a result, most of the 6 million Syrian refugees will have little incentive to return home and Syria will remain a severely weakened state.

Beginning of the Conflict, 2011–14

Encouraged by the success of popular protest movements in Tunisia and Egypt, hundreds of thousands of Syrians began demonstrating in

March 2011, demanding an end to security force abuses and government corruption. Beyond the influence of television coverage of the revolts in Tunisia and Egypt discontent about the government's response to the drought that beset Syria from 2006 to 2010 was another underlying cause of the uprising. Poor economic circumstances among climate refugees in shantytowns around big cities encouraged more young people to seek change by taking to the streets. The majority of protests in the spring and early summer of 2011 were peaceful. The Syrian government quickly responded with arrests and shootings, leading soldiers who had defected from the army to return fire against Syrian security forces repressing the demonstrations.

The violence escalated quickly and widely. By autumn 2011, insurgents had seized whole neighborhoods of several towns and cities across Syria. The government further escalated with tanks, artillery, and warplanes. By autumn 2011 the nature of the conflict had changed as well, becoming a battle not only for accountability but for power. The fight also became markedly more sectarian with a growing presence of Sunni extremists fighting alongside more moderate elements of the opposition. In response to the armed opposition's gains in 2012, Iran in 2013 began mobilizing tens of thousands of foreign Shi'a militiamen to fight on behalf of the Assad government. In the spring of 2013, when Assad's hold on power was weakening, Iranian-backed Lebanese Hezbollah's critical intervention turned the tide in Homs Province. In 2014–15, Iran's Quds Force, the foreign and clandestine wing of the Islamic Revolutionary Guard Corps (IRGC), led by the late General Qassem Soleimani, sent fighters from Iraqi Shi'a militant groups such as Asa'ib Ahl al-Haq and Kata'ib Hezbollah to fight in Syria. It also organized Afghans and Pakistanis into the Afghan Fatemiyoun and Pakistani Zainebiyoun brigades, which it sent to Syria. By late 2013 the influx of pro-government militia fighters, and severe shortages of money and supplies among the armed opposition that aggravated its leadership problems, led to a war of attrition. Shifts in control of territories between the many armed opposition factions and the Syrian government and its allies were marginal from late 2013 until spring 2015.

Western governments, shocked at the scale of bloodshed and fearful of growing extremist elements in the Syrian opposition, urged negotiation of a transitional national unity government. Along with Turkey and a few Gulf states, they provided limited material aid to client groups among the armed opposition in order to press the Assad government to come to the negotiating table. They avoided direct military intervention in this phase of the war. Notably, President Barack Obama rejected retaliating against the Assad government after it used chemical weapons in a ground assault in the eastern suburbs of Damascus in August 2013 that killed hundreds of civilians. Obama concluded that a wave of limited strikes could put America on a slippery slope toward more direct involvement in the war.[1]

Failed Negotiations

Each effort at finding a negotiated settlement between the Syrian political and armed opposition and the Syrian government collapsed due to the latter's rejection of any compromise on power sharing or even confidence-building measures such as prisoner releases and humanitarian aid access.

Getting to Failure in Geneva, 2012–14

The foreign governments backing the Syrian opposition did not seek immediate regime change in Syria. When President Obama said that Assad should step aside on August 18, 2011, he emphasized that the United States would not impose a transition on Syria and would instead leave to the Syrian people the choice of their leaders. The Obama administration did not want to intervene too heavily in Syria in 2012–14; it did not want to "own" the conflict. The administration's policy was to cut entanglements in the Middle East, not add to them. Thus, Washington aimed at securing some kind of negotiated settlement, ideally under the auspices of the United Nations (UN), and pushed its allies into at least formally acquiescing to that goal. The Geneva 1 communiqué that the United States and Russia negotiated with the UN, Turkey, and Arab League states on June 30, 2012, called for a cease-fire and negotiation between the Assad government and the opposition for a national unity, transition government.

It took the Americans and their allies a year and a half to herd the main elements of the factious political and armed opposition to the negotiating table in Geneva in January 2014; only direct intervention from Turkey and Qatar that month secured the informal acquiescence of hardline but non-jihadi Islamist rebel groups to the Geneva talks. Although the opposition delegation offered in writing to the UN in February 2014 to negotiate each position in a transitional government, including the status of President Assad, the Syrian government delegation rejected any political discussion. The talks promptly foundered. The Assad government's military position in early 2014 was relatively stable and the Russian government pointedly declined to put any pressure on it to negotiate political compromises. The disunity within the Syrian armed opposition due to leadership conflicts and arguments about the allocation of supplies ensured that military pressure on the Assad government was slow to build.

More Fighting, More Failed Talks, 2014–17

The war of attrition between the foreign-backed armed opposition on one side and the Syrian government, supported by Iran and, to a lesser extent, Russia, on the other turned against the Syrian government in the spring of 2015. Idlib Province in northwestern Syria fell to the rebels and the rebel groups advanced south and west, bringing Latakia, a bastion of government support, within artillery range. In July 2015 President Assad acknowledged publicly that the Syrian army suffered from a serious manpower shortage and thus had to withdraw from some important areas. In August the late Iranian General Soleimani flew to Moscow to urge the Russians to intervene militarily given the increasingly dire situation facing the Syrian government.[2] Moscow rapidly moved warplanes to a base in western Syria and began combat support operations at the end of September 2015. Moscow said it was bombing ISIS and al-Qaeda terrorists, but most of its initial targets were Free Syrian Army (FSA) groups whose commanders had accepted in principle a negotiated political deal.[3] The Russian intervention gradually shifted the balance on the ground back to the Syrian government's favor.

A new round of Geneva peace talks in 2016 stalled as the Syrian government again rejected any political discussions, believing that with Russian and Iranian help it could secure more on the battlefield than at the negotiating table. Moreover, by this time, the American focus had shifted away from pressuring Assad to negotiate. Obama declined to respond to the Russian escalation in western Syria and instead focused on fighting ISIS in Iraq and eastern Syria. While the Russians pounded the anti-Assad opposition in western Syria, the Americans pounded ISIS in eastern Syria. Most notably, the Syrian army scored a major victory with the recapture of rebel towns in the southwestern suburbs of Damascus in August 2016, followed by a bigger victory with the recapture of East Aleppo in December 2016. Following the government victory in Aleppo, Russia convinced Iran and Turkey to join it in convening political talks outside the formal UN process in 2017 that started in Astana, Kazakhstan. In 2017 the three states of the Astana process with UN and American backing called for four cease-fire zones in western Syria. The more moderate armed opposition elements, with their backs to the wall, accepted the zones, but the Syrian government with help from Russia, Iran, and Hezbollah attacked and captured three of the four zones, one by one, in 2016–18. Idlib Province in northwestern Syria is the only of the four left, and its future is hotly contested (see below).

The UN special envoy, Staffan de Mistura, meanwhile convened two more rounds of UN talks in 2017, but these made no notable progress. As its enemies' strength diminished, the Syrian government had little incentive to compromise at UN talks. De Mistura in December 2017 publicly blamed the Syrian government for refusing to negotiate with the opposition and urged Russia to put pressure on Assad to make some concessions. The Western mantra dating to 2011 that there was no military solution to the Syrian conflict was wrong. It only made sense if one side's escalation in the war was matched by escalation on the other side. The Americans and allies opposed to Assad declined to match the Iranian and Russian escalations, enabling the shift in the military balance starting in late 2015 in favor of the Assad government. Thus, the American strategy of resolving the Syrian conflict through negotiations without applying some kind of powerful, persuasive military pressure on Damascus failed badly.

Lost Opportunity

Some analysts argue that the American strategy of achieving a negotiated settlement through a UN process combined with limited military pressure was mistaken from the beginning.[4] They assert that the Assad government could never have accepted reforms or subsequent calls from elements of the Syrian opposition and their foreign backers for a genuine transitional, national unity government. These analysts note that any genuine power sharing would be completely anathema to Assad and his security apparatus. They also argue that while Assad was, in fact, losing in the war of attrition by 2015, the Iranians and the Russians would never have allowed his government to collapse. The American intervention, and that of the other pro-opposition foreign states, they conclude, merely forestalled Assad's victory and thus prolonged the war. They do not, however, address the splits within the Syrian government leadership that more pressure would have produced. For example, a bombing in 2012 killed several top Syrian government officials in an operation most believe was an inside job.[5] Similarly, sharp economic pain was causing audible complaining within the ruling circle in 2020. Meanwhile, Moscow and Tehran would have faced challenges managing the domestic political sensitivities from greater casualties and costs of greater escalation on their sides. Their ability to escalate indefinitely in the face of increased rebel strength was unclear, and it would have been further at risk politically if the armed opposition had pushed to win over elements of the Syrian government's support base in return for greater external assistance. Furthermore, the ill-coordinated manner in which foreign state backers funneled aid to armed opposition groups—in particular the Turkish-Qatari aid to Islamist extremist armed groups—prevented the Syrian opposition from effectively reaching out to elements of the Syrian government political base or from coalescing into a united military command.[6] The opposition failed to entice key segments of the Syrian government's support base and most external aid to it, with the big exception of Turkish assistance, diminished sharply by 2017.

Dynamics of the Fighting, 2018–21

Direct military intervention by foreign states, especially Russia, the United States, and Turkey, has shaped the latest phase of the civil war. Most notably, their interventions led to Syria's current division into three zones, each of which enjoys an umbrella of external protection.

By 2018, the Syrian army and its Iranian-led militia allies, backed by powerful Russian air support, were consolidating their hold over most of western Syria. They recaptured the eastern suburbs of Damascus in the spring of 2018. In July 2018 the Russians brokered an agreement, backed by the United States and Israel, that required armed opposition elements in Daraa in southwestern Syria to surrender their heavy weapons and allow a limited Syrian government presence. In the summer of 2021 opposition elements in Daraa reacted against increasing Syrian government encroachment in their local governance and openly rebelled against the government again. Russian backing for a Syrian government siege ultimately led in September 2021 to a rebel surrender and recognition of a bigger Syrian government presence in Daraa.[7] Of the four cease-fire zones agreed upon between Russia, the Syrian government, and the opposition in 2016, only parts of the last zone, in Idlib and northern Aleppo Province, remained in opposition hands. Frequently the Syrian army launched limited offensives north into Idlib, again with Russian airstrikes in support. By 2020 it had secured control of the highway linking Damascus to Aleppo. Syrian assaults into Idlib also aimed at recapturing the highway that links Aleppo to Latakia on the coast. The Russians supported that goal and negotiated a deal with Turkey in September 2018 to allow for joint Russia–Turkey patrols along that highway. However, Turkey did not keep the road secure from rebel groups, provoking Russian charges that Turkey was reneging on their agreement.

Eastern Syria

Fighting ISIS was never a Syrian government priority, and the government made quiet deals to buy oil and food from the Caliphate.[8] The great bulk of Syrian and Iranian-backed militias were deployed in fighting in western Syria, and prior to 2017 scattered Syrian army units in central Syria did little to resist ISIS. However, operating under the Russian air umbrella that stretched from the Mediterranean to the east bank of the Euphrates River starting in late 2015, the Syrian government, backed by Iranian-backed militias, exploited the collapse of ISIS in the lower Euphrates Valley in the second half of 2017. It recaptured the parts of Homs, Hassakeh, and Deir ez-Zour provinces on the west side of the river. In 2021 Russian ground units began to deploy in these areas as well at the invitation of the American-backed Syrian Kurdish People's Protection Units (YPG) militia to deter deeper Turkish incursions into northeastern Syria. Elsewhere, small Russian units deployed along the Euphrates River to compete for control with Iranian-backed militias. In 2021, therefore, the Syrian government, backed by its sometimes competitive Russian and Iranian allies, controlled almost 70 percent of the Syrian territory, including all of the major population centers. Within that area the Russian military has built up its airbase in western Syria as well as its long-standing naval facility at Tartous.

Syrian government control could not extend east beyond the Euphrates River because of the ongoing American military presence.

Spurred by public revulsion of the ISIS murder of American hostages, by autumn 2014 the Obama administration was emphasizing the defeat of the ISIS and moved the effort to resolve the broader Syrian Civil War to the back burner. The American air force first intervened to help the Syrian Kurdish YPG militia defend the Kurdish town of Kobani at the end of 2014 and into 2015. Over the next several years the Americans developed a relationship with the YPG militia, providing training and military supplies to enable it to assume the largest share of the ground battle against ISIS in eastern Syria. The Americans initially deployed small teams of special operators to coordinate airstrikes. Regular army forces eventually joined them in helping the YPG militia, alongside Arab fighters, to take back ISIS territories step by step, culminating in the capture of the last ISIS controlled town in March 2019. The fighting against ISIS was often very tough; the mixed Kurdish–Arab fighting force, called the Syrian Democratic Forces (SDF), lost about ten thousand fighters.[9]

The national security rationale for the continued deployment of about two thousand American soldiers in eastern Syria after the last ISIS bastion fell was then less clear. Military operations, especially ones led by Syrian Kurdish commanders not local to the area, were not stopping a trickle of recruitment for ISIS, which maintained an ability to conduct occasional assassinations and small-scale ambushes. Some officials stated that the continued American military presence would pressure the Assad government to negotiate a compromised political deal and restrain Iranian influence in Syria. Notably, the American military controlled the junction of the Syrian, Jordanian, and Iraqi borders to block Iranian utilization of the main highway crossing from Iraq into Syria. However, the lack of any movement on the UN-led political talks and the steady stream of Iranian material into Syria by air and through secondary roads under Syrian government control showed that the United States presence would not achieve its new objectives. President Donald Trump had campaigned in 2016 on fast victory against ISIS in the Middle East and then withdrawal. He announced via Twitter in December 2018 that the American forces would leave Syria. Officials at the State and Defense Departments scrambled to reverse the president's decision and convinced him to leave about half the troops in Syria to continue helping the YPG-led SDF and guard oil wells in eastern Syria. Trump remained unenthusiastic and in response to a major Turkish incursion in October 2019, he ordered American forces to redeploy away from the Turkish border in northeastern Syria. This decision caused a small uproar in Washington and led to the resignation of Defense Secretary James Mattis and the senior anti-ISIS coalition coordinator Brett McGurk. Presidential candidate Joe Biden, who had backed the Obama administration's withdrawal of forces from Iraq in 2011, in October 2019 called Trump's refusal to push back against Turkish pressure on the YPG in Syria a shameful sellout of American allies that would enable ISIS to regain strength and attack America.

Turkey

Turkey has a clear priority national security objective in Syria: forestall the formation of a Syrian Kurdish state. Ankara initially was determined to see the Assad government removed and its allies in the political and armed opposition, including groups connected to the Syrian Muslim Brotherhood, prevail in the civil war. However, since 2015, when the Russian air force intervened to boost Assad, and the United States ramped up the fight against ISIS in the northeast using the Kurdish YPG militia as its main ground force in that fight, Turkey's key objective has shifted to forestalling the establishment of a Syrian Kurdish entity in northern Syria. Because of historic and social ties between Turkish and Syrian Kurds, Ankara fears even a small Kurdish state in northern Syria would boost terrorism inside Turkey and pose longer-term risks to Turkish national unity. Turkey to no avail protested American help to the Syrian Kurdish YPG militia, highlighting its organic ties to the Kurdistan Workers' Party (PKK) in Turkey (see below). American efforts in the Obama and Trump administration to make tactical security arrangements along the Turkish-Syrian border to diminish Turkish antagonism toward the YPG could not address the strong, underlying objections in Ankara to the rising YPG-controlled statelet in northern Syria. The American alliance with the YPG drove Ankara to find accommodation with Russia. Turkey succeeded in gaining Russian acceptance of limited Turkish intervention in northern Syria to block YPG westward expansion. Its first direct ground intervention, called Operation Euphrates Shield, seized territories in northern Syria in 2016–17 to block the YPG's push into northwestern Syria. As the YPG statelet grew stronger in northeastern Syria under American military protection, Ankara redoubled efforts to preempt the statelet from taking further root. The Turks launched two more military operations against the YPG-led Kurdish administration in northern Syria. The first, Operation Olive Branch, seized the area around Afrin in north-central Syria in 2018. The next, called Operation Peace Spring, in 2019 seized territories east of the Euphrates along the border and further segmented areas dominated by the YPG. Washington was unhappy that these Turkish operations distracted YPG attention away from the battle against ISIS as Kurdish fighters redeployed to defend Kurdish locales along the border. Without American combat air support, the YPG militia fighters cannot hold ground against concerted Turkish military attacks. Therefore, in 2019 to limit Turkish incursions connected to Peace Spring the YPG invited the Russians and small Syrian army detachments to deploy into YPG-controlled spaces along the northeastern border with Syria. The result is that the Syrian–Turkish border in northeastern Syria regularly sees Syrian government, Russian, Turkish, and American military units operating in very close proximity with occasional confrontations. There is a deconfliction mechanism between the Russian and American forces, but this did not prevent occasional face-to-face stand offs between their soldiers in far northeastern Syria in 2020 and 2021.

No Negotiated Political Deal in Prospect, 2017–21

The shift in the military balance between 2015 and 2018 removed any remaining incentive for the Assad government to make compromises in a political negotiation. Russian and Iranian officials warned that the opposition would not gain a political victory at the UN negotiating table that eluded it on the battlefield. In the face of total Syrian government rejection of negotiation for a new government, the dogged UN envoy De Mistura dropped any further discussion of a transition government and instead sought to convene talks between the Syrian government and parts of the Syrian opposition about changes to the constitution. This effort, too, faltered in 2018. De Mistura resigned in October 2018, replaced by Norwegian diplomat Geir Pedersen. Pedersen dutifully convened multiple sessions with the government, political opposition, and members of Syrian civil society from 2020 into 2022 to negotiate changes to the constitution. In October 2021 at the end of another failed round of discussions, Pedersen indirectly blamed the Syrian government for not engaging constructively.

Bringing the Conflict to a Close

Syrian Government

The Syrian government has been the main protagonist since the beginning of the conflict and the balance of power in western Syria strongly favors the government in Damascus. Most important, the government's hold on the major population centers of Damascus, Aleppo, Homs, Hama, Latakia, and Daraa is secure. President Assad insists on controlling all major institutions and rejects power sharing with the opposition or any effort to impose change or reform from the outside. This government thus enjoys a relatively unified command structure and functions as a state. President Assad has had steady support from his military and the government's four capable, ruthless intelligence services. Dire economic circumstances have driven the government to extract revenues wherever it can. This caused some cracks among the ruling elite, most notably a very public squabble between President Assad and his wealthy businessman cousin, Rami Makhlouf, in 2020 over payments the Assad government demanded. Makhlouf ultimately had to comply, as Assad's hold on power is firm and the government's coercive power still strong. Nonetheless, the long conflict has weakened the state substantially. Its manpower resources are exhausted and the government's desperate search for more fighting men empowered local warlords who, while nominally loyal to Damascus, led fighters who were little more than irregulars exploiting neighborhoods they control for money and plunder. In the absence of any considerable countervailing pressure, the strong but brittle Assad government at most might eventually accept a few cosmetic changes to the constitution and perhaps a few small changes in the cabinet. Constitutional changes mean little when the Syrian government has never been subject to the rule of law. The weak Syrian political opposition negotiating team working with the UN has little incentive to accept a watered-down national deal. Meanwhile, Islamist extremist elements have never evinced any interest in a negotiated settlement. Russia, Iran, and the Syrian government insist that these jihadi elements cannot be included in any political deal and must instead be destroyed. Therefore, a national political deal under UN auspices or some other mechanism that dramatically stops the remaining fighting is unlikely. There will be no Appomattox moment that concludes the Syrian civil war.

Rather than negotiating a new political order, Assad's government aims to recapture, gradually, all of the opposition-controlled territories. Damascus will depend heavily on help from its allies and has signaled that Russian and Iranian forces will remain in Syria over the long term. Damascus retains some agency; it has occasionally, gingerly, resisted Russian pressure to be more forthcoming on humanitarian aid deliveries, political reforms, and confidence-building measures. It has also publicly rebuked Iran for taking too much credit for battlefield successes. The Syrian government also welcomes moves from some regional states to gradually normalize relations. Jordan has been particularly vocal about the need to work with the Assad government, and President Assad visited the United Arab Emirates to meet de-facto ruler Crown Prince Mohammed bin Zayed and Dubai ruler Mohammed bin Rashid in March 2022. There is even discussion of a pipeline that would go from Egypt through Jordan and Syria to Lebanon and from which the Syrian government would receive either gas or cash. Washington has indicated it will waive its sanctions to allow the project to move forward.

This gas project is but one example of how resolving the Syrian civil war and reconstruction involves not just the Syrian government's terms for the opposition, but also necessarily involves foreign state interests given the heavy intervention by regional and international powers. The balance of power in western Syria means that any near-term political agreement between the Assad government and the remaining Syrian opposition will be on Assad's terms. Only long-term force commitments from the Turks and the Americans would enable the remaining Syrian opposition elements in Idlib, Afrin, and eastern Syria to hold the Syrian government and its allies in check. Washington and Ankara sharply disagree about the proper local allies and most desirable outcomes in Syria, however. Thus, Damascus, Moscow, and Tehran hold an advantageous position as the war winds down.

Russia

Russia is the key foreign state that can help bring the long conflict to a close. Only Moscow has steady diplomatic contacts with all the other actors in Syria. It will likely maintain bases and an upgraded military presence even after the guns all fall silent. Moscow doesn't control Assad's decision-making but it has influence and it shares with Assad a vision for the conflict's end state. Russian President Vladimir Putin has not wavered in pursuing a result to the war that leaves the Assad government in power and in some manner sovereign. Russia also uses its military success in Syria to highlight its reliability as an ally and to showcase some of its weapon systems.

Beyond its military assistance, Russia provides important diplomatic cover for Syria at the UN. Putin has a broader message to Western countries through his involvement in the Syrian conflict: Moscow rejects foreign states intervening against autocratic governments on behalf of domestic opposition movements. Bitter about the Western exploitation of UN Security Council Resolution 1973 to intervene militarily in Libya to overthrow Muammar Gaddafi, the Russians have resisted Western efforts to pressure Assad for major political concessions or even his departure. In a sense, Putin has drawn a red line in Syria against Western support for domestic opposition movements in countries that might one day include Russia. Notably, the Russians have stressed that foreign forces (with the exception of the Russians) should eventually withdraw from Syria.

Sensitive to potential domestic backlash against his Syrian war effort, Putin deploys Russian air units while limiting the use of ground forces to a few special operations units and Russian mercenaries that fight on Assad's side. The overall Russian effort has been relatively low cost to Moscow. So far, however, the Russians have not been able to translate military success into a political settlement. The Russians now seek to use the Astana group that it organized in 2017 to promote, with the UN, a minimal political resolution of the civil war focused on constitutional amendments. Assad has largely stiffed the Russians, but Russian leverage with the Syrian government is stronger when Assad has to face not just fragmented opposition groups but also Turkish or American troops that Syrian forces alone cannot defeat in a conventional battle.

Ending Foreign Troop Deployments in Syria: Turkish Zones

While the Russians may decline to employ their air force against either the Turks or the Americans, Moscow will not legitimize their long-term presence on Syrian soil either. Instead, it is more likely that Russia will protect Assad's hold on western Syria while pressing for a series of separate negotiations to enable Syrian forces to redeploy further into the Turkish and American zones. One set of negotiations would aim to convince Turkey to withdraw its military units from Idlib, Afrin, and the Peace Spring border area between Tel Abyad and Ras al-Ayn, allowing reestablishment of formal—albeit weak—Syrian government control over these areas and the borders. This will be a difficult negotiation involving the future of Turkish-backed Syrian rebels as well as Islamist extremists operating in northwest Syria and the future of millions of internally displaced civilians and perhaps millions of refugees too.

Refugees and Internally Displaced Civilians

According to UN estimates, there are approximately four million civilians in Turkish-controlled areas in northern Idlib and Aleppo provinces. Ankara wants to forestall any massive rush by these civilians to enter Turkey as refugees. This Turkish national security interest transcends political divisions inside Turkey, especially as the 3.6 million Syrian refugees already in Turkey are becoming a bigger social, political, and economic problem. As a result of the public unhappiness with the large refugee population, the Turkish government essentially closed its border to refugees in 2015. Ankara ideally would like millions of refugees already in Turkey also to leave. To date very few of these Syrian refugees have agreed to return to homes in government-controlled areas to the south. Ankara therefore keeps trying to conclude a durable agreement with Moscow that would restrain Syrian-Russian attacks on Idlib. Russian and Syrian forces regularly strike Idlib targets, but have made only limited gains on the ground. Without a deal with Russia that restrains Syrian ground incursions and Russian air attacks, Turkey faces the real prospect of big new waves of refugees. In the wake of its Ukraine debacle, Moscow needs good relations with Turkey, thus strengthening the Turkish position in Syria for the next several years.

Finding a means of reassuring civilians under Turkish protection in northwestern Syria that they can remain there safely in the short- and medium-term after an eventual Turkish withdrawal will be vital to convincing Ankara that a withdrawal will not jeopardize Turkish interests. So far, the Syrian government has evinced little interest in promoting the rapid return of Syrian refugees or the internally displaced persons (IDPs). Instead, it has in many instances appropriated their land for redevelopment by loyal businessmen. A Russian observer force charged with protecting civilians from the Syrian security forces likely will not be sufficient given resentment among large segments of the local population against Russia because of its brutal air campaign and the Russian record of not enforcing limits to Syrian government depredations in southern Syria. The Arab League gained Syrian government acceptance to deploy a very small and ultimately ineffective force in late 2011 at the start of the uprising and the UN likewise gained Security Council approval for a very small and ultimately ineffective observer force in 2012 that was withdrawn after only four months. It might be possible to find a multinational observer force that wins approval from Damascus if there are firm assurances that the force is not permanent and does not infringe on international recognition of Syrian government's sovereignty over zones from which the Turkish forces withdraw and the observer forces deploys. Its operational effectiveness against Syrian government arrest campaigns among the civilian population would be open to serious question, however, in the face of an unrepentant Syrian government.

Syrian Non-Jihadi Opposition

The other issue to be negotiated between Turkey, Russia, and the Syrian government in northern Syria is the fate of the opposition groups there that are not jihadis. Under the Turkish military umbrella in northern Syria the political opposition Syrian National Coalition operates an interim government that governs areas not controlled by jihadis or the AANES. Very loosely connected to it are non-jihadi armed opposition factions that originally started operating under the loose umbrella of the FSA in 2012. The Syrian opposition was always split between liberals and Islamists; there was never an agreed vision of the future state. The Islamist spectrum of the armed opposition was further split between religiously conservative groups that would accept negotiation with the Syrian government and jihadi groups that reject any negotiation and insist on fighting to stand up an Islamic state of some kind. There are dozens of factions that Turkey has sought to unify, but these rebel groups jealously guard a high degree of autonomy. Much of the political and security scene in northern Syria swirls around these factions' collaboration and conflict. They depend on Turkish aid and function essentially as Turkish proxies; Ankara has even sent some to fight on its behalf in Libya. These non-jihadis had sparred with jihadi fighters in Idlib, but they lost all major battles against them. Their weakness on the ground against the jihadis has seriously hindered Turkey's ability to placate the Russians and forestall further assaults on Idlib. These Turkish proxies also sometimes fight against the YPG militia, frequently at Turkish instigation. The United States placed several of the groups under sanctions because of their constant human rights violations; one group murdered a Syrian Kurdish political activist they captured in 2019. The final status of the non-jihadi rebel groups and the Syrian opposition civil administration in these Turkish-controlled zones depends heavily on Turkey and Russia. In the deal that restored opposition-controlled Daraa to Syrian government control, the Russians incorporated former armed rebels into a Russian-backed and commanded "Fifth Corps" while other rebel fighters agreed to surrender their heavy weapons and maintained nominal control of their former stronghold. The Russians in other locales have also negotiated demobilization and "reconciliation" deals between the Syrian government and former rebels. The Assad government might promise to reconcile with the non-jihadi rebels and political opponents in northern Syria, but the history of such agreements suggests that over time the Assad government reasserts full authority and arrests opponents as it gathers strength and peels away opposition on the ground. Aware of this, and with no place left to go, as part of any Turkish withdrawal agreement these opposition factions will demand safety in Turkey or likely will choose to fight deployment of Syrian forces into their zones.

Jihadis in Turkish Zones

The most important jihadi opposition group still controlling territory in Syria is the Organization to Liberate the Levant (Hayat Tahrir al-Sham or HTS). It evolved from the Nusra Front, which had been an offshoot of the Islamic State in Iraq, itself having been a spin-off from al-Qaeda. HTS has proven far more agile politically than its Iraqi forbearer. It often makes tactical alliances with non-jihadi organizations, breaking them when needed in order gradually to hold military predominance in northwestern Syria. HTS operates in Idlib Province in close proximity to Turkish military positions and non-jihadi groups. In large parts of Idlib it now operates the Salvation Government, an administration that manages schools, government offices, and utilities. HTS aims to extract itself from global terrorism lists and with Turkish encouragement claims to have broken all ties with al-Qaeda. (However, the US government rejected its claims and has classified it as a terrorist organization since 2012.) HTS has also cracked down on foreign fighters in territories it controls in Idlib Province. The Syrian government emphasizes that it considers HTS a terrorist organization. The Syrian army won't be able to defeat HTS fighters easily without strong Russian air support, however. The Russians have negotiated cease-fire agreements in Idlib that require Turkey to disarm HTS, and they complain that Turkey has not kept its promises. The Turks have hesitated to fight HTS directly and some observers think Turkey hopes to make HTS "disappear" by merging it with non-jihadi opposition factions. The future of Idlib and that of HTS depend mainly on Russian–Turkish negotiations about their bilateral relationship, a discussion that extends well beyond issues relating to Idlib itself. Moscow needs good relations with Turkey and will keep giving Ankara a margin to maneuver in its dealings with the Syrian fighters in Idlib. In the end, however, the Russians and Syrian government will insist that HTS be destroyed and Turkey will not go far to defend its leadership and fighters.

Resolving Eastern Syria

Eastern Syria is an even more complex challenge to resolve than the Turkish zones because of the greater number of actors, notably Iran, the United States, and a strong local Syrian administration. The Syrian Kurdish leftist political party, the Democratic Union Party (PYD), has dominated eastern Syria since 2012, backed by its seasoned militia, the YPG. When the Syrian army withdrew from most of eastern Syria to concentrate its efforts in western Syria, it handed over key sites to the PYD and its YPG militia. The PYD allowed Syrian government intelligence services to maintain a few sites under their watch in Qamishlo and Hassakeh. Anxious for American support, the YPG in 2015 readily accepted the American demand that Arab fighters join with the YPG militia to create the SDF. The YPG remains the backbone of the SDF, and their commanders lead it. Similarly, the PYD dominates the AANES. The PYD and YPG militias are not democratic and have harassed political opponents and compelled young men to serve in the SDF. The AANES manages local governance ranging from taxation and budgeting to health care, education, and agriculture. Following the PYD emphasis on populist governance and decentralization, the AANES devolves some responsibilities to municipal councils as well. The Americans work with it on stabilization projects. After much confusion in Washington about an American withdrawal from Syria in late 2018 and 2019, the PYD/YPG worry about the long-term American commitment in eastern Syria. The PYD therefore carefully maintains ties and contacts with Russia and the Assad government even though it has not been able to secure concessions from Damascus that would ensure its local autonomy would continue.

The PYD/YPG has organic links to the Turkish PKK, which both Turkey and the United States consider a terrorist group. Notably, the commander of the SDF, Shahin Cilo, aka General Abdi Mazloum, is a YPG fighter with connections to the PKK, and many YPG fighters hail from other PKK groups. These ties ensure continued Turkish animosity toward the AANES. Moreover, the PKK's conflict with the Kurdistan Region of Iraq's government sometimes spills over to aggravate relations between the PYD and the Kurdish Regional Government in Erbil. By contrast, the American position is one of pragmatism: Washington perceives the YPG-led SDF as the best force to contain ISIS in eastern Syria.

The Syrian government that wants to reestablish its authority over eastern Syria promotes an old-style Ba'athist ideology that gives no space for decentralization. Thus, Damascus has consistently resisted Russian encouragement for the Syrian government to reach an agreement with the AANES that would allow the latter to maintain its local governance. Still, the AANES and its colleagues in SDF uniform are adept at using external actors to protect them. They rely on the Americans to ensure the Syrian government doesn't try to retake oilfields vital to their budget. They rely on Russian and Syrian government protection to deter deeper incursions into their territories by the Turkish army. With SDF and American acquiescence, the Russians are gradually expanding their military presence east of the Euphrates River. After the Turkish Operation Peace Spring in 2019, the Russians began patrolling the eastern-most portion of the Turkish border with small Syrian government detachments, ostensibly to deter the Turks. Moscow began deploying warplanes at Qamishlo airport in late 2021.

As pro-government military forces very gradually increase in northeastern Syria, the focus there turns to what Washington will do. By early 2019, the Trump administration's policy had evolved into protecting its proxies in eastern Syria and trying to strangle the Assad government economically. The Americans couldn't translate real successes degrading ISIS and asserting control over eastern Syria into political concessions from Assad. Instead, the Americans are largely shut out of the key UN talks about political reforms that include the UN, Russia, Turkey, and Iran. President Trump, anxious to declare victory and end major commitments in Syria, insisted to a reluctant Pentagon and State Department in 2018 and 2019 that most US forces withdraw from the country. The Biden administration has emphasized that without major reforms in Syria it will maintain harsh sanctions against the Syrian government and will not support reconstruction. The third pillar of the Biden administration's publicly stated approach is to push for humanitarian aid access to Syrian civilians, notably IDPs in Idlib and northern Aleppo. The administration has limited its public remarks about the roughly nine hundred US troops in eastern Syria to confirming that their mission with the SDF against ISIS continues. It has not defined timelines or even benchmarks that would indicate when the troops might withdraw. American patrols often move through towns in the AANES closer to Turkey as a show of support for the YPG in those areas; ISIS has never operated in those spaces. The Americans also hold a pocket of desert inside Syria at Tanf, near the junction of the Syrian–Jordanian–Iraqi borders, where they block Iranian access to a road coming out of Iraq.

The American position has its vulnerabilities. As ISIS no longer controls any territory in Syria, the legal justification under the UN Charter for the American military presence is more problematic. Eastern Syria is not economically viable. The Biden administration restarted a $50 million stabilization assistance program with the AANES, and it budgeted $125 million for 2022. Small amounts of American economic aid won't resolve the growing economic problems in the AANES areas, such as price inflation and fuel shortages. Damascus seems little inclined to grant the PYD/YPG more than legalization of wider use of the Kurdish language and some other gestures in the cultural/social domain. Damascus, in fact, could make more concessions to the PYD/YPG about autonomy to convince them to demand the Americans withdraw their remaining forces. Such a call would make any continued American presence east of the Euphrates River impossible. (The Syrian government's commitment to keep its promises after the Americans depart would be a different question.) The Americans also must confront tougher security conditions over time—the longer they remain in eastern Syria, the more time hostile intelligence services and extremists will have to discover security vulnerabilities. A January 2019 suicide bombing in Manbij, a city supposedly pacified, killed four Americans. A drone attack against the American base at Tanf in October 2021 caused no casualties but demonstrated how America's opponents can target its forces. In September 2021 a resolution in the House of Representatives demanding a specific authorization for a continued US troop presence in Syria failed. It did, however, garner a majority of Democratic members of the House and signaled the political difficulties of an indefinite deployment.

Thus, Russia in the years ahead could find opportunities to negotiate with the Americans about the future fight against ISIS elements east of the Euphrates River. Moscow will also spearhead future negotiations involving the Syrian government and the PYD/YPG and local Arab figures about the future of the AANES and the SDF; Turkey and the United States might implicitly be consulted in those negotiations. The Syrian–Russian goal would be the formal reestablishment of Syrian government control. Negotiations about the AANES's future status, which necessarily will involve substantial PYD/YPG concessions, will be difficult and prolonged. Only when the Americans stand aside, as they did in 2018 when the YPG faced Turkey at Afrin in Operation Olive Branch, or in October 2019 when the Americans withdrew before a Turkish incursion with Operation Peace Spring, does the YPG accept the Syrian army deployments into towns under its control. If the Russians can convince the Americans about a sustained Syrian government-Russian fight against ISIS, the Syrian government is tactically clever enough to conclude a deal with the Syrian Kurdish PYD/YPG about local autonomy if it perceives a long-term interest in doing so. It knows that with the passage of time it could reimpose its authority fully as it regathers strength. Arab ethnic chauvinism would play to its advantage, although the fate of Arab fighters who joined the SDF will be at risk when the Syrian security forces deploy into their towns. An eventual Syrian government clampdown on the AANES's Kurdish elements would enjoy Turkish support.

Iran

The Americans might try to delay their withdrawal until Iranian forces also withdraw from Syria. The Russians would likely welcome an Iranian withdrawal, as would Arab states beginning to normalize relations with Damascus. However, the Assad government is unlikely to ask Iran to withdraw all its forces. Iran's proxy militias provided most of the manpower that enabled Damascus to prevail on the battlefields of western Syria, and they help in the ongoing fight against ISIS in central Syria. Outside analysts estimated that Iran provided as many as eighty thousand foreign Shi'a fighters to support Assad.[10] These Iranian-backed foreign Shi'a militias, under IRGC command, are deeply embedded into the broader Syrian security force order of battle and command network.[11]

Going forward, Iran's principal goal is to ensure the survival of the Assad government, which in turn provides strategic depth to Lebanese Hezbollah and the Iranian-backed "resistance front" against Israel. (This front seeks to deter Israel from carrying out a direct attack against Iran, and the confrontation with Israel gives Iran and its allies at least a nominal claim to regional leadership.) The Iranian government has repeatedly asserted that forces under its command will remain in Syria, while denouncing the presence of American forces in eastern Syria as well as American support for YPG militia and local Arab fighters. Iranian manpower losses have not been great, as Iraqi, Lebanese, Afghan, and Pakistani fighters bore the brunt of losses under Iranian command. Iran's difficult economic circumstances are hindering its activities in Syria, as is Russian pressure on Iran to reduce its presence near Israel. Tehran nevertheless is firmly committed to a long-term presence in Syria, in particular to establish bases for missiles which could reach Israel.

Damascus and Tehran have little incentive to accept linking an American withdrawal to the removal of all Iranian forces. They more likely would wait out the Americans. The Assad government, with Iranian backing and probably Turkish and Russian support as well, would likely use nonconventional tactics to harass American and SDF forces to weaken American resolve. Syrian intelligence and the Iranian Quds Force already operate throughout eastern Syria aiming to generate anti-foreign occupation fighters with money and arms. They will seek to utilize car and roadside bombs, assassinations of local allies, ambushes, and small-scale indirect fire attacks, as well as drone attacks, to cause casualties and undermine American domestic political support for a prolonged American presence in Syria. These locally generated hostile forces could even include Islamist extremists, a tactic the Syrian government used against the Americans in Iraq in 2004–9. Such asymmetrical tactics would impose fewer manpower costs on the tired communities that support Assad's government. It is not clear that Washington has the patience to withstand occasional casualties and long, drawn-out talks over the future of eastern Syria. It has no particular strategy to compel Syrian and Iranian concessions beyond harsh economic sanctions. As neither the Syrian nor Iranian government's top interest involves their population's economic welfare, how sanctions would compel concessions in any foreseeable timeframe is an open question.

Israel

Israel will also have a role in diminishing the violence in Syria because of its insistence on rooting out Iranian forces from Syrian soil. Without an end to Israeli airstrikes against Syrian and Iran-backed forces in Syria, there won't be a definitive end to the violence in the country.

Prior to 2011, Israel had occasionally struck targets in Syria, but these targets were usually connected to Hezbollah. And in fact, Israel took a relatively circumspect stance toward the Syrian Civil War until 2017. It provided small-scale assistance to a few opposition elements near the Israeli border but limited its intervention. The buildup of pro-Iranian militias and IRGC Quds Force elements in Syria in 2016 and 2017 provoked alarm inside the Israeli government. In 2018, the Israelis launched a series of sharp, limited airstrikes against Iranian and Syrian targets. Anxious not to engage the Russian air force, which is also operating in western Syria, Jerusalem set up a deconfliction mechanism with Moscow to avoid any air combat. Israel has maintained a steady dialog about Syria with President Putin under Prime Ministers Benjamin Netanyahu and Naftali Bennett.

Netanyahu first sought that Syria respect the 1974 cease-fire lines and confirm the demilitarized zone on the Golan. Since 2018 Jerusalem has aimed to secure Russian pressure to compel Iran to remove all of its military forces and the associated militias it had sent into Syria. Jerusalem is particularly sensitive to Tehran's attempts to build up missile bases after the pounding Israeli cities took from Iranian-supplied Hezbollah missiles launched from Lebanon in the 2006 war. Jerusalem also has encouraged Washington to take a tough line on the Iranian presence in Syria; the Israelis would be delighted to see American forces in eastern Syria tangle with nearby Iranian forces. President Trump in March 2019 noted the American presence at Tanf aims at impeding an Iranian buildup in Syria and thus helping address Israeli security concerns. This presence, however, is not stopping Iran from airlifting men and material to western Syria as it has done for the past thirty years, and it also uses secondary roads connecting into Syria from pro-Iranian militia bases in western

Iraq. Iran appears not to want a major confrontation with Israel in Syria and has been restrained in response to repeated Israeli airstrikes against its forces in Syria. As there is little prospect of Iran withdrawing or Israel standing down, an Israeli–Iranian confrontation thus remains another potential flashpoint in Syria.

ISIS Presence

While ISIS lost its remaining territories in March 2019, it continues to operate as an insurgent group able to strike in both central Syria, controlled by the Syrian government, and eastern Syria, controlled by the Americans and the SDF. Syrian government forces face regular ambushes along the western bank of the Euphrates River in Deir ez-Zour province, and occasional attacks farther west in Homs and Suwayda provinces. Similarly, the group, operating in small bands, conducts ambushes of SDF fighters on the eastern side of the Euphrates River as well as assassinations of local leaders. ISIS conducted a serious attack on a prison holding ISIS prisoners in Hassakeh in January 2022. American backing for the SDF has not stopped a trickle of new recruits joining ISIS that enables the group to continue fighting in eastern Syria. While these attacks threaten neither Syrian government control over its territories, nor that of the SDF in the east, Washington will be reluctant to withdraw until it is assured there is a capable force on the ground to contain ISIS after American soldiers depart. The Syrian army lacks the manpower by itself to adequately police this vast space in southern Hassakeh and Deir ez-Zour provinces east of the Euphrates River and the Russian army would need to send substantial reinforcements. The force best able to confront ISIS over the longer term are Arab fighters now organized in the SDF but how they would be integrated into the Syrian army is an open question to be negotiated. The Syrian government has so far taken a hard line against the SDF remaining a distinct military force.

Reconstruction Stalled, Refugees Stranded

Over half of Syria's prewar population has been displaced in the war, with roughly 6.5 million Syrians living as refugees, mostly in Turkey, Lebanon, and Jordan, and another 6 million internally displaced. Meanwhile, the World Bank estimates that by 2019 economic activity had declined by more than 50 percent from the levels of 2010.[12] A March 2021 report undertaken by Frontier Economics consultancy and the aid organization World Vision estimated that the Syrian economy had suffered a total of about $1.2 trillion in losses during the first ten years of the civil war.[13] The United States enacted an unusually severe set of secondary sanctions called the Caesar Act in the first half of 2020 that penalize any foreign entity doing business with a long list of proscribed Syrian figures and economic sectors. The tighter American sanctions aggravated shortages of imported fuel and deterred outside investment, including from Russia, China, and the Arab Gulf states. The sanctions and the banking crisis in Lebanon in 2019 triggered a steep decline in the Syrian pound, adding to already rising prices; the UN estimated that by February 2021 basic food prices had risen more than 200 percent in a single year.[14] As a result, UN estimates from early 2021 showed that 90 percent of the population lived below the poverty line and half the population needed humanitarian aid, 4.65 million were in acute need. Although Washington said that its Caesar sanctions have carve-outs for humanitarian aid, their disruption of import financing and investment added to unemployment and rising food costs. Rising world food prices in the wake of the Ukraine war will aggravate food shortages throughout Syria.

Estimates for the cost to reconstruct Syria vary widely but range in the hundreds of billions of dollars. The government's 2021 budget was less than $7 billion, and only a small fraction of that was devoted to reconstruction. The costs of reconstruction are also far beyond the means of Russia and Iran, and the Chinese have invested little in Syria since the war began. Russia has pushed the Europeans in particular to be more forthcoming on aid financing for the Syrian economy, highlighting the needs of internally displaced civilians and refugees. The European Union and its member states, as well as the United States, stress that they will dismantle sanctions and enable help for Syrian reconstruction only when there is genuine political reform inside Syria.

With Assad remaining in power, there is little prospect of such reform and hence the sanctions will remain in place indefinitely. Some Arab states have restored full diplomatic relations but sanctions are likely to deter almost any Gulf or other external investment, even from many Russian and Chinese firms. Corruption, always a problem in Syria, is worse now because resources are so scarce and this will further hinder investment. Indicative of the corruption, illegal production and trade in drugs overseen by Assad allies had become the largest Syrian export by the end of 2021.[15] Beset by weak investment, chronic energy shortages and infrastructure shortfalls, and a precipitous drop in real wages, the Syrian economy will not regain much vigor even as the fighting diminishes in the years ahead. In this environment, few refugees have much to return to. (They would also face security risks in many cases.) How best to aid the huge Syrian refugee communities in Jordan, Lebanon, and Turkey will be a major challenge for the international community for years to come.[16] Increasing resentment and hostility toward refugees among host populations in those countries will only aggravate the refugee problem. Forestalling recruitment by extremist elements among dispirited refugee communities will be a related challenge as well.

Conclusion

As the Syrian conflict winds down, Syria is emerging as an economically broken state whose northern and eastern territories are occupied by foreign powers. The weakened government, in control of the key parts of the country, is unrepentant. Turkey's position is uncomfortable and the Turkish government hasn't found a way out of its Syria quagmire, but it will revolve in part around the fate of the millions of Syrian civilians in northern Syria. Russia's problems in Ukraine may give the Turks a respite from Russian and Syrian government pressure. Turkey's ultimate stance in Syria also depends on the future of the PYD/YPG-administered statelet in northeastern Syria. That statelet's future in turn depends in large part on the Americans. Washington will eventually withdraw as eastern Syria is not strategically vital for American national security. The American public is ill informed about the role of US forces in Syria and incidents that cause significant US casualties will undermine support for the current policy. The United States should recognize that it cannot expel Iranian forces from Syria with the minimal resources Washington is willing to devote to the task. Likewise, it is unlikely that America's Gulf allies will be able to use restored diplomatic relations and promises of investment to downgrade the Syrian government's relations with Iran. Instead, Russia and Iran will compete for influence in Syria, and Israeli strikes and American sanctions on Iran will help Russia in the contest. Meanwhile, the Americans and their Gulf and European allies will not be able to fix the economic, social, and political problems that drive extremist recruitment in Syria, and the Kurdish YPG militia also cannot. A residual extremist problem is certain, therefore. The Syrian government will not allow independent economic aid actors, while funding government entities ensnares donors into the web of government favoritism and corruption. Reconstruction, thus, is far off. The best that outside states can do to reduce Syrian suffering and diminish future extremist recruitment is to focus resources on the six million Syrian refugees whose living conditions often are precarious. In these camps and informal settlements, especially in Lebanon and Jordan, outside help can alleviate the harshest conditions. It will also be important to ensure that extremists operating inside Syria cannot reach outside the country to strike America and its allies. This will require a new, more detailed level of security cooperation, particularly with Turkey, Iraq, and Lebanon.

Notes

1 Phil Gordon, *Losing the Long Game: The False Promise of Regime Change in the Middle East* (New York: St. Martin's Press, 2020), 228–30.
2 Laila Bassam and Tom Perry, "How Iranian General Plotted Out Syrian Assault in Moscow," *Reuters*, October 6, 2015.
3 Robert Mackey, "Parsing YouTube Evidence of Russian Strikes in Syria," *New York Times*, September 30, 2015; Zack Beauchamp, "Russia Says It's Bombing ISIS in Syria. This Map Shows It's Lying," *Vox*, October 7, 2015.
4 Sam Heller, "America Had Already Lost Its Covert War in Syria—Now Its Official," The Century Foundation (July 21, 2017); Aron Lund, "How Assad's Enemies Gave Up on the Syrian Opposition," The Century Foundation (accessed October 17, 2017).
5 See, for example, Sam Dagher, *Assad or We Burn the Country* (New York: Little, Brown, 2019), 312–13.
6 Lund, "How Assad's Enemies Gave Up."
7 Abdullah al-Jabassini, *Dismantling Networks of Resistance and Reconfiguration of Order in Southern Syria* Policy Brief, no. 44 (Robert Schuman Centre for Advanced Studies, European University Institute, October 2021).
8 Chloe Cornish, "The Men Making a Fortune from Syria's War," *Financial Times*, October 3, 2019.
9 Luke Mogelson, "America's Abandonment of Syria," *New Yorker*, April 27, 2020.

10 Richard Spencer, "Iran's 80,000 Militia Men in Syria Prime Powder Keg," *The Times*, May 5, 2018.

11 Tobias Schneider, "The Fatemiyoun Division: Afghan Fighters in the Syrian Civil War," Middle East Institute (October 15, 2018).

12 World Bank Overview of Syria, October 12, 2021. Available online: https://www.worldbank.org/en/country/syria/overview#1 (accessed October 14, 2021).

13 World Vision and Frontier Economics, "Too High a Price to Pay: The Cost on Conflict for Syria's Children," March 2021. Available online: https://www.wvi.org/sites/default/files/2021-04/Syria%2010th%20Anniversary%20Global%20Policy%20Report_Revised_0.pdf (accessed October 14, 2021).

14 World Food Program, "Twelve Million Syrians Now in the Grip of Hunger Worn Down by Conflict and Soaring Food Prices," World Food Programme (wfp.org), February 17, 2021. Available online: https://www.wfp.org/news/twelve-million-syrians-now-grip-hunger-worn-down-conflict-and-soaring-food-prices (accessed October 14, 2021).

15 Ben Hubbard and Hwaida Saad, "On Syria's Ruins, a Drug Empire Flourishes," *New York Times*, December 5, 2021.

16 UNHCR, "Eleven Years on, Mounting Challenges Push Many Displaced Syrians to the Brink," March 15, 2021. Available online: https://www.unhcr.org/en-us/news/briefing/2022/3/623055174/eleven-years-mounting-challenges-push-displaced-syrians-brink.html (accessed October 14, 2021).

6 FROM EMIRATE TO EMIRATE

Afghanistan's Twenty-Year War

Marvin G. Weinbaum

Introduction[1]

The Afghan civil war that began late in 2001 ended on August 15, 2021, marking the failure of an experiment with democratic constitutional government and of a multinational military mission led by the United States. Over a period of fifteen weeks, Taliban insurgents seeking to restore an Islamic Emirate overran a succession of provincial capitals and, with little bloodshed, captured the seat of government. As the foot soldiers of the insurgency were about to flood into Kabul, President Ashraf Ghani and his closest advisors fled, and most of the officials associated with the Ghani regime either scrambled to find flights out of the country or went into hiding. That the Islamic Republic of Afghanistan's days were numbered had been apparent for several months, but the speed at which the Afghan National Security Forces (ANSF) disintegrated was wholly unanticipated. The US intelligence sources had given the government at least three months. The country's warlord-led provincial and local ethnic militias, which had been expected to provide a last line of defense against the Taliban, also lost their will to fight, at least sparing Afghanistan an extended, almost certainly bloody civil war.

Doubts had always been expressed about the capability and reliability of the security forces. Including both regular army and militarized police, the largely US-funded defense forces were slated to number at least 350,000. In reality, at no time were its ranks close to being filled. Recruitment lagged and desertions grew increasingly common. In the closing weeks of the regime, possibly fewer than a quarter of government troops were still in the field.[2] There was general recognition that the ANSF was riddled with corruption and saddled with incompetent, divided leadership.

The fate of the Ghani government and the political system was as much determined at the negotiating table as on the battlefield. In late February 2020, in an agreement reached with the Taliban without the participation of or consultation with the Kabul government, the Trump administration promised the withdrawal of all American troops by May 1 of the following year. The deal was met with deep disappointment by the ruling circles in Kabul and the military, and many Afghans at first refused to believe that the Americans, who had invested so deeply in their country's future, were about to abandon it. Moreover, the February agreement stoked hopes that the conflict could be brought to an end politically rather than militarily. The Taliban had agreed to negotiate, though not directly with the Ghani regime, with a delegation of broadly representative Afghans. Those talks in Doha did not begin, however, until after more than six months and then only after the Kabul government, under strong pressure from the United States, was forced to make difficult concessions to get the Taliban to the table. Once begun, the discussions over procedural issues never progressed to substantive negotiations and by January 2021 were suspended by the Taliban.

By then the insurgents had made steady gains in consolidating their control over much of rural Afghanistan. Although not yet in possession of any provincial capitals, by capturing districts surrounding the country's population centers, including Kabul, the Taliban were well positioned to overrun government garrisons. What had been a two-pronged strategy, simultaneously pursuing military and diplomatic paths to secure power, had by early 2020 become dedicated almost exclusively to a military route to victory.

The full weight of the decision to leave Afghanistan and the beginning of the end for the government and the political system did not come until April 2021 when the new American administration confirmed the United States's intention to leave. The announcement by President Joe Biden that US troops would be fully gone from Afghanistan by September 11 if not sooner set in motion events that made the government's collapse almost inevitable. Kabul was assured of continued military funding for the ANSF but perhaps the most valued component of the American support, the provision of close air support, was to be withdrawn.[3] With this decided, all US military allies in the fight, most of whom depended on the tactical support of US forces, also declared their full intention to soon leave. So too did the thousands of American and other private contractors who were providing the Afghans valued equipment maintenance and training. By May 1, with the United States then in violation of the February 2020 agreement, the Taliban began in full earnest their final assault at a pace that may have surprised even them.

With the loss of confidence in the military and civilian leadership, and in its ability to stand without a foreign military presence, Afghan forces, low on morale and ammunition, surrendered themselves and their equipment. Except for some scattered, short-lived pockets of resistance, the Taliban, now ascendant, were left to decide the kind of country they wanted. On August 19, just four days after taking Kabul, the Taliban officially declared the Islamic Emirate of Afghanistan, reviving the name under which they had previously ruled the country from 1996 to 2001.

Perpetual Afghan Civil Wars

The concluded conflict in Afghanistan with the return of the Taliban and the United States withdrawal was only the most recent in a series of wars and episodes of civil strife that have engulfed the country over the past four and a half decades. At least six periods of almost continuous conflict can be distinguished. The first followed the communist coup in April 1978, when Islamist insurgents mounted a guerrilla campaign aimed at disrupting and ultimately bringing down the Moscow-backed government in Kabul. The Islamic-centric insurgency widely expanded and intensified in a second phase with the December 1979 military invasion of the Soviet Red Army in support of the Kabul regime, and the intervention of regional and international actors backing *mujahedeen* opposition forces. A third phase of civil war came with the exit of the Red Army in 1989 and a surviving communist regime facing direct combat with the insurgent groups. With the fall of the Kabul government in the spring of 1992, a fourth stage saw several of the victorious mujahedeen parties turning their weapons against one another in a destructive contest for political power in Kabul while the rest of the country was left subject to regional strongmen and their rapacious militias. Into this nearly anarchic state, the Taliban, a movement of militant Afghan students out of the madrassas in Pakistan, crossed into Afghanistan, captured Kandahar and with a slow but relentless offensive began a fifth phase of civil war. A sixth phase followed the US military intervention to punish al-Qaeda and their Taliban protectors for the September 11, 2001, terrorist attacks in New York and Washington, DC.

These phases share some key features. All saw foreign actors through material support to proxies actively fueling the conflict. Each period, moreover, was marked by the leading roles of militant groups seeking a regime committed to establishing an ultraconservative Islamic political order. Also, in every case, the forces of ethnicity contributed to intensifying the conflict. And none of these Afghan civil conflicts ended in a political settlement; all were eventually decided militarily.

Deeper Historical Context

Most of the underlying causes of the most recent Afghan conflict predate the 2001 US intervention. They contain echoes of the past, including missed opportunities and lessons. The 1978 coup marked the beginning of state failure and civil strife in Afghanistan. The regime in Kabul and its Soviet supporters carried out a brutal purge of religious leaders, civil society, intelligentsia, tribal leaders, and all domestic opposition. The new government also introduced radical political, economic, cultural, and social reforms that were largely antithetical to Afghanistan's predominantly religious and traditional society—triggering a nationwide antigovernment and anti-Soviet rebellion.

To suppress the uprising and rescue its struggling Afghan client state, the Red Army resorted to dreadful tactics, including indiscriminate aerial strikes and depopulation strategies, sparking major internal displacement and forcing five million Afghans to take refuge in neighboring countries, predominantly in Pakistan and Iran. This period of the conflict led to the killing of about fifteen thousand Soviet military personnel and more than one million Afghans over the next decade.[4]

Many of Afghanistan's religious fundamentalists settled in Pakistan, where they received a warm welcome and extensive support. As part of the Cold War, the United States, Saudi Arabia, and their allies provided financial aid and weapons to the mujahedeen.⁵ These fundamentalist leaders, who harbored strong anti-communist and anti-capitalist sentiments, created seven parties—collectively known as "the mujahedeen"—to wage war against the Kabul government and its Soviet allies. They also established close ties with transnational Sunni extremist groups, including future leaders of al-Qaeda. Indeed, most of the Taliban leaders, including Mullah Mohammad Omar, were formerly members of the mujahedeen.

Unlike the most recent civil war, the Soviet war culminated in a deadlock, with Soviet and Afghan government forces holding the urban regions and insurgents commanding much of the rural areas. When Mikhail Gorbachev came to power in 1985, he questioned the possibility of a military victory in Afghanistan. In line with his "new thinking" foreign policy doctrine, he decided to gradually end the occupation of Afghanistan, which he had described as "the bleeding wound."⁶ The new Soviet leader instructed the Kabul government to negotiate peace with the opposition and form an inclusive power-sharing government. While troop drawdown did not begin until February 1988, Moscow's announcement unnerved the Kabul government, whose survival depended on Soviet military and financial assistance. Therefore, in December 1986, Afghan President Mohammad Najibullah announced a reconciliation program designed to broaden the government's support base and seek peace with the insurgents. He offered unilateral concessions, including a six-month cease-fire, a new constitution recognizing Islam as the state religion, the promise of general elections, a reversal of some of the socialist economic reforms, amnesty for opposition leaders, release of sixteen thousand political prisoners, and half of the posts in a national unity government for insurgent leaders.⁷

Emboldened by the Soviet decision to withdraw, however, mujahedeen leaders rejected Najibullah's peace offer and doubled down on efforts to topple the government militarily. "The counter-revolution is aware of the strategic decision of the Soviet leadership to withdraw the Soviet troops from the DRA [Democratic Republic of Afghanistan]," a Soviet official noted. "The counter-revolution will not be satisfied with partial power today, knowing that tomorrow it can have it all."⁸

In addition to a lack of interest and political will by the international community to bring peace to Afghanistan, the lack of sincerity about a negotiated settlement by all external parties to the conflict also contributed to the failure. On April 14, 1988, for example, Afghanistan, Pakistan, the United States, and the Soviet Union signed the Geneva Accords, which had been under on-and-off negotiations since 1983 and were concluded only when the interlocutors agreed to a "negative symmetry" that called on Moscow to cut its military aid to the Kabul regime, and Islamabad and its allies to stop interfering in Afghan affairs. As required, the Soviets had entirely withdrawn their troops by the following February. However, in what became "positive symmetry," Moscow maintained support to the communist government, while Pakistan continued to aid the Afghan mujahedeen seeking to depose the Kabul government.[9]

The Soviet experience in Afghanistan and the announced and then actual withdrawal of the Red Army did not encourage the insurgents to make peace with the Kabul government. Quite the opposite, the mujahedeen intensified military operations to seize Kabul. Facing internal divisions and financial hardship after the 1991 collapse of the Soviet Union, the Kabul government fell to the mujahedeen in April 1992. There followed a devastating civil war between competing armed groups that paved the way for the emergence of the Taliban in 1994 in southern Afghanistan and the seizure of Kabul in 1996. As with the communist government's collapse and the Taliban's ascent, regime change with the Taliban's ousting in 2001 and return in 2021 had profound consequences for societal freedoms, the nature of governance, and regional and global security.

Parties to the Conflict

Arrayed in the post-2001 conflict to bring down the new Kabul government were a wide array of armed groups. Spearheading the insurgency was the Quetta Shura Taliban (QST) composed of Afghan Taliban commanders, established in the winter of 2002 in Quetta, the capital of Pakistan's Baluchistan province, which borders southern Afghanistan. These Taliban were closely aligned with the more cohesive Haqqani Network, perhaps the insurgency's most effective terrorist force. QST carried out strikes against coalition and Afghan security forces, mainly in the form of suicide attacks undertaken in cooperation with Pakistani militant groups.[10] Also of importance as a party to the conflict was the Islamic State-Khorasan Province (ISKP), established in January 2015 in eastern Afghanistan. This movement emerged mainly from among dissident elements of both the Afghan and Pakistani Taliban, joined by foreign terrorist groups, most notably the Islamic Movement of Uzbekistan (IMU).[11] Unlike in Iraq, the war in Afghanistan was not formed along sectarian lines, but ISKP was determined to change that by selectively targeting the Shiite Hazara minority. The cast of anti-state players also encompasses the remnants of al-Qaeda and supporting militant groups in Pakistan, notably the Tehrik-i-Taliban Pakistan (TTP), Lashkar-e-Jhangvi (LJ), and Lashkar-e-Taiba (LeT), that have also been engaged in terrorist attacks against India.[12] All sought the downfall of the Kabul government and the ouster of foreign forces from Afghanistan. They have had their own agendas, however, and in some cases are in direct competition, none more so than the QST and the Haqqani Network pitted against ISKP.

The primary foreign party to the conflict was the United States. But over the course of this UN-sanctioned mission, its NATO allies also contributed by providing troops and financial assistance. Although not direct parties in the war, Pakistan, Iran, and India felt they had a significant stake in the outcome of the conflict, as did to a lesser degree several other regional countries, including Russia, Saudi Arabia, the UAE, Qatar, and several Central Asian states. There was a general concern among Afghanistan's neighbors that an outright Taliban victory could expand Islamic insurgency beyond the country's borders. Frequent regional meetings dedicated in recent years to promoting Afghanistan's development also attested to the widespread perception of Afghanistan's centrality to regional economic connectivity and stability.[13]

Throughout the conflict, regional states retained their diplomatic ties with the Kabul government, finding it preferable to the Taliban in providing for a stable, peaceful, and prospering Afghanistan. Yet virtually all regional states favored reaching a negotiated political resolution of the Afghan conflict that provided for some kind of power sharing with the Taliban. At the same time, there was a lingering lack of confidence among neighboring or near-neighboring states in the eventual outcome, and most developed links to the Taliban leadership as hedging strategies in the event of the failure of the Kabul regime.

For the Taliban and other insurgent groups, establishing their own versions of an Islamic government in Afghanistan both motivated and rationalized their waging war against government and foreign forces seen as occupiers. There was a range of opinion among the Taliban leadership about how this might be achieved. The ascendant view was that there is no reason to discuss compromising on their principal aims when military success remains achievable. Others in the senior leadership seem prepared, however, to explore political negotiations as an alternative or complementary means of realizing political ascendance.[14] Despite occasional conciliatory signs to the contrary, negotiations with the Taliban confirmed that whatever the differences in strategy among the Taliban senior leadership, there were no differences in an unwillingness to yield on their core beliefs.

The typical Taliban field commander and foot soldiers were less motivated by Islamic ideology than by patriotic appeals calling for an Afghanistan free of foreign occupation and foreign cultural influences. Many were also driven by the profits of extortion, kidnapping, smuggling, drugs, and other criminal activities.[15] For many fighters, alienation from Kabul's rule could be traced to a sense of injustice born from contact with government agencies, including, above all, state judicial institutions rife with corruption. In the absence of alternative employment opportunities, the relatively generous salary paid to Taliban foot soldiers was also a motivating factor. Much of the public viewed the Taliban as less corrupt than predatory warlords and government officials. In general, although all Afghans sought a stronger economy and many held the government responsible for not bettering their lives, anger over socioeconomic conditions did not play an important role in explaining the Taliban's military gains.[16] Few, if any, Afghans expected the Taliban would strengthen the economy or provide better public services as a reason for backing the insurgents.

Phases of the Twenty-Year War

The conflict that began with the routing of al-Qaeda and their Taliban hosts in Afghanistan late in 2001 can be broken down into five phases, one blending into the next. The first covers the period following the Taliban's disintegration in Afghanistan and their finding sanctuary in the border regions of neighboring Pakistan. Excluded from amnesty initiatives and negotiations over the formation of a new Afghan government, the movement's largely intact leadership soon began to rebuild by recruiting and training many new fighters, mainly from among Afghan students in Pakistan's borderland madrassas. The Taliban also reestablished their close relationship with al-Qaeda and renewed their ties to the Haqqani Network, a tightly knit group of veteran fighters whose leader, Jamaluddin Haqqani, rejected an invitation to align with the new government.

Pakistan's border tribal agencies also provided safe haven for fighters aligned with Gulbuddin Hekmatyar, another former mujahedeen leader, and with exiled insurgent groups from Chechnya, China, and Uzbekistan. In 2002, the number of American troops totaled 5,000 and would grow to 8,000 over the next two years, mainly as directed by the George W. Bush administration to engage in counterterrorism, including searching out senior members of al-Qaeda and the Taliban, a task left mainly to US Special Forces and CIA operatives. What counterinsurgency was necessary was left almost entirely to Afghan warlords.

Three key factors prepared the ground for the Taliban reemergence. First, three decades of war had fragmented Afghan society and crippled the country's civilian and military institutions.[17] As a result, the new Afghan government, led by President Hamid Karzai, struggled to govern effectively and expand its writ across the country. President Bush's pledge of a "Marshall Plan" for Afghanistan did not materialize; the country received only $52 per capita in foreign assistance for the first two years of post-conflict reconstruction, substantially less than Bosnia ($1,390) and Kosovo ($814) did during similar periods in their reconstruction.[18]

Second, the United States and its allies initially had a small footprint in Afghanistan, and they largely relied on local warlords and power brokers to provide security and governance, fueling corruption and lawlessness and leaving a security vacuum that could be filled by the insurgents. Furthermore, the 2003 invasion of Iraq distracted Washington from state-building and stabilization efforts in the war-ravaged country. The CIA and the United States Central Command considered the Taliban a "spent force" and diverted key military and intelligence assets to Iraq, limiting the military mission in Afghanistan to counterterrorism operations against the remnants of al-Qaeda.[19]

Third, the Taliban leadership, including the group's leader, Mullah Omar, relocated to Pakistan, where they received support from state and non-state entities to reestablish the Taliban as an insurgent movement. During the regrouping phase following their escape from Afghanistan, Pakistan served as a valued source of financial and logistic support. Then and later, the Haqqani family, whose links to the Inter-Services Intelligence (ISI), Pakistan's premier intelligence agency, dated to the 1980s, received special favor. In Pakistan's tribal regions the Taliban were also able to establish ties and gain the protection of newly forming anti-state militant groups that would coalesce in 2007 to form the TTP.

By late 2005 the conflict entered a second and more confrontational stage marked by changed Taliban tactics and a willingness to take greater risks. Having infiltrated back into Afghanistan in far larger numbers, they had established a strong presence, particularly in the country's south and southeastern provinces. Suicide attacks became more prevalent, as did the widespread use of improvised explosive devices on roads and in the fields. There was concern in 2006 that the Taliban might undertake a major Tet-style offensive centered on Kandahar Province. Despite increases in the troop levels from seven thousand in 2006 to more than twenty-five thousand by 2009, the United States did little to reassess its overall military strategy, preoccupied as it was for much of the time with the war in Iraq.[20] By 2009, American and Afghan casualties had risen sharply, and there were growing convictions within the US military command that the Taliban were on their way to winning the war.

A third stage beginning in 2010 followed from the decision by President Barack Obama to order a surge that called for US forces to rise to 100,000, which together with allied NATO-led troops brought the number close to 140,000. The campaign focused on Helmand and Kandahar provinces, the two where the Taliban had become most deeply entrenched. The surge was intended to rout out the Taliban through counterinsurgency military operations that also emphasized advising and equipping Afghan forces. These military actions were expected to be followed up by a major effort by the Kabul government to implement more effective provincial and local governance measures. An accompanying counterterrorist strategy was designed to "disrupt, dismantle and defeat al-Qaeda in Afghanistan and Pakistan."[21] Drone attacks succeeded in destroying many of the remaining al-Qaeda safe havens in tribal areas of Pakistan. As planned, the surge in Afghanistan concluded in 2014 with only 9,800 troops left in Afghanistan

The fourth stage of the conflict beginning in 2014 was one of transition. The American administration was determined to further reduce its military footprint in the country while creating a larger and more capable Afghan army and police force. The United States had committed to this task in 2005 but had not seriously followed through. Training and advising now became central as all the fighting was slated to be handed off to Afghan forces. Although by 2016 only 8,600 American troops remained in Afghanistan, the US air campaign against the Taliban grew.[22] This stage also marked a more concerted effort to explore the potential for a negotiated end to the conflict. While the prospect of serious negotiations remained a possibility, the Taliban senior leadership in Quetta, known as the Rahbari Shura, was not targeted. The United States also drew back from attacking Taliban fighters except when air power was used to come to the aid of hard-pressed Afghan government troops. It was during this period that ISKP entered the conflict and soon became a prime target of the US air campaign. An offshoot of the ISIS movement in Syria and Iraq, ISKP succeeded in occupying territory in the country's northeast. Its combatants numbered well short of 10,000, mostly drawn from the ranks of disaffected Afghan and Pakistan Taliban joined by several thousand foreign insurgents. Meanwhile, as the Taliban continued to expand and tighten their grip on the countryside, the number of fighters under their command grew from an estimated 20,000 to 60,000.[23]

A fifth stage began with the February 2020 agreement to remove all American forces from the country in fourteen months. For all that the deal seemed to foretell, Washington's determination to exit militarily did not at first fully register with the Afghan government and national security forces. Even with intra-Afghan talks having effectively broken down and prospects dashed for a negotiated power-sharing government, it was not until Biden's April announcement of his intention to have all US forces out of Afghanistan no later than September 11, 2021, that the war's outcome became more or less inevitable. Morale within the Afghan military and among the civilian leadership then began its rapid descent. Within weeks the Taliban commenced their spring offensive, capturing a series of provincial capitals, and completing the country's takeover in eleven days in early August as Afghan defense forces melted away.

Shaping the Conflict

Perhaps no single factor better accounts for the course and outcome of the Afghan conflict than *the determination, resilience, and patience of the Taliban*. Despite internal divisions over leadership, there was a unity of purpose in achieving the ousting of all foreign forces and the reestablishing of an Islamic Emirate. The government had nothing to match the inspiration provided Taliban fighters and the popular appeal of the insurgency's assertion that the country was in the hands of foreign occupier enemies of Islam. In the belief they were fighting for a righteous cause and were destined to ultimately prevail, the Taliban were willing and able to wait out their adversaries. Clashing ambitions among senior

Taliban leadership and operational differences between the movement's political wing and its field commanders were at times in evidence. But to a surprising degree the leaders proved able to reconcile their differences sufficiently to avoid threatening organizational cohesion, and the hierarchical structure of the movement remained largely intact through the conflict.

These features stood in strong contrast to the *Afghan Republic's political elites*, whose public displays of disunity contributed to an erosion of public faith and confidence in the country's leadership. The bitterly disputed presidential elections were only the most visible demonstration of the badly divided ruling class. Even leaders with largely similar political orientations struggled to find common ground. There was little sense of urgency to draw together even while facing the direst possible outcomes. Those at the helm of government frequently revealed arrogance, insensitivity, and inflexibility, leading to serious misjudgments, even delusional thinking about the course of the war. Without taking credit away from the Taliban, whose well-designed military, political, and communication strategies were to prove crucial to their ultimate success, the failure of the Islamic Republic resulted more from disappointment with the Kabul government than from the appeal of the insurgency.

No country contributed more than *Pakistan in sustaining the Taliban in their insurgency*. While neither entirely trusted the other, their interests largely coincided. Most importantly for Pakistan, the Taliban offered an insurance policy that if the Afghan state were to fragment, a force of friendly Pashtuns could provide Pakistan a security belt of border provinces in Afghanistan. And were the Taliban to return to power, a beholden Taliban movement could be expected to exclude India's presence and influence. For its part, Pakistan offered the insurgents a lifeline. With the assistance of Pakistani ISI operatives, Taliban foot soldiers were able to cross between the two countries largely unimpeded.[24] The safe haven provided an opportunity for them to recuperate and receive medical care. Taliban leaders and those of the Haqqani Network were also helped with recruitment and in raising funds. Less clear or consistent was the extent of Pakistan's role in military operations and in shaping the Taliban's diplomatic strategies. The close relationship between ISI operatives and the Taliban movement's leaders, especially with the insurgency's Haqqani wing, was unmistakable but likely not decisive in achieving the Taliban's military successes.

Pursuing a dual foreign policy on Afghanistan, Pakistan also influenced the course of the war by its willingness to accord land and air rights to the US military. The transport of military equipment from the port of Karachi across Pakistan to Afghanistan depended on the approval of successive Pakistan governments. Without a land route, it would have been immensely more difficult and certainly far more costly to provision American troops and allied forces. Handsome financial assistance incentivized Pakistan's military to join with the United States in intelligence sharing and to allow the use of Pakistan's air space for US military aircraft overflights and landing rights. At least for a time it also provided access to bases in Pakistan from which the United States could launch drones in support of ground operations and for the targeting of believed terrorists.

The decision to pivot American *military efforts from Afghanistan to Iraq* had a profound effect on the war. Even as the air campaign in Afghanistan began in 2001, preparations were already underway for an invasion of Saddam Hussein's Iraq. Resources and personnel were very soon redirected in preparation for the attack on Iraq. At a time when US forces needed the intelligence and drones to confront a strengthening and increasingly aggressive Taliban, those assets were being transferred. Some of the CIA's most qualified people were reassigned to Iraq.[25] The Taliban's building challenge to the United States and NATO forces in Afghanistan coincided with what was in 2006–7 the most difficult period for the US military in the Iraq war. It took a successful troop surge in Iraq and the election of a new American president to refocus American attention on Afghanistan.

The decision in late 2009 to undertake *a military surge in Afghanistan* brought a new intensity to the conflict against the Taliban and also ended any remaining thoughts that the Taliban insurgency could be defeated militarily. The US campaign, designed to reverse the Taliban's momentum, was joined by NATO forces and numbered at its height 140,00 troops. From the outset it labored under a presidentially imposed time constraint that called for a troop drawdown to begin in less than three years and be completed by 2014. The US mission was most heavily focused on two southern border provinces, Kandahar and Helmand, where the Taliban were in firm control of key districts. It was thought that if US forces achieved sustained victories in the two most militarily challenging provinces, these successes would have a demonstration effect and soften up several strategically important provinces in the southeast for American forces. But surge forces never had the opportunity to extend their operations. The Taliban fiercely resisted in fighting that accounted for the majority of American lives lost during the entire war.[26] Importantly, plans that called for the Kabul government to bring to reoccupied districts a "government in a box" of basic services and administrative reforms never materialized. The Taliban had only to wait out the surge.

With the failure of the surge, there began a basic strategic reorientation in the conduct of the war with the planned *transfer of military operations* to Afghanistan's own security forces. Its success hinged on the capacity of the Afghan army and police to wean themselves from their dependence on foreign military personnel. The US and NATO troops dropped to 20,000, with subsequent withdrawals leaving 9,800 in the country by the time that Obama left office in early 2017 and 5,500 on the ground during most of the Trump administration.[27] For a variety of reasons, the ANSF failed to live up to expectations. Plagued by desertions and recruitment difficulties, the defensive forces never succeeded in sustaining the projected troop levels. The Afghan army and police were riddled with corruption. Salaries often went unpaid, and money was frequently syphoned off by payments to nonexistent soldiers. Officer positions were bought and individuals appointed who were unqualified even at the highest ranks. Use of authorized local defensive forces had mixed results. A unit of Afghan Special Forces, more extensively trained, stood apart for its successful operations. But despite plans to expand it, the force never numbered more than 20,000 and was spread too thin to be effective.

With the military picture looking increasingly bleak, there began a more serious effort *to find a political solution* to ending the conflict. The US and European officials sought out those Taliban in positions of influence thought to be amenable to political compromise in a conflict being portrayed as a "hurting stalemate." The move toward diplomacy also impacted the way the war would be fought against the Taliban and other insurgents. There were opportunity costs as the United States gradually adjusted its military operations. While the United States accelerated its air attacks particularly against ISKP, its support of ground actions against the Taliban became increasingly more defensive in nature as it was seeking to lure the Taliban leadership to the bargaining table. As a result, all but the country's more populated urban areas were gradually ceded to the Taliban.

The mistaken belief in the possibility of a negotiated compromise peace agreement stemmed from a *failure of the United States and others to understand the Taliban movement's true aims*. Washington badly underestimated the Taliban's determination to monopolize power in pursuit of an idealized Islamic state, raising false hopes for a political settlement. The war involved clashing value systems, the species of conflict in which compromise is generally impossible and where one side or the other ultimately prevails. In Afghanistan it has been a struggle between two competing visions of the state: one promising a democratically elected, pluralistically tolerant, constitutionally governed Afghanistan, the other offering a theocratic state that rejects the idea of popular will or any guidance except that provided by Koranic scripture as interpreted by an emir and religious council. This incompatibility doomed any peace process among Afghans that was predicated on realizing reconciliation through power sharing.

The US and Western governments along with the Kabul government nevertheless continued to put their faith in being able to end the conflict through negotiations. Even after a failure to make any progress, they insisted that the Taliban leaders' refusal to compromise in the Doha talks only demonstrated that they were hard bargainers. The Taliban correctly judged that it would be the US and Kabul regime, in their determination to find a political outcome to end the conflict, that would be willing to make all the concessions. That aside, the Taliban were unshaken in the belief that they were destined to return to power and that compromise would be viewed as a betrayal by many field commanders as well as a violation of their religious mandate.

Thus, the conflict was never destined to end with a grand bargain struck in a Geneva- or Doha-style international conference. The only agreement the Taliban signed on to was not an Afghan peace deal but an exit agreement with the United States. And in the process of excluding the Kabul government from the deliberations, the United States accorded the Taliban a long-sought legitimacy, demoralized the Afghan civil and military leadership, and paved the way for a Taliban military takeover.

For much of the twenty-year war, US intentions were to manage the conflict rather than to defeat the Taliban militarily. Although there were brief periods when completely crushing the insurgency may have seemed an achievable goal, American efforts were mostly aimed at keeping the enemy at bay. Too often, the US military command engaged, together with civilian leadership, in *self-deception, deliberate obfuscation, and disinformation* in describing the war's progress and justifying their decisions.[28] This undoubtedly contributed to the distrust that built up over time with members of the Afghan government, the Afghan people, and—when media reports and testimonials of returning troops portrayed a different reality—the American public.

Fateful Decisions

A possibly alternative track for the Afghan conflict required a long-term military commitment that the last three US presidents were determined to avoid and that a disillusioned US Congress and American people had become increasingly unwilling to endorse. The war's fate was sealed when the Biden administration, whose options had been narrowed by the previous administration's troop drawdowns and withdrawal commitments, decided to frame the American presence as a choice of "all in" or "all out." With the first ruled out as highly dubious militarily and also politically risky, the second dictated a complete military withdrawal. The timing of a departure was justified as there "never being a good time to leave."[29] The decision declined to employ in Afghanistan a strategy that has for decades kept thousands of American military forces deployed across the globe. These troops have been engaged mainly in stabilization operations, not with the expectations that they could set things right but to keep worse things from happening. For Afghanistan there was a broadly shared view among the US senior commanders that with between 2,500 and 4,500 troops and a similarly small number of NATO troops, stabilization could be achieved for an extended period of time at an acceptable level of danger to American forces and sufficiently low political risk.[30] A residual US force could have denied the Taliban what had always been the centerpiece of their strategy to reclaim power: the removal of all foreign forces.

The ease with which the Taliban consolidated power in the summer of 2021 did at least avoid a likely prolonged civil war. The supposedly well-armed militias belonging to regional strongmen that were widely expected to stand as a second line of defense for the regime very quickly dissolved in the face of the Taliban's final offensive. The region was spared the kind of conflict that might have, as in the 1990s, involved neighboring countries in a proxy-driven war.

For the United States and its NATO allies Afghanistan was a strategic failure. Their military mission left the country with essentially the same government in power as the one overthrown in 2001. There was success in eliminating Osama bin Laden and for a generation no catastrophic terrorist attack on the United States has occurred. But there can be no assurance that with foreign forces departed, global terrorist organizations will not enjoy a revival in a Taliban-ruled Afghanistan. Despite promises by the Taliban to deny any group an opportunity to use Afghan soil as a platform to attack other countries, there is reason to question the Taliban's intention to block al-Qaeda's rebuilding or the burdened regime's ability to prevent ISKP and other Islamic terrorist groups from strengthening. The process of withdrawal has also taken a heavy toll on the credibility of the United States as a reliable military partner and global leader. The war's outcome stands as a political setback for the United States and its European partners in their efforts to nurture the growth of viable Afghan democratic institutions under difficult circumstances on difficult soil.

There are many postmortems on what went wrong on Afghanistan. Some point to a failure to understand sufficiently the country's history and culture, affecting among other things the ability to establish relations with traditional leadership. Many lay the blame on the burden of having to defend a disunified, uncoordinated, corrupt, and incompetent regime. The frequent rotation of US military personnel is often faulted for the failure to build trust relations in rural areas. A large body of thinking also believes that there was a fundamental error in having trained the Afghan military to fight the wrong kind of war. The United States is criticized for trying to stand up a military that resembled as much as possible its own capabilities and ways of fighting rather than preparing the nation's security forces to match up to the Taliban's guerrilla-style conflict. Afghan soldiers and police, a great majority of them barely literate, often lacked the skills to operate technically advanced weapons and were too dependent on foreign contractors to service the equipment.

In totally withdrawing, the United States and its military partners appeared largely indifferent to the loss of the impressive growth in human and social capital they had helped to create, notably in Afghanistan's urban centers. So too were handsome gains made in creating a free media exemplified by the profusion of TV channels and radio stations. The substantial expansion of health services, one of the major accomplishments of the previous regime, was also bound to suffer. Predictably, the international withdrawal of financial and development assistance to the new Taliban government would bring a collapse of Afghanistan's economy and a meltdown of its financial system. Together with the country's severe drought and endemic food insecurity, a humanitarian crisis of major proportions became unavoidable.

The question now naturally arises as to the sustainability of the Taliban regime. Will it any time soon itself be faced with insurgency, adding one more to the long succession of Afghan civil conflicts? It seems that the overwhelming majority of Afghans, however disapproving they may become of the Taliban regime, will be reluctant in the near future to back armed revolt. Most Afghans are exhausted from more than forty years of nearly continuous conflict, and the most aggrieved are more likely to try to flee the country than to take up arms against the Taliban regime. Economic protests and pockets of militant resistance, as well as terrorist attacks by ISKP, will probably persist but are unlikely, at least in the near future, to pose serious threats to the Taliban's hold on power. If the regime begins to unravel, it is most likely to arise from dissension within a factionalized Taliban leadership and in conjunction with popular discontent with a disastrous economy.

Afghanistan's twenty-year-old Islamic Republic would have been for some an earnest, if faulty, undertaking, and for others a costly, misguided mission in state building. Uncontestably, the war has been most of all a tragedy for the Afghan people. Tens of thousands of civilians have died and the hopes of millions for a better life in a liberalizing society and modernizing economy are now gone. The war's most immediate legacy is a humanitarian crisis, unlikely to be relieved without a massive international intervention. Over time, a barely functioning economy and a Taliban regime ruling but doing little governing will leave Afghanistan a minimal state, assuring that it remains one of the world's poorest countries and also conceivably setting the stage for the next round of civil conflict.

Postwar Prospects

Whether the Taliban's restored Islamic Emirate finds it possible to overcome the multiple challenges it faces or will in time succumb to political instability and renewed conflict ultimately hinges on the choices it makes in governing. The regime's longevity and the country's stability are likely to be determined by whether its rulers, guided by ideology and concerns about solidarity, can also embrace policies that more fully recognize the country's social and political diversity. An Afghan public denied a voice by a Taliban leadership fixed on retaining power is bound to become increasingly restless and alienated from the Kabul regime. Notwithstanding popular distaste for renewed civil conflict, a continued failure of government to deliver most basic services will eventually engender widespread protests, giving rise to enough armed resistance to fragment the Afghan state.

As the fledgling Afghan state faces trying to govern, it is up against formidable stumbling blocks, many of its own making. Despite claims to have learned from its previous incarnation in power, the Taliban seem intent on reintroducing many of the same repressive social policies and harsh judicial and extra-judicial practices that once earned them wide condemnation from the global community. Success on the battlefield has not prepared the Taliban for the task of governing a country very much different from the one lost in 2001. The population has more than doubled since the Taliban last took power, and over years the return from abroad of millions of refugees, together with the influence of foreign money and ideas and a more educated generation of Afghans, has produced people with far higher expectations of their government. With few Taliban skilled in the management of a bureaucracy, the inherited civil service was decimated with the collapse of the republic. Replacing a government dependent on foreign financing for three-quarters of its budget, the new regime must cope with an Afghan economy in freefall, starved of funds by the cutoff of support from international loan agencies and the freezing of billions of dollars in Afghan state bank assets parked in US banks.

The region's countries have much at stake in the stability and viability of a postwar Afghan state. An Afghanistan at peace opens up new opportunities for regional economic integration. A stable and secure Taliban regime could better enable Afghanistan to fulfill its long-sought role as a crossroad for trade and energy transfers needed to spur regional economic growth. It might also create incentives among regional powers for political cooperation that lowers existing trade barriers and encourages controls against drug production and trafficking.

For the time being, however, the region is forced to deal with the disruptive effects of the abrupt United States exit. A largely predictable humanitarian crisis has accelerated a mass migration that could have serious economic and security implications for the neighboring countries. These states share a common interest in having Islamic insurgency contained within Afghanistan and together worry about the transnational appeal of ISKP, the implacable enemy of the Taliban. But all stake-holding countries, occupied mainly with pursuing their own interests in a post-conflict Afghanistan, were quick to separately establish ties with Taliban, effectively legitimizing the new regime.

Pakistan seeks to redeem its years of covert support of the Taliban insurgency by Kabul's excluding Indian influence and through cooperation in defusing the threat of cross-border TTP terrorism. It also requires an Afghanistan free of armed conflict to allow unimpeded commercial traffic and the trans-Afghan transmission of energy resources from Central Asia. With the security vacuum left by the United States, China can be expected to engage increasingly in Afghanistan and put greater pressure on the Taliban regime to sever all ties to Uyghur insurgents. The prospect that China can become Afghanistan's economic savior—through incorporation into China's Belt and Road Initiative, and with renewed investment in tapping Afghanistan's mineral resources— greatly enhances Beijing's influence. But both developments will have to wait until the Chinese are assured of a stable, conflict-free Afghanistan. Russia, Iran, and the neighboring Central Asia states will be pushing the Taliban for cooperation in closing down drug trafficking routes and keeping Islamic insurgent groups in check. Iran is also anxious for the new regime to do more to stem the flow of refugees and shield its Shiite coreligionists from terrorist acts. India, previously staunchly opposed to the Taliban, appears prepared to offer Kabul generous development assistance as a counter to Pakistan's grip on Afghanistan and as a reward for a less ideological Taliban foreign policy.

Left with little other means of leverage, the region's states, along with the rest of the international community, will for a time use their withholding of political recognition and economic aid to influence the new regime's behavior. Though willing to finance programs intended to relieve Afghanistan's humanitarian crisis, these countries express concern that funds not be used to strengthen the Taliban's hand in pursuing domestic policies with which they disagree. None of these states are likely to actively pursue weakening the Taliban regime. Only an Afghan government that has consolidated its control is likely to be in a position to rein in those foreign terrorist organizations still nesting in Afghanistan. Domestic unrest can leave ungoverned space that is conducive to these groups' regrouping and launching attacks in the region and beyond. For the United States whose strategic interests in Afghanistan has narrowed to avoiding the export of global terrorism, the Taliban's cooperation in the form of on-the-ground intelligence will be vital to the success of many counterterrorist operations. This will require building the needed trust between the United States and a Taliban whose bonds with al-Qaeda remain unbroken.

America's military withdrawal from Afghanistan has undoubtedly forced a broad reassessment across the region of the US reliability as a partner and resolve as an adversary. It will lead some states to consider new security alignments and find ways to strengthen old ones. The impact of the US. decision on Afghanistan is already profound, but its full effects regionally and its bearing on great power strategic relations in Southwest Asia rest heavily on the direction Afghanistan now takes. The postwar Afghan state has inherited many of the same unresolved social, economic, and political problems that plagued its predecessor. The Taliban have added new concerns also liable to have both significant regional and global consequences. For all of the US determination to geographically refocus its foreign policy priorities, the perils of global terrorism, nuclear proliferation, humanitarian crises, and mass migration are likely to restrain the United States from turning its back on Afghanistan and its region.

Notes

1 Portions of this chapter are adopted from an earlier edition coauthored with Ahmed Khalid Majidyar.
2 Susannah George, "Afghanistan's Military Collapse: Illicit Deals and Mass Desertions," *Washington Post*, August 16, 2021. Available online: https://www.washingtonpost.com/world/2021/08/15/afghanistan-military-colla pse-taliban/ (accessed October 18, 2021); Idrees Ali and Jonathan Landay, "Taliban Surge Exposes Failure of U.S. Efforts to Build Afghan Army," *Reuters*, August 15, 2021. Available online: https://www.reuters.com/ world/asia-pacific/taliban-surge-exposes-failure-us-efforts-build-afg han-army-2021-08-15/ (accessed October 18, 2021).
3 Thomas Gibbons-Neff, Helene Cooper, and Eric Schmitt, "Pentagon Struggles to Wean Afghan Military off American Air Support," *New York Times*, May 6, 2021. Available online: https://www.nytimes.com/2021/05/06/ us/politics/afghanistan-withdrawal-biden-milley-austin.html (accessed September 17, 2021); Carla Babb, "Centcom Head Says US Will Not Support Afghan Forces with Airstrikes after Troop Withdrawal," VOA News, June 14, 2021. Available online: https://www.voanews.com/a/usa_

voa-exclusive-centcom-head-says-us-will-not-support-afghan-forces-airstri
kes-after-troop/6206992.html (accessed September 17, 2021).

4   Mail Foreign Service, "Russian Soldier Missing in Afghanistan for 33 Years
    Is Found Living as Nomadic Sheikh in Remote Afghan Province," *Daily
    Mail*, March 5, 2013.

5   Steve Coll, *Ghost Wars: The Secret History of the CIA, Afghanistan, and Bin
    Laden, from the Soviet Invasion to September 10, 2001* (New York: Penguin
    Books, 2005), 237–9.

6   Svetlana Savranskaya and Thomas Blanton, "Afghanistan and the Soviet
    Withdrawal 1989," *National Security Archive*, February 15, 2009.

7   Ibid.

8   Ryan Evans, "The War Before the War: Soviet Precedent in Afghanistan,"
    Foreign Policy, April 3, 2013.

9   David B. Ottaway, "Agreement on Afghanistan Signed in Geneva,"
    Washington Post, April 15, 1988.

10 Jeffrey Dressler and Carl Forsberg, "The Quetta Shura Taliban in Southern
    Afghanistan: Organization, Operations, and Shadow Governance," Institute
    for the Study of War (December 21, 2009).

11 Borhan Osman, "The Islamic State in 'Khorasan': How it Began and
    Where it Stands Now in Nangarhar," Afghanistan Analysts Network (July
    27, 2016).

12 Congressional Research Service, "Terrorist Groups in Afghanistan,"
    August 17, 2021. Available online: https://sgp.fas.org/crs/row/IF10604.pdf
    (accessed February 10, 2018).

13 Emily Carll, "An Afghanistan at Peace Could Connect South and Central
    Asia," *Atlantic Council*, June 7, 2021. Available online: https://www.atlantic
    council.org/blogs/new-atlanticist/an-afghanistan-at-peace-could-conn
    ect-south-and-central-asia/ (accessed September 27, 2021).

14 Robert D. Lamb, Mehlaqa Samdani, and Justine Fleischner, "Afghanistan's
    National Consultative Peace Jirga," Center for Strategic and International
    Studies (May 27, 2010).

15 United Nations Security Council, "Taliban Finances and Connection to
    Criminal Activity" Section, in *Twelfth Report of the Analytical Support
    and Sanctions Monitoring Team Submitted Pursuant to Resolution 2557
    (2020) Concerning the Taliban and Other Associated Individuals and Entities
    Constituting a Threat to the Peace Stability and Security of Afghanistan,*
    June 1, 2021, 14–16. Available online: https://undocs.org/pdf?sym
    bol=en/s/2021/486 (accessed October 9, 2021).

16 Agence France-Presse, "Afghans Angry at Government After Kabul Suicide
    Attack," *The National*, April 23, 2018.

17 Barnett Rubin, *The Fragmentation of Afghanistan: State Formation and
    Collapse in the International System*, 2nd ed. (New Haven: Yale University
    Press, 2002).

18 James Dobbins, John G. McGinn, Keith Crane, Seth G. Jones, Rollie
    Lal, Andrew Rathmell, Rachel M. Swanger, and Anga R. Timilsina,

"Afghanistan," in *America's Role in Nation Building from Germany to Iraq* (Santa Monica: Rand Corporation, 2003).

19 David Rohde and David E. Sanger, "How a 'Good War' in Afghanistan Went Bad," *New York Times*, August 12, 2007

20 Carter Malkasian, *The American War in Afghanistan: A History* (New York: Oxford University Press, 2021), 199.

21 "Remarks by the President Barack Obama in Address to the Nation on the Way Forward in Afghanistan and Pakistan," December 1, 2009. Available online: https://obamawhitehouse.archives.gov/the-press-office/rema rks-president-address-nation-way-forward-afghanistan-and-pakistan (accessed October 9, 2021).

22 Ibid., 395.

23 Steve Coll, "Looking for Mullah Omar," *New Yorker*, January 23, 2012.

24 Seth G. Jones, *In the Graveyard of Empires: America's War in Afghanistan* (New York: W.W. Norton, 2010), 257–58.

25 Interview with Robert Grenier, November 2007, in Seth G. Jones, *In the Graveyard of Empires: America's War in Afghanistan* (New York: W.W. Norton, 2010), 127.

26 Carter Malkasian, *The American War in Afghanistan: A History* (New York: Oxford University Press, 2021), 301–2.

27 Ibid., 384.

28 See Steve Coll and Adam Entous, "The Secret History of the U.S. Diplomatic Failure in Afghanistan," *New Yorker*, December 10, 2021. Available online: https://www.newyorker.com/magazine/2021/12/20/ the-secret-history-of-the-us-diplomatic-failure-in-afghanistan (accessed December 15, 2021).

29 Remarks by President Biden on the End of the War in Afghanistan, August 31, 2021. Available online: https://www.whitehouse.gov/briefing-room/ speeches-remarks/2021/08/31/remarks-by-president-biden-on-the-end-o f-the-war-in-afghanistan/ (accessed October 19, 2021).

30 Helene Cooper and Eric Schmitt, "Military Officials Say They Urged Biden against Afghanistan Withdrawal," *New York Times*, September 29, 2021. Available online: https://www.nytimes.com/2021/09/28/us/politics/milley- senate-hearing-afghanistan.html (accessed October 26, 2021).

7 THE ORIGINS OF THE LIBYAN CONFLICT AND THE PATH FOR ITS RESOLUTION

Jonathan M. Winer

Introduction

For forty-two years, Muammar Gaddafi drove all of the important decisions about Libya. Even as he told Libyans that every one of them was equal and a king, Gaddafi alone allocated the country's only meaningful source of revenue, the proceeds from its oil production, to the people and for whatever he deemed Libya might need, for infrastructure, goods and services, and investment.

With Gaddafi's overthrow in 2011, Libya lost the driver of its engine. It faced a choice between moving forward to achieve mutual accommodation and inclusive government, or renewed civil conflict. Mostly, its leadership has avoided making the choice. Fragmented by geography, tribe, ideology, and history, Libyan's leaders have resisted anyone, foreign or local, telling them what to do, largely shrugging off efforts to rebuild institutions at the national level, and seeking instead to maintain control locally when they have it, often supported by foreign patrons.

Prior to April 4, 2019, when General Khalifa Hifter launched his effort to take Tripoli by force from the internationally recognized Government of National Accord (GNA) under Prime Minister Fayez al-Sarraj, the outcome had been an unstable stability, or a stable instability, in which each faction was in a position to limit the influence of others, but not to take control of Libya as a whole. Functional impasse inhibited further progress on most issues of importance.

General Hifter's effort to conquer the country sought to correct history by replacing Gaddafi's personal rule with his own new military dictatorship. His reckless ambition in turn led to the introduction into Libya of tens of thousands of foreign mercenaries and military forces. The initial foreign militarization of Libya was led by Russia and its mercenary forces from the Wagner Group, the United Arab Emirates, and Egypt in support of Hifter as he sought to take Tripoli by force. But in keeping with Newton's Third Law of Motion, these were met by countervailing forces introduced by Turkey to fight for the GNA as of January 2020.

When Hifter's "easy war" stalled out amid mounting atrocities, the foreign forces and Hifter's fighters pulled back from Tripoli to bases further south and east. The risk of regional war between Egypt and Turkey abated. But the result for Libya was a status quo ante with everything worsened: more than four hundred Libyans newly dead; some two hundred thousand Libyans displaced by the war; and the seemingly permanent, or at least long-term, presence of foreign militias and military forces on Libyan territory.

Over the course of two international conferences convened in Berlin by German Chancellor Angela Merkel, the foreigners negotiated a road map for a transition away from conflict to elections. By October 2020 a cease-fire took hold. In February 2021, a group of seventy-five Libyans, handpicked by the United Nations in November 2020 and christened the Libyan Political Dialogue Forum (LPDF), met. The LPDF chose to replace the now tired and unpopular GNA with a second transitional government, the Government of National Unity (GNU), under a new prime minister, Abdul Hamid Dbeibah, in a LPDF vote marred by allegations of bribery. The GNU's principal mission was to maintain peace for the duration of the year to enable Libyans for the first time to vote for the direct election of a president, scheduled for December 24, 2021, to be followed by a further round if no candidate achieved 50 percent of the vote. Notably, parliamentary elections were unilaterally delayed by Libya's existing parliament, the House of Representatives (HoR), until 2022. The fact that it was the current parliament, elected in June 2014, under the control of its speaker, Aguila Saleh Issa, which decided contrary to UN and international pressure to defer the elections of any successor, underscores the vulnerability of these processes to would-be spoilers that undermined the scheduled election process throughout 2021.

The fragile election process slowly collapsed over the course of December 2021, amid the sudden early departure in mid-December of UN Special Envoy Ján Kubiš and the UN secretary-general's decision to replace him with former US diplomat and former acting Special Representative Stephanie Turco Williams to act as his personal advisor on Libya, after Russia indicated its intention to stall any formal successor.

As Williams takes on the job of trying to make Libyan elections happen, she faces an array of potential internal and external spoilers who may prefer that Libyan institutions remain weak and subject to their manipulation. While Libya has a concrete opportunity to choose its first democratically elected president, there remains considerable risk of renewed instability. Libyans who have benefited financially or politically from the status quo may prove unwilling to acquiesce to change. Foreign forces, in particular those directed by Russia and Turkey, may resist early departure from the country.

Libya's best chance for progress requires near complete alignment among international actors. For elections to transform into an elected government with the ability to exercise sovereignty throughout the country, international actors must press their clients to accept the elections and their consequences, as the alternative to active conflict or an uneasy status quo. Sustainable governance will require geographic balance on the location of Libya's main institutions, agreement on economic reforms that include a solution to the massive debt built up by Libya's internationally unrecognized eastern government, and a national security structure that integrates the forces from the west and east that have been engaged in a "5+5" negotiation process sponsored by the UN.

Achieving success is not impossible. It will just likely be very hard.

Historical Factors

Over thousands of years of history, the territory that comprises the modern state of Libya has been divided between north and south. City-states in the northern coastal area have been dominated by conquerors from elsewhere in the Mediterranean, while in the south nomadic tribes

(Tuaregs, Tubu) living in pastoral economies have had little involvement with, let alone interference from, those in the north.

As Jacques Romani observed in *The Middle East Journal*, Libyans before Gaddafi tried and failed to forge national unity through governments based on pan-Islamism and pan-Arabism. In the end, they succumbed to persistent colonialist rule until the country became an independent federalist state with an ineffective national government under the monarchy of King Idris in 1951.[1]

Until Gaddafi's overthrow in the February 17, 2011 revolution, just two regimes had ruled Libya since independence: King Idris from 1951 to 1969 and Gaddafi from 1969 to 2011. King Idris's government of 1951–69 was minimalist in practice, adjudicating disputes with a light touch, and with only nascent national institutions. Oil was discovered during his reign, in 1959, and Libya subsequently went from being among a handful of the world's poorest countries per capita, to one with a broad social safety net.

Following the 1969 September revolution, in which Gaddafi and the Free Officers Movement deposed King Idris in a coup and abolished the monarchy, Gaddafi built a rentier, socialist society in which essentially all basic needs (water, electricity, cheap energy, cheap food, health care, and education for both sexes) were met by the state.

But these basics were provided by a government which extended no meaningful political rights in practice and in which wealth beyond the basics was divided between the "haves" (those favored by Gaddafi) and the "have-nots" (everyone else).

Under Gaddafi's rule, elites included people from historically prominent families, plus his own, the small and previously uninfluential tribal group called the Qadhadhfa; successful importers, those trained as engineers and involved in infrastructure, and local tribal leaders. The technocrats, who were part of the Gaddafi system, stayed out of politics. They were generally competent, their capabilities typically enhanced by stints abroad studying in any of the world's best universities, paid for by the Libyan state.

Have-nots included the people of Cyrenaica east of Benghazi, whose territory produced most of Libya's oil wealth, which departed from terminals in their region; the peoples of the Saharan interior; and Islamists, resentful of Gaddafi's purely secularist governance. They also began to include commercial and educated classes in Libya's most prosperous cities, such as Misrata and Benghazi, whose elites felt politically marginalized despite their affluence.

Throughout Gaddafi's forty-two-year rule, Libyans were told that power rested in the hands of the people under a system Gaddafi called *Jamahiriya*—the so-called state of the masses. In theory it was supposed to provide social justice, high levels of production, the elimination of all forms of exploitation, and the equitable distribution of national wealth. Instead of parliaments, Libya was supposed to have direct democracy, achieved through self-government, by the people through popular committees, rather than any form of intermediation. In practice, Gaddafi decided everything that mattered. In the words of James Gelvin, it was "an Orwellian nightmare," as "rule by the masses" in principle meant control by "Gaddafi & Co," backed by repression to keep the system going.[2]

Gaddafi's radical socialism is laid out in some detail in his 1975 manifesto, "The Little Green Book,"[3] which states that Libya's wealth belongs to all of its people equally, and they can decide how to manage it by participating in popular committees, congresses, and conferences. For the forty-two years of Gaddafi's rule, they met, and he decided, especially after 1984, when he responded to an attempted military coup with a brief reign of terror. (In all, there were at least six attempted coups over the course of Gaddafi's tenure.[4])

The country's political institutions were underdeveloped and immature. Political parties were banned in 1972, and "rule by the people" was in practice limited to rule at the local level. There, where everyone knew everyone, Libyans had experience in adjudicating compromise as families and tribes could generally find solutions that made sense within the community. But Gaddafi had prevented this from ever happening on a national level.

Gaddafi centralized the functioning of the state and built a limited number of essential institutions: the National Oil Corporation (NOC); the Central Bank; the Great Man Made River and associated water infrastructure; the Libyan General Electric Company; and the Libyan Post, Telecommunications, and IT Holding Company. Each of these institutions was fundamentally technocratic, not political, and functioned reasonably well, even in an economy beset by corruption at the top and hobbled by subsidies at the bottom, which together inhibited the development of a broader economy beyond oil.

Gaddafi's oft-generous social policies and infrastructure projects bought him a measure of support inside Libya, despite ideological limitations that for many years inhibited the development of an economy beyond oil exports and imports of foreign goods. Restrictions on the right to have a private business were in place until 1988. Until then, postcoup Libyan commerce was run almost entirely by "revolutionary committees," a structure that led to substantial shortages of consumer goods.[5]

Gaddafi's erratic foreign policy had long alienated other Arab leaders and left him increasingly isolated from other governments in the region. Within Libya, his domestic policies were also increasingly seen as arbitrary, as well as repressive. While he shared enough wealth to take care of the basic economic needs of most Libyans, his regime increasingly came to be seen as a corrupt kleptocracy that benefitted Gaddafi, his family, and his minions first.

A never-to-be-forgotten inflection point was the 1996 massacre at Abu Salim Prison, in which some 1,270 prisoners, including a number of Libya's best and brightest political activists, were slaughtered and buried on the spot, before their bodies were exhumed and then ground into dust to leave no trace of what had happened. For this, influential Libyan families who lost fathers, brothers, sons, and cousins never forgave Gaddafi and his regime.[6]

More than four decades on, the young, handsome, and inspiring Gaddafi of 1969 had long since given way to an eccentric, embarrassing, and dangerous "crazy uncle" with an ostentatious lifestyle, given to wearing florid uniforms and making long, boring speeches. Initial civil protests in Benghazi exposed the long developing cracks in the social contract between Gaddafi and the Libyan people, which rapidly built into the earthquake of the February 17 Revolution in 2011.

By then, Gaddafi's support was a mile wide, but an inch deep: within a week of the February 17 Revolution, most of Libya was reported to be under the control of opposition groups, with Gaddafi's forces holding only Tripoli, Sirte, and Sabha. The first Libyan independent government, the National Transitional Council, established itself in Benghazi for public affairs purposes on February 27, less than two weeks after the rebellion began. Once Gaddafi organized a response, his forces took back about half the country. Nonetheless, NATO's aerial bombardment soon turned the tide against him. With his death on October 20, 2011, the Council suddenly was required to exercise power in reality, not just in name.[7] Libya's salvation had come, but its troubles were just beginning.

Primary Domestic Actors

Gaddafi's ouster created new opportunities for a range of Libyans who previously had been foreclosed from exercising political power. For the first time, without any previous experience, Libyans as a society would determine how their oil wealth (some $25 billion a year) and national savings ($150 to $200 billion) would be spent.

As a result, from early 2012 on, numerous contestants vied for control of governance, territory, money, and oil resources. These included a wide scope of contesting forces, some more politically focused, and some principally military.

Political Groups

- Political elites who had done well under the Gaddafi regime, including successful importers of foreign goods, government contractors, and some technocrats.

- Local politicians spread across Libya's coast representing largely local interests, such as the Misratan business community.

- Tribal leaders from important families at the local level, along the coast, and representatives of the Tuareg and Tubu in the south. The role of these was elevated under Gaddafi as a foundation for society as a whole, especially to dispense patronage and to adjudicate disputes.

- Heads of nascent political parties of varying ideologies, including political Islamists.

- Highly educated Libyans wanting to exercise political freedom for the first time, including highly educated Libyan women who had more in common with Italian women of their generation than with Libyans living more traditional lives.

Security Forces

- Remnants of the Libyan Army under Gaddafi, some of which coalesced in the east over the summer of 2014 under the leadership of General Hifter, with Egyptian and Emirati backing, and aided by Russia deciding to print and deliver some ten billion dinars of Libyan currency from its state printer, Goznak, to the east from 2016 to 2018.

- Heads of militias, whose continued power depended in no small part on their ability to deliver salaries to anyone who had been a member or could claim that they had. (The number of the latter ballooned dramatically due to these payments, from around 30,000 that actually fought against Gaddafi's forces in 2011 to an estimated 250,000 by 2014.[8])

- Local Salafist Islamist extremists and terrorists, including but not limited to Ansar al-Sharia and the groups that coalesced into the Benghazi Revolutionaries Shura Council in 2015. Elements of at least the former were among those responsible for the death of US Ambassador to Libya Christopher Stevens and three other Americans in Benghazi in September 2012.

- International terrorist groups with Libyan components, including al-Qaeda in the Islamic Maghreb and later, ISIS. These included foreign fighters with ideologies and experiences derived from beyond Libya who applied a level of violence and brutality that went well beyond the limited blood-letting between other competing Libyan forces.

- Petroleum guards with tribal ties, seeking to extort a greater share of revenue from the oil they were responsible for protecting, in both the west (Zintan) and the east (Ajdabiya).

- Criminal gangs, including kidnappers and smugglers.

Instead of institutions to govern the country, what Libya had was a lot of oil wealth and many contenders seeking to claim it, none with uncontested legitimacy at the national level, or the ability to enforce it through control of coercive force. (Libya's national army was largely destroyed by a combination of bombing by NATO forces and militia seizures during the ten months of civil war in 2011.)

Generally, with the exception of the criminal and terrorist groups, who were typically hated throughout Libya, no one was particularly more legitimate than anyone else. Competition over power and resources, with no arbiter, brought Libya increasingly weak governments. Whoever emerged from negotiations over the exercise of leadership in Libya's transitional governments was inevitably a compromise candidate, chosen precisely because they would be unlikely to affect the balance of power among all forces participating in the political process. A description of the National Transition Council's chairman, Mustafa Abdul-Jalil, in office until summer 2012, could stand in for a description of Libya's appointed leaders generally: "Most Libyans agreed … he was a man of principle, but it was frequently unclear what, if anything, he did."[9]

Unprincipled persons also found positions of power, which were used as leverage to gain more and to oust opponents. A critical watershed came after the legislature in Tripoli was established in July 2012, when it was intimidated into enacting a political lustration law in May 2013, preventing anyone with even a remote connection to the Gaddafi regime from holding public office during the country's transition.[10] The action was widely seen as vengeance and one-sided justice by "Islamists" aiming to deal a fatal blow against anyone competing for power who they could label as "Gaddafites." The lustration law covered anyone who had worked for Gaddafi, even if they had participated in and supported the revolution. In practice, it meant that those subject to the law were both delegitimized and removed from politics. It allowed those responsible for enacting the law, which occurred while armed guards from local militias helpfully watched over the proceedings, to consolidate their power by wiping out their opponents. This action paved the way for the civil conflict that followed a year later.

Western diplomats working on Libya generally agreed that their biggest collective mistake after the revolution was the failure to take action in May 2013 to refuse to recognize the lustration law for what it was—a power grab. It was a period in which the US policy had yet to recover from the death of Ambassador Stevens eight months earlier, and no ambassador was yet in place. Things were not made better by the American absence.

Primary Foreign Actors

Broadly speaking, the involvement of international powers and regional actors contributed to dividing the country and made it more difficult to undertake a credible process of national reconciliation.[11] While France, the UK, and the United States were all deeply engaged in the air war to oust Gaddafi, thereby functionally destroying his ability to contain the revolution, at the end of the conflict, these and other European powers largely retreated and did not seek to exercise control over events in Libya. Instead, they offered a broad menu of assistance programs in every sphere (political, economic, and security), essentially all of which failed. It was left to private sector interests to exploit the contracting opportunities, which first blossomed amid an orgy of Libyan spending, and then quickly withered.

By contrast, regional actors developed favored clients, based on a mixture of ideological and geographic ties. Egypt, Saudi Arabia, and the UAE on one side and Qatar and Turkey on the other helped fuel the conflict by covertly providing military support to their clients. Qatar supported Islamists with money and military aid through Sudan. Turkey engaged in relationships going back geographically to Ottoman times with friendly groups, primarily in Misrata and Tripoli. And from the summer of 2013 onwards, Egypt and the UAE, with support from Saudi Arabia and Jordan, worked with forces which previously had been associated with Gaddafi and against anyone who smacked of Mohammed Morsi's Muslim Brotherhood in Egypt, ultimately becoming the political and security backers of General Hifter's Libyan National Army (LNA), operating from bases near Tobruk, close to the Egyptian border.

The competition between forces backed by Qatar and Turkey on the one hand, and by Egypt, the UAE, Jordan, and Saudi Arabia (and later Russia) on the other hand, played a substantial role in the ultimate splitting of the country into two governments in June 2014, neither of which controlled much territory outside their respective capitals of Tripoli in the west and Tobruk in the east. The decision by ISIS to enter Libya soon thereafter and to supplement the largely domestic al-Qaeda entities and their affiliates with foreign fighters from Syria and Iraq focused the attention of these regional actors. It also played a role in Algeria becoming further involved in efforts to reach a political accord, which in turn led to greater engagement from Morocco on the same mission. The ongoing competition between the governments of these two countries played out in a constructive fashion for Libya, as both saw a stable Libya as in their national interest. For Algeria, this was a matter of protecting its border from terrorism and Islamic extremism, as well as reducing the risks of foreign military intervention. For Morocco, engagement brought with it an earned "equality" with Algeria on Libyan matters.

Underlying Conditions Fueling Conflict

After four decades of highly personalized, centralized rule under Gaddafi and given a near total lack of developed national institutions, Libya was undoubtedly unpromising ground in which to sow a democratic revolution, even though this was almost certainly the desire and aim of most Libyans when Gaddafi was overthrown. Initially, the Libyan revolution resulted in the distribution of armaments widely throughout the country as militias raided military depots. Afterwards, these self-selected militias all received continuing cash payments from the state as revolutionary *thuar*.[12] The Libyan army under Gaddafi had never had very strong leaders because he had ensured no one became powerful enough to challenge him. Once the security apparatus was destroyed by the revolution and NATO bombing, instead of having a unified coercive force subservient to the will of a dictator, Libya's post-revolutionary security institutions were fractured along local, tribal, ideological, partisan, personal, and regional lines.

Libya's politicians were ill-equipped to govern, let alone lead. Its transitional political institutions struggled to do their work amid competing theories of legitimacy with no simple means to resolve them. As late as 2014, the judicial system was generally respected, as demonstrated when Libyans honored the ruling of the Supreme Court on the selection of a prime minister from two candidates nominated by competing governments.[13] But increasingly, court decisions, too, were ignored by the losers.

The big prize of Libya's oil wealth became increasingly contested, as different groups began to use their control of oil (from oil fields to pipelines to terminals) as a weapon to extort funds. This tactic had the predictable result of reducing oil production, in the process, slowly and then more rapidly, consuming Libya's national wealth and beggaring the country.

Precipitating Events Leading to Open Conflict

Over the course of 2014, there were a series of provocations by competing interests in the west and the east. First, on February 14, General Hifter, recalling Gaddafi's own 1969 coup, announced on TV that he had taken control of Libya's main institutions that morning, and was suspending the GNC, the government, and the Constitutional Declaration in the name of the people. In response, the government ordered his arrest, which was as chimerical as his coup.[14] In May, General Hifter initiated Operation Dignity to reclaim Benghazi from Islamist forces, which in turn prompted the creation of Operation Dawn by those forces and others in the west to oppose him. In June 2014, after elections were held, the new HoR made the fateful decision not to convene in Benghazi as had been agreed but instead to move further east to Tobruk. That decision ruptured any sense of unity among Libyans in the west, prompting its predecessor, the GNC, to unilaterally decide to ignore the elections and declare it was still Libya's legitimate parliament. Over the duration of 2014, conditions further deteriorated, leading to the period of two ineffective and minimally legitimate governments. Each claimed to control all of Libya, but in practice held little territory. Meanwhile, military forces aligned with each competed on the ground for control of Benghazi and a limited number of other areas.

During this disastrous period, Libya's historical grievances became current ones. East–west divisions intensified; oil production rapidly dropped, creating massive deficits that ate away at Libya's national savings; and space became increasingly ungoverned. Following fighting between Zintanis and Misratans, among others in Tripoli, and growing violence and criminality, the United States and most other international embassies quit the country entirely by mid-summer. Regional actors doubled down on support for their clients, providing funding, weapons, and in some cases overt military support. For example, Sudan, seeing an opportunity, sold Soviet-era Russian weapons to both sides, with funds and facilitation coming, respectively, from the Saudi–Emirati–Egyptian camp on one side, and the Turkey–Qatar camp on the other.[15] As the UN Mission in Libya (UNSMIL) sought to find a path to initiate talks, the country moved toward a low-intensity, but potentially broadening civil war.

Mitigating Factors

Yet even amidst the crisis of two governments in 2014, beyond Benghazi, Libya did not descend into widespread civil war or anarchy. A number of mitigating factors came into play that helped stabilize the country even as it was largely ungoverned. The most important included the decision by the Central Bank to continue to pay all the salaries that had been established following the 2011 revolution. This had ensured continued payments to a wide range of constituencies, including militias now fighting one another in Benghazi. These payments helped to maintain a foundation of a welfare state even under the terrible conditions of 2014, making it less of an economically driven existential battle.

Other factors included minimal sectarian differences within Libya. Almost all Libyans are Sunni Muslims of the Maliki school of jurisprudence. The country has little tradition of sustained Libyan-on-Libyan violence, with 2011 being the exception, not the norm.

The entire country retains a national interest in continued oil production, due to the geographic spread of its oil reserves and infrastructure from interior to coasts, making all mutual hostages and no one in a position to capture it all. Libya's licit economy is almost entirely based on oil production,[16] and oil has been, and for the foreseeable future will remain, its only significant revenue source. This reality requires its problems to be addressed nationally and inclusively, as any division of Libya would be inherently incomplete, unstable, and incompatible with maintaining even a minimally functioning state.

Most Libyans appear to believe conflict is in neither their local nor the national interest. By 2015, regional actors recognized that they had enough to deal with in Syria, Iraq, and Yemen without adding an unstable Libya to the mix. Western actors realized that they had a real stake in stabilizing Libya to counter the growing flow of migrants through Libya to Europe, and in preventing it from becoming a safe haven for terrorists who would export terrorism elsewhere.

Indeed, within Libya, an additional and often underappreciated restraint on intra-Libyan warfare was the ugly presence of ISIS, which by 2015 had taken over the coastal city of Sirte and a substantial crescent to its south, as well as the eastern city of Derna. To cite the famous adage of British writer Samuel Johnson, "the prospect of a hanging concentrates the mind." Libyans and foreign actors alike saw the beheadings of Egyptian Copts by ISIS, terrorist attacks on tourists in Tunisia carried out from safe havens in Libya, and a lethal assault on one of Tripoli's major international hotels and concluded that geographic control of any portion of Libya by ISIS was not something that any of them could tolerate.

Ironically, ISIS's presence in Libya proved to be a major mitigating factor that enabled international actors to bury their differences and work in common to promote a national Libyan Political Agreement (LPA), as was eventually reached in December 2015 in Skhirat, Morocco, with the help of essentially every regional and international actor with any relationship to Libya.[17]

The Skhirat Process Leading to the LPA

UNSMIL began its work after the revolution with the goal of helping Libya through its transitional period from post-conflict to a permanent government. It simultaneously had reconstruction, humanitarian, human rights, security, and political missions under UN Security Council Resolution (UNSCR) 2009, enacted in September 2011. Over the course of the two-year tenure of its second leader, Tarek Mitri, from 2012 to 2014, UNSMIL's mission narrowed in practice to aiming to resolve the political crisis, eventually stalling out amid Libyan boycotts and the June 2014 Tripoli–Tobruk split into divided governments.

Meanwhile, the ISIS threat, together with the development of systematic criminal activity to smuggle migrants into Italy by local militias on the coast, especially in western Libya, drew renewed focus by Italy, France, and the UK, as well as the United States. Combating terrorism was not an academic concern for the United States after the tragic murder of Ambassador Stevens and three other Americans at the United States consulate in Benghazi on September 11, 2012.[18]

Mitri's successor, Spanish diplomat Bernardino Leon, appointed in September 2014, focused his efforts on forging a political agreement to create a new transitional government to replace the two competitors (Tripoli and Tobruk) that had emerged by June 2014, and thereby to curtail the civil war that had developed over the course of 2014. Over a period of fifteen months, he picked representatives from a range of Libyan groups to join what he called the Political Dialogue. He assembled relevant international actors, including both neighbors and Western countries, and overcame recurrent Libyan boycotts. Through a round-robin of meetings in Algiers, Berlin, Cairo, Geneva, London, Paris, Rome, and Tunis, among other locations, as well as interminable iterations in Skhirat, Morocco paid for by the Moroccan government, Leon was able to create a framework which became the LPA. The agreement was signed at Skhirat in December 2015 a few weeks after his departure and replacement by German diplomat Martin Kobler.

Notably, the LPA depended entirely on securing the full alignment of major international actors. Egypt, the UAE, Saudi Arabia, Qatar, and Turkey all contributed to getting reluctant and oft-truculent Libyan clients to participate in the talks. Among the greatest difficulties in achieving international alignment was the conviction by Egypt and the UAE that the Qataris and the Turks were providing arms to the "Islamists," and the "Muslim Brotherhood," and the equal conviction of the latter that Egypt and the UAEs were providing them to General Hifter and the "Gaddafites." Russia, despite complaining about NATO's role in having removed Gaddafi in the first place, also supported Leon's activities. China did the same without reservation. Everyone involved also agreed to cease supplying funds and weapons to their clients, pulling them back from using force to change geographic areas of control.

The Post-Skhirat Balance of Power

The GNA established through the LPA created a geographically and ideologically balanced nine-person Presidency Council (PC) as well as two legislative bodies, the State Council in Tripoli and the HoR in Tobruk, and extended the tenure of the latter, which otherwise had run out in the fall of 2015. It established a process by which the HoR was supposed to consult with the State Council, and endorse a cabinet selected by the PC, whose ministers would reflect appropriate horse trading among Libyan constituencies.

In practice, the requirement of a functioning HoR proved to be the Achilles' heel that ensured the GNA would never be effective. The HoR's speaker, Aguila Saleh Issa, rejected the idea that anyone outside of his control should exercise power from Tripoli. He told those close to him that the east had only just started receiving benefits after suffering for decades under Gaddafi and should try to retain as much power as possible. When his faction saw that a majority of the HoR would endorse a cabinet proposed by the PC in June 2016, they turned off the electricity in the building and locked the doors to prevent a vote.[19]

Over time, the fractious nine-person PC transitioned into a more traditional form of governance. The head of the PC, Fayez al-Sarraj, acted as prime minister; other members, including two representing the easterners and one from the Tuaregs, resigned. A few PC members carved out concrete portfolios, especially Ahmed Maiteeg from Misrata, who focused on practical issues such as securing the coastal highway. Prime Minister Sarraj elevated his status domestically through frequent meetings with foreign counterparts. His cabinet, appointed but not confirmed, functioned at various levels of competence, including several Gaddafi-era technocrats who knew what they were doing.

Western governments with their own interests in Libya's economy supplemented UNSMIL's efforts by establishing working groups to bring together Libya's economic institutions so that basic decisions could be made about expenditures despite Speaker Aguila's functional boycott. Prime Minister Sarraj made the brave decision in March 2016 to take up residence in Tripoli in the face of threats issued by the self-proclaimed head of the previous government in the capital displaced by the GNA. He was supported in this decision by the Italian government, as well as Maiteeg, who had friendly forces available to help. He then built-up sufficient support to enable the government, however shaky, to remain there and provide some basic stability to the country. Despite this stability, the country remained beset by power shortages, crumbling health care facilities, a banking crisis, a more than two year long struggle for control of Benghazi that damaged much of the city's physical infrastructure, and the takeover of Sirte and its surrounding region by ISIS.

The United States and allies worked closely with the Sarraj government and military forces from Misrata and Tripolitania to oust ISIS from Sirte in 2016, at the cost of hundreds of Misratan lives. At the same time, the UAE, Egypt, and France provided various forms of support to General Hifter's LNA forces in the east. This enabled him ultimately to take Benghazi in July 2017 after years of fighting and to establish military governorships along many of the coastal cities east of Benghazi, even as his efforts to take Derna from Islamist extremists continued to face fierce resistance. Equipment provided earlier through the UAE and continuing support from Egypt played a key role in enabling General Hifter to take military action in September 2016 to push out Ibrahim Jadhran and the National Petroleum Guards at Ras Lanuf, al-Sidra, Zuwaytina, and Brega in the so-called oil crescent along the coast, both confirming his position as Libya's strongest military force and enabling oil production to resume by ending Jadhran's extortion racket.

In June 2018, Jadhran once again tried to retake the oil crescent. In response, General Hifter pushed back and declared that from then on the oil would be distributed by the "eastern NOC," rather than the national NOC, required under Libyan law and by applicable UNSCRs.[20] In the short term, the result was to take hundreds of thousands of barrels of Libyan oil off the market, denying the revenues to the Central Bank, which continues to pay salaries to millions of Libyans, including soldiers serving in General Hifter's LNA.

The ability of the HoR to defy international demands that it endorse a cabinet and work with the GNA was facilitated by the provision in spring 2016 of billions in ersatz Libyan dinars by Russian state printer Goznak. These dinars went to a separatist "eastern Central Bank" operating under Speaker Aguila. Due to the liquidity crisis, neither the official Central Bank governor, Sadek al-Kabir, nor Prime Minister Sarraj, took steps to declare the currency to be counterfeit. This resulted in General Hifter and Speaker Aguila having very large sums available to them with no accountability or oversight, enabling them to ignore international pressure for the most part.[21]

Russia has never explained its reasons for issuing the fake currency. However, in this period, it also undertook public efforts to promote General Hifter, meeting with him in several venues and treating him as a near head of state. This had the predictable result of enabling him to ignore demands from the United States, Italy, the UK, France, and others to deal with Prime Minister Sarraj and the GNA until pressure from Egypt and the UAE (as well as France and Italy) ultimately enabled the two to meet.

Periodically, General Hifter declared his intention to take over the entire country by force and by popular acclaim, mimicking the 1969 coup against King Idris.[22] But in practice, he has lacked sufficient support both to take further territory and to hold it. Recurrent health problems, infighting, and allegations of corruption have further inhibited his ability to act unilaterally, especially in light of the recognition by his sponsors that Egyptian security depends on a stable, unified, Libya with national institutions, which General Hifter alone cannot provide. And yet, with foreign backing, he has remained the only plausible candidate to become a purely military successor to Gaddafi.

During its first two-and-a-half years of existence, the GNA experienced an array of crises. These included multiple resignations at the PC, the replacement of the head of the State Council in Tripoli, struggles over control of the Central Bank and NOC, multiple claimants to Libya's sovereign wealth fund, periodic terrorist attacks, and turf wars among militias. Despite these challenges and others, including ongoing power outages and runs on the banks, Libya's institutions have successfully avoided both progress and collapse. It has remained in the interests of those who hold power to maintain the status quo rather than to take chances on change.

The transitional government was widely disliked, due to its reliance on militias, liquidity shortages, and inflationary pressures, the last of which was due in substantial part to the introduction of what ultimately amounted to some fourteen billion or more in counterfeit Libyan dinars printed by Russia, which gave them to a Benghazi-based branch of the Central Bank of Libya for distribution by General Hifter, Aguila, and those working with them to expand their influence. Nevertheless, there was sufficient stability to enable Libya to pump one million barrels per day (bpd) or more much of the time, generating sufficient revenues to meet its near-term needs in terms of salaries and necessities until General Hifter initiated his war, wreaking havoc on the country's economy too.

One continuing problem throughout the transition was that much of the revenue generated from oil was squandered on patronage networks, cash payments to large numbers of Libyans who did not actually do any work, militia-related bribes and corruption, and anyone able to obtain letters of credit from the Central Bank. This system facilitated enormous profits on the black market, alleviated to an extent in the last years of the transition by partial reforms that taxed those purchasing letters of credit based on the difference between the official and black market rates. Libya's patronage networks are extensive: in the west, the militias receive official salaries (guaranteed by the Central Bank and the GNA) and are also well-positioned to extract extortion of various kinds from their territory and assets (like airports); in the east, General Hifter's LNA is sustained in similar ways, while HoR Speaker Aguila has used government contracting and the counterfeit Russian dinars, among other tools, to build out his system.

Moving Beyond Skhirat: Political Agreement or Stalling for Time?

After securing the Skhirat Agreement during his first weeks in office through vigorous diplomacy, UN Special Representative of the Secretary-General (SRSG) Kobler had to deal with the reality that major stakeholders, in particular Speaker Aguila and General Hifter, would not accept the GNA's authority. In practice, he was unable to make much further progress over his remaining eighteen-month tenure.

In the summer of 2017, a new UN secretary-general appointed a new UN SRSG, Ghassan Salamé. Like SRSGs before him, he began with great enthusiasm and a new political road map. First, the road map would reduce the PC's membership from nine to a more manageable three to address widespread frustration and resignation of many council members. These three would make political decisions to be implemented by a separate prime minister on an interim basis until the country could hold elections. Second, the UN would convene a democratic national assembly so that many Libyan voices could be heard on the country's future. Third, there would be a vote on a constitution, so that Libya could move beyond a transitional government to a permanent one. Finally, elections, including both a direct popular vote for the new position of president of Libya and elections for a new parliament, would take place.

Over the following nine months, whenever the Salamé road map gained traction, one or more major Libyan actors boycotted, retreated, prevaricated, reinterpreted, or otherwise failed to take the necessary steps, blocking progress due to a lack of trust or good faith and divergent regional, political, and personal interests.[23] Then, on May 29, 2018, after intensive consultations involving the participation of a wide range of international actors, French President Emmanuel Macron was able to convene a meeting in Paris attended by Libyan Prime Minister Sarraj, General Hifter, Speaker of the House Aguila, and Head of the State Council Khaled Meshri. At its conclusion, President Macron announced that the Libyans present had agreed in principle to support the Salamé plan, including a national conference, a vote on a permanent constitution, and elections on a president and parliament by December 10, 2018.

This appeared to be a hopeful, and important, moment. But implementation of this plan required Libya's leaders to be uncharacteristically willing to put aside personal ambitions for the good of the country. Characteristically, it was immediately followed by General Hifter and Aguila telling their followers that they had agreed to nothing in Paris. Moreover, diplomats were privately saying that France had given General Hifter too much attention and he was taking the Macron initiative as a sign that France was ready to join Russia, the UAE, and Egypt to support him taking power by force, if necessary.

In practice, the Paris Agreement triggered military action on the ground. Within days of the meetings, a militia group affiliated with disgraced former National Petroleum Guard force leader Jadhran sought to reclaim control over the heart of Libya's oil crescent. In response, General Hifter retook it. Following that, Speaker Aguila's self-appointed eastern "government" issued a statement authorizing sales by representatives of the eastern NOC. Such efforts to take and sell the oil without regard for existing contracts, Libyan law, or applicable UNSCRs remain a fundamental threat to the country's survival.

While General Hifter was able to gain control over the oil in the east, this did not enable the eastern NOC to sell the oil, as neither it nor the eastern government are recognized internationally. But blocking the oil deprived Libya of revenue and risked widespread criticism. Accordingly, UN mediation resulted in the oil returning to NOC control. Libya's unified oil production and sales system has been a central factor in keeping the country from splitting apart, and any effort to grab it threatens to break civil accord more broadly.

Coming right after the Paris Agreement, the episode highlighted the ongoing struggle for control of Libyan national resources. Implicitly, it begged the question of whether everyone would honor the results of any future national election—or instead, would see it as an occasion for groupings to claim power locally through taking whatever opportunities may permit regardless of the impact on the country as a whole.

The War on Tripoli and Its Aftermath

Although micro-skirmishes over territory were common, at a macro level Libya achieved some stability under the first thirty-six months of the GNA, despite growing criticism, especially of Prime Minister Sarraj's dependence on militias in Tripoli. However, that near-term stability did not resolve the issues over grievance, greed, power-sharing, separatism, and the personalities fracturing the country since Gaddafi's fall. An example of that type of violence took place at the end of August 2018, when competing militias attacked one another in Tripoli's suburbs with heavy weaponry, killing dozens of civilians, prompting international warnings, and the further need for Libya's government to pay protection money to the militias, thereby further ensconcing them into the fabric of Tripoli's security.

General Hifter pointed to the militias providing Tripoli's security as the justification for his decision to overthrow Libya's internationally recognized government and his April 2019 assault on the capital. In reality, he initiated the war, having secured nonobjection from then-US National Security Advisor John Bolton and in a presidential phone call with then-US President Donald Trump, precisely because UN processes were coming to a critical inflection point, with the prospect of new rounds of negotiations among Libyans that could lead to a settlement and elections. General Hifter's goal was to take Tripoli in a blitzkrieg backed by foreigners, and establish a dictatorship. Reality then intervened.

The invading forces began the war on Tripoli in an effort to soften up resistance through the use of drones supplied by the UAE and intelligence, logistics, and sniper support provided by a few hundred employees of Russia's Wagner Group, characterized as "mercenaries" to enable President Vladimir Putin to deny Russian state sponsorship. These entered Libya in violation of the UN arms embargo, with the Trump administration ensuring that the UN took no action in response. Following the death of hundreds of Libyans over the first month of fighting and the displacement of tens of thousands from Tripoli, the initial blitzkrieg degenerated into a typical war of attrition, amid the introduction of an ever-growing range of foreign actors, including mercenaries from Sudan and Chad as well as Russia in support of General Hifter's assault, and Syrian fighters brought in by Turkey against Hifter's forces. For about eight months, Hifter's forces dominated, largely due to their ability to control the airspace with Emirati drones and Russian fighter jets, despite the importation of some twelve thousand Syrian fighters by Turkey to aid in the resistance.

By December 2019, Turkey had developed the ability to use signals intelligence to obtain precise information on General Hifter's forces, from his troops to his headquarters. This enabled the security forces defending Tripoli to use Turkish drones to target and destroy General Hifter's artillery and drones, while Turkey supplied the GNA with its own heavy artillery and rocket launchers, which together swiftly changed the balance of forces to one favoring the defenders. The first Berlin conference took place the following month, in which each of the major foreign actors again pledged their cup to the cause of peace, and to the principle of cease-fire. From there, it was largely a matter of facts on the ground slowly conforming themselves to the international political as well as the domestic military realities. With widespread recognition that General Hifter would not be able to conquer Tripoli, his forces and the foreigners supporting them pulled back from Tripoli in late May 2020 in a precursor to what became a full and publicly declared cease-fire in October 2020.

General Hifter's failure was accompanied by a resurrection of traditional diplomacy, and a recognition by a wide range of foreign actors that Libyans needed to resolve their differences through political means, rather than by force. Egypt and the UAE appeared to recognize that their support for General Hifter had backfired, increasing the influence of their Turkish adversary. President Putin had found, like others before him, that General Hifter was not susceptible to foreign direction or control, and was, moreover, not going to succeed in his dream of dictatorship. The US foreign policy had returned to its pre-Trumpian goal of securing international alignment in support of an inclusive Libyan government that would achieve stability through economic and political reforms that in turn would enable a sustainable security environment. Under the leadership of a new acting SRSG, Stephanie Turco Williams, UNSMIL developed a plan to turn the Berlin declarations into the reality of a further transition government, the GNU, with elections to follow on December 24, 2021.

The road to war had been tried. The war had failed to resolve Libya's crisis. All that was left was to try the alternative road of peace.

A Pathway to Peace

Libyans are experts at boycotting initiatives designed to help them achieve progress in governance.[24] For a decade after Gaddafi's death, no one within Libya had the ability, the position, and the will to act as a convener of a national process. Whatever chance the UN had to do this depended on international actors reaching an agreement, convening in some city outside of Libya (Rome, Paris, Berlin, Skhirat), and convincing Libyans that a negotiated settlement and elections are the only viable way forward, rather than a military dictatorship, partition, or civil war.

Then something remarkable happened. With the collapse of Hifter's war, Libyans began to decide that continued conflict was not merely against the national interest—but their own. This recognition was sped by Libya's compounding economic misery. In 2020, Libya's economy had its worst performance in its modern history, according to the World Bank, which found its economy shrank by 31 percent, after a nine-month blockade of oil terminals and oil fields that reduced the country's oil output to about 228,000 bpd, around one-seventh of its capacity. Oil and gas revenues still constitute some 60 percent of Libya's total economic output and provide more than 90 percent of the country's revenues and exports. Shutting down the oil in turn reduced government spending and the combination cratered purchasing power, as well as Libya's ability to provide basic health services as Covid-19 took hold.

By late 2020, both Libyans and the patrons alike had had enough, leading to a formal cease-fire in October 2020 under UN auspices, and the creation of the "5+5" talks between the eastern and western military forces, aimed at de-escalating the risk of any further conflict between them and confidence building, with the goal of ultimately unifying the forces into a national body that could in turn take on the militias. The UN created a new political mechanism, the LPDF, to get beyond the political impasse that reflected not only the differing political interests of diverse Libyan groups, but hardened political antipathies, including those between Aguila and then Prime Minister Sarraj. Aguila cut a deal with GNA Interior Minister Fathi Bashagha to run as a tandem ticket for president and prime minister in a short-term interim government. To the surprise of many, a patronage-savvy Dbeibah narrowly emerged as the winner of voting for the new interim PM in February 2021, entering office despite credible claims that a few of the seventy-five delegates had been bribed to vote for him, and that the bribes had made the difference in his narrow victory over the Aguila-Bashagha ticket that was expected to win. The transitional Dbeibah government was immediately accepted internationally, and conditions improved somewhat domestically, without further east-west conflict.

On October 21, 2021, international actors came to Tripoli to meet in a stabilization conference initiated by the government of Libya, not the UN, let alone any foreign country. With senior officials from the UN, Arab League, African Union, European Union, and some thirty foreign countries in attendance, including those who had previously sponsored one side or the other in Libya's civil war, the Tripoli conference expressly affirmed the permanent and firm commitment of the Libyan government to the country's sovereignty and territorial integrity, the goal of having elections take place on December 24, 2021, and ultimately, the intended resolution of Libya's security divisions under the UN sponsored "5+5" process.

Thus, General Hifter's failed war and the ensuing economic misery had perversely set the stage for a potential, if still uncertain, pathway to peace and to the establishment and enablement of a permanent, rather than transitional, government.

To actually get there, Libya will need the acquiescence of the current head of the HoR, Aguila, the master staller, who has now outlasted every Libyan effort to form a functional government that is not under his thumb for the past seven years. While Aguila agreed in October, after months of delay and international pressure, to allow the scheduling of the December 24 presidential elections, he simultaneously refused to allow the scheduling of the parliamentary elections until an undefined later date. He also enacted an election law that required the winner to obtain more than 50 percent of the vote, making a second run-off vote all but certain after the initial round of elections. These provisions, which were unilaterally attached by Aguila and those aligned with him to the conditions for the vote, would have provided Aguila room to negotiate with whoever might emerge as the potential president following a first round of voting.

Instead, in the end, the Aguila plan, designed to give him the maximum negotiating room in 2022, played an important role in undermining the trust of other Libyans that any election process would wind up producing a new president and parliament with sufficient legitimacy to manage the risk of social and political unrest or conflict in the wake of the elections, especially if such controversial figures as Hifter or Seif al-Islam Gaddafi wound up on top.

With the election processes delayed, Dbeibah, as head of Libya's current transitional government, the GNU, also has special cards to play. If the election process continues to stall out, he may seek to retain his current position, through using the resources he controls in that position as tools for providing patronage and securing support for continuing the transition. A weakened General Hifter also retains the potential to spoil progress. It is not unimaginable to think he could denounce any Libyan elections that actually take place as having been fraudulent or rigged, echoing the claims of those in other countries, such as Donald Trump, who did not like the outcomes of a vote. In the case of General Hifter, such objections could be accompanied by a refusal to end military rule in the eastern coastal cities where he has established it, from Benghazi to Tobruk.

It is unlikely that elections alone will be sufficient to establish stability in Libya. They almost certainly must be accompanied by some form of a deal that simultaneously addresses political, security, and economic issues.

For a political settlement to be possible, there must be continuing unified foreign support for the Berlin road map further endorsed in the October 2021 Tripoli conference and the one that followed in November 2021 in Paris. Those undertaking efforts to prevent Libya from moving forward in government formation following the December elections need to face consequences from foreigners withdrawing support from them.

Whoever is elected president will need to demonstrate that they will govern with competence and inclusiveness, initiate economic and security reforms early, and provide economic benefits not only to every region in Libya but also to the foreign actors who have been most present in Libya, in particular, Egypt and Turkey alike. Among the thorny issues facing a reunified Libya will be addressing the billions of dinars in spending undertaken by Libya's "eastern government," based in Tobruk, which borrowed substantial funds from eastern-based banks, essentially swallowing their capital and replacing it with worthless IOUs. Overall debt incurred by the eastern government has been estimated by the World Bank to amount to about ten billion dinars a year.

Getting oil revenues to reach their potential remains essential for the country's economic recovery. Libya has proven reserves of forty-eight billion barrels, the largest in Africa.[25] Up to 2011 its output was as high as 1.6 million bpd. With investment, it could return to that level again, or even top it, reaching as much as 2.1 million bpd.[26]

Any change of power in Libya, including through elections, poses a threat to the patronage networks of Libyan's existing leaders. Whatever their promises in principle, such figures often prove loath to give up power in practice. For progress to be made, all of these constituencies and more must receive some share of Libya's wealth. Elections, therefore, are not alone sufficient—sharing resources is essential.

For elections to have legitimacy, Libyans must agree on the structure of the government and measures to ensure its inclusiveness. Geographic balancing is likely to be essential in practice for elections to move forward. An obvious compromise would be to distribute some key national functions to Benghazi, historically Libya's second city, where security is now provided by General Hifter's forces, as well as some other key agencies such as the NOC headquarters.

To achieve security for the long run, Libya requires national security institutions that include a national army as well as local police forces to supplant militias. Building these necessitates reconciliation through the UN "5+5" process. Some form of military council would promote inclusion and alignment, accompanied by some additional force to reduce the risk of a coup. Militia members willing to give their allegiance to the state would be allowed to join local police or the national army on an individual basis. One could create incentives to make this possible by introducing a salary differential for those entering legitimate state institutions in lieu of militias, and then phasing militia salaries out over time. Inflation, through the devaluation of the Libyan dinar, can assist in this process. One fundamental barrier to such plans has been that they have not been in the interest of any of the leaders of Libya's militias, or those who rely on them.

There are economic reforms that would make a huge difference for the Libyan economy and create jobs and opportunity for the Libyan people. While Libya has readjusted the value of the dinar to a more realistic number in relation to the US dollar, a floating exchange rate would serve the country better by eliminating the distortions arising from the difference between the formal rate and the black market one. The government should eliminate fuel subsidies to counter smuggling and the black market; make cash payments to individuals and families who have been verified through the national ID system to offset the loss of money due to the elimination of subsidies; increase salaries of those who actually do real jobs and who agree to accept the civilian authority of a new president; agree on a formula for revenue sharing with municipalities on a per capita basis to give them a stake in a united, productive Libya; and undertake new contracting activity to rebuild national infrastructure and to provide jobs and opportunities.

A government taking these steps would see Libya's economy rapidly grow and foreign investors and companies return. More oil could be identified and extracted; natural gas resources could be properly exploited; and Libya's location and comparatively smaller population would again enable it to become a destination for workers from neighboring countries in need of jobs.

While a stable Libya would have more winners than losers, the losers will not fold their tents and disappear into the desert. A new government will still have to address the Turkish and Russian military presence through what would be at best a sequential, phased withdrawal. It will also have to find a way to bind together new security arrangements sufficient to address Libya's domestic terrorist threat. Those focused on countering terrorism might remember that ISIS was able during the period of divided government and civil war in 2014 to secure control of some 150 miles of Libya's coastal region around Sirte, and was extirpated there in 2016 not by the forces of General Hifter, but by those aligned with the Tripoli government, with whom the US military combatant command for Africa, AFRICOM, has stayed in close touch.

Should the path to peace fail, with forces in the east remaining unwilling to accept the results of elections, transitional government and de facto partition would pose a continuing threat to not only Libyan but also to regional security. A Libya divided and weakened by civil war and nursing unresolved grievances would risk again becoming a receptive host for terrorism. As the country works to move beyond transition to an elected government, Libya remains riddled with landmines from the decade of division that followed its successful uprising against Gaddafi. When such landmines blow up, they serve as reminders of just how much must be overcome for Libya to successfully navigate the path to security, stability, and peace. Whatever the outcome of elections and whenever they are ultimately concluded, Libya will need help from foreigners in removing the concealed explosive devices that already litter its landscape, both literally and metaphorically, rather than their assistance in laying new ones.

Notes

1 Jacques Roumani, "Review of The Libyan Revolution and Its Aftermath," ed. Peter Cole and Brian McQuinn, *Middle East Journal* 69, no. 3 (Summer 2015): 484.
2 James L. Gelvin, *The Arab Uprisings* (Oxford: Oxford University Press, 2012), Chapter 3.
3 Muammar Gaddafi, *The Green Book* (Government of Libya: Libya, 1975).
4 Kamel Abdallah, "The Libyan coup that Never was," *Al Ahram Weekly*, February 26, 2014.
5 "Background Notes: Libya," *U.S. Department of State* 5, no. 8 (July 1994): 3.
6 "Libya: June 1996 Killings at Abu Salim Prison," Human Rights Watch (June 27, 2006).
7 For a detailed day-by-day account of the ten months of revolution, see Landen Garland, *2011 Libyan Civil War* (Delhi: White World Publications, 2012).
8 The decision to pay all who had fought against Gaddafi made being a "thuwar" one of Libya's prime sinecures. See Jason Pack, Karim Mezran, and Mohamed Eljarh, "Libya's Faustian Bargains: Breaking the Appeasement Cycle," Atlantic Council (2014).
9 Linsey Hilsum, *Sandstorm* (London: Penguin Press, 2012), chapter 10.

10 Mark Kersten, "Libya's Political Isolation Law: Politics and Justice or the Politics of Justice?" Middle East Institute (February 5, 2014).

11 Karim Mezran and Arturo Varvelli, "Foreign Actors in Libya's Crisis," Atlantic Council (July 2017).

12 The US ambassador to Libya from 2013 to 2015, Deborah Jones, trenchantly told me in early 2014 that if Libya had issued an edict providing continuing cash payments to people who had been taxi drivers during the civil war, rather than fighters, instead of militias now fighting over turf with guns, Libya would only have a traffic problem.

13 The decision to accept the verdict of the Libyan court and step aside later made Misratan real estate developer and politician Ahmed Maiteeg a logical choice for selection as one of the deputy prime ministers in the GNA.

14 Ashraf Abdul-Wahab, "General Hafter Announces Coup; Politicians React with Scorn, Order His Arrest," *Libya Herald*, February 14, 2014.

15 Letter dated March 4, 2016, from the Panel of Experts on Libya established pursuant to resolution 1973 (2011) addressed to the President of the Security Council, UN Document S/2016/209.

16 The illicit economy, dominated by smuggling, is a different matter, and exists outside—but alongside—the state, with its comparative importance ebbing and flowing based on how well or poorly Libya's governance and formal economy are doing otherwise. Its significance has been and is likely to remain especially substantial for Libya's Saharan peoples, as well as for criminal groups operating in Libya's coastal region west of Tripoli.

17 After the Skhirat accord, I separately contacted each of the nine newly minted members of the Presidency Council and asked them whether they would support US airstrikes against terrorist camps in Libya. Without hesitation, each of the nine, including the so-called Islamist members, told me Libya needed the United States to take out foreign fighters based in Libyan camps, and we had their permission to do so.

18 While I was Special Envoy for Libya, what the United States wanted most in Libya was a stable government it could rely on to partner in counterterrorist activities. Despite all of its limitations, once the GNA was created, the United States could call the prime minister, ask for permission to carry out strikes against terrorists, and receive it.

19 Over time, it became clear to me that Speaker Aguila's goal was to maneuver his way into becoming president of Libya, with the ability to handpick his own prime minister. By late 2016, even Egypt, which had been his prime sponsor, threw up its hands, with senior officials from Egypt's national security services telling me his word could not be relied upon.

20 France, Germany, Italy, Spain, the UK, and the United States Joint Statement on Libya 2016.

21 In the spring of 2016, I pressed the Sarraj government to declare publicly that the Russian dinars were counterfeit and would not be honored.

I warned that their circulation would exacerbate the devaluation of the currency, increase the power of the black market, and decrease the purchasing power of ordinary people. I also expressed the view that the ersatz currency would provide the parallel structures in the east established by Speaker Aguila and General Hifter the means to expend Libyan funds to whomever they wished, without oversight, and thereby make it easier for them to ignore political processes aimed at making the GNA work. I have been told that the Russia provided a total of 10 billion Libyan dinars to the East between 2016 and 2018, and another 1.9 billion Libyan dinars to General Hifter and those aligned with him in early 2019. This has provided the foundation for a vast patronage system for General Hifter, but did not address his hard currency needs. See Humanitarian Access Team, "Libya's Shadow Economy," *Mercy Corps* (April 2017).

22   When he met with me in the summer and fall of 2016, General Hifter rejected talks with Prime Minister Sarraj to unify the country, and stated it was his intention instead to conquer enough territory so that the rest of the country would agree to make him president by acclamation. Libya's politicians were no good, he said, and he would eliminate them by abolishing the legislature and political offices and placing technocrats in charge of things like health care and education. He would then rid the country of the men he called "the beards," and "Muslim Brotherhood," leaving them the choice of prison, exile, or "the graveyard." He stated that of the three places, everyone would agree the graveyard was the best.

23   Speaker Aguila became notorious for failing to show up at agreed upon meetings. Late in 2016, after the United States elections, he invited me to meet him in Morocco, embraced me, and seemed anxious to get US support for reforms to the GNA that would enable him to support some kind of Libyan government. In early January 2017, he asked me to meet him in Cairo. I demurred—I was a lame duck, and did not see the point. His representative said Speaker Aguila really wanted to meet me one more time to see if progress was possible. I had his word that he would make it worth my time. I agreed to make the trip to Cairo, but on arrival, I was told Speaker Aguila had changed his mind and would not show up. During my years as a diplomat, I never saw anyone behave quite like him.

24   During my tenure as Special Envoy, we never knew when a Libyan boycott would occur, or what might prompt it. At the 2015 UNGA in New York, Libyan delegates from the "Tripoli side" suddenly walked out of a UN discussion on Libya to protest the fact that they had to go through metal detectors, a rule applied to anyone who had not been badged regardless of nationality. It turned out they were also upset that they had been forced to get taxis rather than provided limousines to get them to the meetings, and that it was raining. By the time they were prevailed upon to return, the UN secretary-general and many other dignitaries had already left the scene.

25   "Libya," Organization of Petroleum Exporting Countries, 2018.

26   "Libya Crude Oil Production 1973–2018," *Trading Economics*, chart.

8 IRAQ

A Conflict Over State Identity and Ownership

Randa Slim

Introduction

Iraq is not technically engulfed in civil war. In fact, there are more hopeful scenarios for Iraq than for any other case covered in this book, including Syria, Yemen, Libya, or Afghanistan. Recent governments have focused on trying to stabilize the country after a period of upheaval and the liberation of significant swaths of territory from ISIS rule. They have tried to play down the historical tensions between Sunni, Shi'a, and Kurds at home while continuing Baghdad's outreach to its Arab neighbors abroad. Iraq has also played a growing role as a mediator in intra-regional conflicts, especially between Iran and Saudi Arabia. But notwithstanding these hopeful signs, Iraq is still incredibly vulnerable and a more negative scenario where the country could return to an open state of civil war is a possibility that needs to be considered, and hopefully mitigated against.

For this reason, it is important to track the arc of the civil war that beset Iraq after the US-led invasion in 2003. At the heart of the conflict in Iraq has been a clash of visions among political and social communities over the identity and ownership of the Iraqi state. State legitimacy has been a contested issue since the establishment of the modern Iraqi state in the 1920s.[1]

At its core, the post-2003 conflict in Iraq was a violent renegotiation of both the political compact in place in Iraq since the 1960s and of the balance of power among regional and international players. Political power in Baghdad was transferred from Sunni-dominated to Shi'a-dominated political elites. The conflict was driven by a violent competition among local political actors over power, territory, and resources. This competition often proceeded along ethno-sectarian divides with Shi'a and Kurds seeking to reclaim ownership of a state that they had long perceived as Arab Sunni-centric.

While these sectarian and ethnic divides were not new, the 2003 invasion created a public space for them to be politicized and militarized, gave rise to an upsurge in political parties and civic associations that were mostly organized along ethnic and sectarian lines, and reshaped the relationship between the state and the Shi'a clerical authority.[2]

In addition to the clash over state identity and ownership, structural factors contributed to the conflict, including, among others, a history of authoritarianism, failed nation-building, historical disagreements between Sunnis and Shi'a on political, theological, and doctrinal issues, and decades of the Ba'athist regime playing up religious and ethnic divisions (1968–2003).[3] Despite guaranteed rights in successive constitutions, Iraqis did not enjoy equal status under the law. Not only were Shi'a systematically oppressed, Sunni Arabs and Kurds who opposed the Ba'ath regime also found themselves at the receiving end of the regime's brutality. During the Iran-Iraq war (1980–8), thousands of Arab Shi'a were expelled from the country, imprisoned, tortured, or killed.

But it is important to note at the outset that as much as the conflict has been Shi'i versus Sunni, and at times, Arab versus Kurd, it was also an intra-Shi'a, intra-Sunni, and intra-Kurdish competition for power.

The 2003 US-led invasion gave a final coup de grace to a state that was in the process of disintegration well before the US invasion. Further, it forced Iraqi society to reckon with its past and its contradictions, and ushered in a competition among Iraq's political and societal components over who defines this new state and who owns its resources.

The relationship between the Ba'athist regime and the Iraqi Shi'a and Kurdish communities was already badly broken well before the US-led invasion. Three developments contributed to this rupture, paving the way for the fragmentation of the Iraqi national identity that was an important pillar of the Ba'athist political order.

First, the assassination of Muhammad Baqir al-Sadr, the ideological founder of the Islamic Da'wa Party, by Saddam Hussein's regime on April 9, 1980, made future peaceful coexistence between Baghdad and the Shi'a clergy virtually impossible. Second, the Shi'a uprising of 1991, and its brutal suppression in the aftermath of the 1990–1 Gulf war, signaled an irreparable break between the regime and significant segments of Iraq's Shi'a communities. Third, the establishment of the no-fly zone in northern Iraq in the aftermath of that same war helped the Kurds make a final break with the regime in Baghdad, giving a boost to their long struggle for self-determination after suffering decades of abuses and multiple displacements under the Ba'ath regime, which killed thousands of Kurds in the Halabja genocide and the wider al-Anfal operation.

In addition to its domestic components, the Iraqi conflict must be contextualized within a regional political order upended by the Iranian Revolution in 1979, which marked the unraveling of a Pax Americana anchored around the monarchical regimes in Iran and Saudi Arabia. This order was further upended by the US-led invasions of Afghanistan and Iraq in 2001 and 2003.

Outside stakeholders pursued their own interests, and the United States and Iran, in particular, saw the invasion as an opportunity to bring Iraq into their respective orbits. While the 2003 invasion eliminated Saddam and his Ba'athist regime, a shared enemy of the Bush administration and the Iranian leadership, Iraq soon became a proxy theater for the decades-old conflict between the United States and Iran. This conflict would crescendo with the killing by the United States of Iranian Quds Force commander General Qassim Soleimani in Baghdad in January 2020 and subsequent Iranian reprisal attacks on Iraqi military bases housing US troops. But the post-2003 political order in Iraq is as much defined by the power plays of Iraqi political and religious stakeholders as it is by the United States-Iranian competition.

In addition to the Americans and Iranians, who were the most influential outside stakeholders in post-2003 Iraq, the fall of the regime of Saddam Hussein also created significant anxieties and vulnerabilities for Iraq's neighbors. Their involvement in post-2003 Iraq is often understood as being motivated by a desire to protect their own interests through the support of different factions in Iraq. For example, the Jordanians feared economic and security vulnerabilities, including the possibility of jihadi activities and networks being exported to Jordan. Turkey and Saudi Arabia gave political support to Sunni factions, but not money or arms.

Through the Arab League, Egypt tried mediating among opposing Iraqi factions (2005–7). Most of the logistical and operational support for Sunni insurgency groups was provided by Damascus. The Assad regime feared the Bush administration was planning another attempt at regime change, this time in Syria, and saw in the former Ba'athist groups and Sunni insurgents an effective tool to bog down American forces in Iraq, preventing them from moving on to Damascus.

The remainder of this chapter discusses the post-2003 conflict in Iraq and focuses on seven key turning points. It examines the principal Iraqi and outside actors who played direct and indirect roles in shaping the trajectory of the conflict, discusses briefly why official and unofficial initiatives aimed at promoting national reconciliation failed, and concludes with recommendations for strategies to move Iraq to a sustainable peace.

Key Turning Points, 2003–17

This section discusses seven turning points in the trajectory of the Iraqi conflict, starting soon after the United States invasion in March 2003 and ending with the expulsion of ISIS from most of Iraq's territory in 2017. This spans a period of fourteen years during which violence ebbed and flowed, sectarianism came to define Iraqi politics, and national reconciliation remained elusive.

Emergence of an Ethno-Sectarian Political System

A first key turning point in the conflict came after the US invasion in 2003 with the introduction of a host of measures by the US-led Coalition Provisional Authority (CPA), under Paul Bremer's leadership. These measures made enemies out of large segments of the Arab Sunni population, who considered the occupying forces as the main culprit in a scheme to criminalize, disempower, and marginalize them. They saw themselves as the losers in this new Iraq, pushing many Sunni leaders and their constituents to reject the post-2003 political order. This set the stage for the rise of al-Qaeda in Iraq (AQI) in 2003–4 and for its successor ISIS in 2014, both of which claimed the mantle of leadership among Arab Sunnis in their quest to upend Iraq's new Shi'a-led political order.

Three measures were responsible for this first key turning point. First was the official elevation of sectarian and ethnic identity as a primary organizing principle in Iraqi politics by apportioning political power based on ethno-sectarian quotas. This measure was initially introduced in July 2003 when the Iraqi Governing Council (IGC) was appointed by the CPA, and was preserved a year later by the interim Iraqi government led by Ayad Allawi and by every subsequent Iraqi administration.[4]

Second, the CPA's decisions to de-Ba'athify government structures and disband the army further contributed to feelings of exclusion among Sunnis. The CPA initially sought to limit the reach of de-Ba'athification, and in some cases, allowed former ranking Ba'ath party members to stay in government jobs. Later on, however, the IGC's de-Ba'athification council, led by Ahmad Chalabi and his deputy Nouri al-Maliki, took a harder stance and reversed all exceptions, while also expanding the ban on public employment to include public activities and positions in civil society institutions, the press, and the media. These three measures created a clear divide between winners of the 2003 invasion (Shi'a and Kurds) and its losers (Arab Sunnis).

Many Arab Sunnis equated de-Ba'athification with "de-Sunnification," as large numbers of Sunnis lost their jobs. Not only did the Arab Sunnis go from controlling the state to holding a minority share of power, they were not even able to effectively wield that minority share. Shi'a and Kurds have always had their own independent political and social structures, which acted as Shi'a or Kurdish interest groups and stepped in to fill the political vacuum created by the implosion of Iraqi state structures in 2003. Sunnis, however, did not have separate political structures as such. They saw their interests and goals as intertwined with state structures, including the army and the Ba'ath party. When the army was disbanded and the Ba'ath party was abolished, they had nowhere else to go. Instead, they were incentivized to fight to reclaim what they had lost.

Third, and relatedly, the Arab Sunni community struggled to come to terms with its place in post-Saddam Iraq. With Saddam gone, the community no longer had a single leader, lacked the cohesive religious leadership the Shi'a had, and the party duopoly the Kurds maintained. Renad Mansour articulated the Sunni predicament best: "Iraq's Sunni Arab majority, making up some 20 percent of the population, went overnight from rulers to ruled. Unlike their Shi'a or Kurd rivals, they were neither prepared nor willing to play sectarian politics."[5]

Post-Saddam, the Arab Sunni community was divided into two camps, one of which was opposed to the United States occupation and the Shiite-led political order in Baghdad. This camp saw the Iraqi insurgency and designated terrorist groups led mainly by AQI (2003–7) and later by ISIS (2014–17) as the main actors able to restore the status quo ante of a Sunni-ruled Iraq. This camp included former Ba'athists led by former deputies and aides to Saddam, one wing of the Association of Muslim Scholars in Iraq (AMSI) led by Harith al-Dari, tribal leaders (some of whom switched allegiance later and allied with the United States coalition forces against the jihadists), Sunni militias, and AQI.

Other Sunni leaders and political entities decided to engage in the political process, trying to chart a new role for themselves in post-2003 Iraq. These included tribal leaders who took part in the US-led troop surge and the Iraqi Islamic Party (IIP). Post-2003, IIP was one of the sole representatives of the Arab Sunnis.[6] Between 2004 and 2018, IIP leaders occupied senior posts including speakership of the parliament, the vice presidency, and ministerial positions.

The CPA's de-Ba'athification order and decision to disband the Iraqi army criminalized and marginalized most of the former members of the political and security organs of the regime. In 2003–7, Ba'athists outside Iraq who were purged from their jobs converged around two former Saddam aides. These two aides, Izzat Ibrahim al-Douri, founder of the Naqshbandi order, and Mohammad Younis al-Ahmad, funded and directed part of the Sunni insurgency against United States and Iraqi forces. Initially both established their presence in Damascus. Moreover, Ba'athists began collaborating with AQI soon after the fall of the regime; however, this collaboration did not last long due to differences between the two groups over control. During the troop surge, some of the ex-Ba'athists allied with the United States occupying forces and turned against the jihadists.

The Sunni religious leaders were split in their approach to the post-2003 order. The most prominent wing was led by al-Azhar-trained scholar Dari of AMSI, who endorsed a militant anti-American line. Dari began organizing clerics to carry out primarily humanitarian missions, and subsequently took on a political focus, operating under the assumption that the insurgents would eventually drive the Americans out and restore the status quo ante. His group, AMSI, praised the insurgents and advocated a boycott of the elections.[7] Many Sunni leaders heeded

Dari's call, and in 2005, a majority of Sunnis did not vote in either the parliamentary elections or the constitutional referendum.

The other wing of the Arab Sunni religious community, headed in 2003 by Adnan al-Dulaymi, a university professor with a history of Muslim Brotherhood activism, represented the Sunni *Waqf* (religious endowment). Dulaymi and Dari were on opposite sides of the political divide. Dulaymi, in contrast to Dari, deemed the new political order and the Iraqi state as legitimate, attended public conferences on Sunni election participation, and organized a fatwa by religious scholars opposed to Dari declaring it a religious obligation for Sunnis to join the army and police.

Over time, after refusing to condemn the growing violence of Salafi-jihadi insurgents, AMSI's political message became increasingly at odds with the mainstream Arab Sunni community. An arrest warrant was issued for Dari, forcing him into exile in Amman, and AMSI's influence over Iraqi Sunnis eventually waned.

By 2004, capitalizing on the fragmented political leadership of the Arab Sunnis and their feelings of alienation under the new political order, AQI was established under the leadership of Abu Musab al-Zarqawi, a Jordanian-born militant who pledged allegiance to Osama bin Laden.

Comprising Iraqi and foreign fighters who made their way into Iraq through Syria, AQI organized suicide bombings targeting Iraqi security forces, government institutions, and civilians. Intending to deepen sectarian conflict, AQI targeted Shi'a mosques, including the 2006 attack on the al-Askari shrine in Samarra. While the 2006 killing of Zarqawi by US forces weakened AQI, the Sunni Awakening Movement in 2007 dealt it a more severe blow by denying it the manpower and the freedom to operate it had formerly enjoyed among Iraq's Arab Sunni population.

In 2010, AQI reappeared on the Iraqi scene, launching coordinated nation-wide bombings. Its reemergence is a testament, in part, to the mismatch in objectives and expectations when it came to Arab Sunni participation in the US-led troop surge. Despite the prevailing perceptions in 2007–10 that Arab Sunnis were finally embracing the new political order in Iraq, political and socioeconomic conditions conducive to resentment and marginalization remained and contributed to AQI's reemergence. In 2011, the Syrian civil war also facilitated the flow of jihadi Salafi fighters, weapons, and money into Sunni tribal areas. Iraq became a staging ground for Gulf Arab states to assist the Sunni opposition in Syria as well.

In 2014, the Naqshbandi Army entered a temporary tactical alliance with ISIS to take over Mosul, but the alliance was short-lived. By 2015, ISIS started targeting these former Ba'athists, who represented a long-term threat to their caliphate project.

Emerging Sunni-Shi'a Violence

The assassination of leading Shi'a cleric Mohammad Baqir al-Hakim on August 29, 2003, was the second turning point in the Iraqi conflict, unleashing a Sunni-Shi'a civil war. Contrary to current analysis of the Iraq War, it was not the 2006 bombing of the al-Askari shrine, a major Shi'a holy site, which triggered the war. Instead, it was this assassination, which was perpetrated by AQI and praised by its leader Zarqawi in several audiotapes, that unleashed the sectarian fight.

The sectarian civil war was in full force by 2004 and elements of AQI were already active in the country. By 2005, Baghdad and many other mixed areas in Iraq, particularly Diyala Governorate, were in the grips of sectarian violence. The al-Askari shrine bombing in Samarra escalated the violence, which culminated in a rising death toll of more than three thousand civilians a month by October 2006.

The main Iraqi protagonist in this fight were Sunni and Shi'a armed groups that filled the post-Saddam political vacuum by providing security and services to their coreligionists and vying for political influence. On the Sunni side, one can identify two major groups, including Sunni tribes and a collection of Sunni armed groups (including AQI) fighting against the Americans and Shi'a political and armed groups. At the time, while some Sunni tribal leaders in Anbar, Nineveh, and Salah al-Din maintained that they could work with the Americans to establish a new government, AQI and other Arab Sunni insurgent groups were seeking to upend the new political order ushered in by the Americans. Instead, they fought the Americans and their alleged collaborators, namely Shi'a and Kurdish political parties and their supporters. They positioned themselves as the protectors of Arab Sunni Iraqis, and tried to harness the narrative prevalent at the time among the Arab Sunni communities that the Iranians and Shi'a Iraqis were working with the Americans to kick Sunnis out of Iraq.[8] There was a perception among Arab Sunnis that the United States had changed its strategic interests in the region to favor Shi'a over Sunni leadership in Iraq. In this context, the de-Ba'athification process contributed to validating these perceptions.

In 2003, Shiite militias also stepped in to provide security and services for their constituents and openly contested for political influence. The Sadrist movement, for example, formally established its own militia, Jaysh al-Mahdi (Mahdi Army), setting up local security patrols and offering social and religious services. The Badr Brigade, established in the 1980s during the Iran-Iraq war, returned to Iraq from exile. Over time, other groups like Asa'ib Ahl al-Haq, which split from the Sadrists, and Kataeb Hezbollah acquired their own support base and resources, and found in Iran a willing patron. In 2014, after the ISIS takeover of Mosul, the *Hashd al-Shaabi* or Popular Mobilization Forces (PMFs), most of whose armed units were Shiite, would be formed to counter ISIS.

The US Surge

The US troop surge of 2007 represents the third key turning point in the conflict. The surge aimed to halt the course of the civil war and to stabilize Iraq using counterinsurgency tactics.

Disillusionment with AQI inspired Arab Sunni support of the surge and led many tribal leaders to join the Awakening Movement, known as *Sahwa*, founded by Sheikh Abdul Sattar Abu Risha. Over time, AQI began to lose much of its support in Arab Sunni communities. It employed tactics that were perceived as blatantly contrary to Iraqi cultural and religious values, and dealt harshly with American and the Iraqi government collaborators, including Sunni tribal leaders and members of the Iraqi Security Forces (ISF). Although AQI claimed to be liberating Iraqis from Americans, Iraqi civilians bore the brunt of their violence.

Operationally, the surge was a success. By January 2009, the Iraqi civilian monthly death toll dropped to 78 compared to 463 in January 2008, while the death toll among police and security forces fell from 140 to 51 over the same time period.[9] By enlisting Sunni tribal leaders in the fight against AQI, the surge aimed to split the Sunni camp, reduce support for the insurgency, and convince Sunnis to endorse the post-2003 political order.

However, Sunni insurgents who joined the Awakening Movement seemed to have different objectives, and they were more likely motivated by a sense of "opportunism" to gain training and weapons. Some were motivated by American promises for employment through incorporation into the ISF. For other Sunni insurgents, endorsing the surge was a way to seek coalition forces' assistance in fighting against Shiite militias. When these objectives were not achieved, many decided to abandon the Awakening Movement. One reading of the reduction in violence after the surge began is that it was a calculated decision by many Sunni insurgents to temporarily lie low because fighting US forces would drain the resources necessary for the long struggle against Shi'a militias and Iran.[10]

At the political level, the objective of the surge was to create the space and security conditions needed to enable reconciliation among Iraq's leaders. Mainly, at the time, this proved difficult because Iraqi political elites viewed national reconciliation as a means to achieve mutually exclusive objectives. For Sunnis, it meant restoration of their power. For Shi'a, it meant redressing injustices carried out by the Ba'athists. For Kurds, it was a means to achieve their autonomy. Yet another complication existed; the United States held onto the mistaken assumption that if the surge reduced violence, the other components of institution building—which would assist with reducing the ongoing competition for power and resources among different Iraqi groups—would automatically fall in place.[11]

The reemergence of AQI in 2011–12 is perhaps a testament, in part, to the mismatch in objectives and expectations when it came to Sunni participation in the surge. Despite the perception that Sunnis were finally being coopted into the post-2003 political order and incentivized to work with the government in Baghdad, conditions conducive for resentment and political marginalization remained and contributed to AQI's reemergence.

Consolidation of Shi'a Control of the Iraqi State

The fourth key turning point in the conflict was primarily engineered by Nouri al-Maliki, former Iraqi prime minister (2006–14), who made a number of decisions during the period between 2008 and 2013 aimed at consolidating Shi'a control of the Iraqi state and consequently his leadership of the Shi'a political class. Maliki's 2008 decision to take on Sadr's Mahdi Army in Basra solidified his leadership position among the Shi'a political elites.

Soon after, Maliki started dismantling Iraqi military structures put in place by the American military, which the United States had insisted include Arab Sunnis and Kurds. He also began establishing parallel security structures staffed by people loyal to him who bypassed the American military and reported directly to him. These structures were often accused of human rights abuses including a notorious 2010 incident in which at least four hundred Sunni men were picked up from Mosul, held without charges, and tortured at an undeclared facility at a Baghdad military airbase.[12]

The United States did not challenge Maliki's unconstitutional power grab in 2010, enabling him to return to the prime ministry despite the fact that his electoral list came in second after Ayad Allawi's Iraqiya list, which enjoyed significant Sunni support. For the Obama administration, which wanted to pivot away from Iraq, challenging Maliki's power grab meant investing time and energy in a country they were eager to exit. The interests of US President Barack Obama and Iraqi Prime Minister Maliki converged around the idea of enforcing an agreement signed by George W. Bush to withdraw forces from Iraq by the end of 2011. Elected in 2008 on a platform to end the Iraq war, President Obama wanted US troops out to tout this achievement in his 2012 reelection campaign. Prime Minister Maliki wanted US forces gone because he saw them as a major obstacle to consolidating his hold on power in Iraq. In this he was assisted by other Shi'a politicians whose constituencies wanted the United States out because of American military excesses as well as pressure from the Iranian leadership, which insisted on a full US military withdrawal.

Had a residual force of 20,000 to 25,000 US troops stayed in Iraq post-2011 as American military officials wanted, would it have changed the conflict trajectory by much? I would argue that given Maliki's sectarian agenda and the Obama administration's unwillingness to invest the time and energy to challenge him, residual forces would not have succeeded in preventing Maliki from continuing his power grab of Iraqi state structures. It is important to articulate three key components of Maliki's sectarian strategy.

Sidelining Moderate Sunni Political Leaders from the Government

Maliki proceeded to remove Sunni political leaders from the government, especially those who had public support, were viewed as moderates, and enjoyed good relations with the international community. In the 2010 elections, the Iraqi electoral commission, which was under Maliki's control, disqualified more than five hundred, mostly Sunni, candidates on the charges that they had ties to the Ba'ath party. In December 2011, Vice President Tariq al-Hashimi was accused of supporting terrorism and a warrant was issued for his arrest. He fled the country and was later sentenced to death. In December 2012, protests erupted in Fallujah after ten bodyguards of Rafi al-Issawi, the finance minister at the time, were arrested on terrorism charges. These protests eventually spread to other Sunni-majority provinces of Iraq, including Mosul, Samarra, and Tikrit. In March 2013, Issawi resigned from the Maliki-led government.

In April 2013, a military attack on a protest encampment in Hawija, west of Kirkuk, led to dozens of deaths, sparking violent attacks by civilian protesters and insurgent groups against government installations and personnel in Sunni-majority areas. According to the UN mission to Iraq, more people died in violent attacks in April 2013 than in any other month since 2008. Two Arab Sunni ministers resigned from the cabinet in protest of the army operations: Minister of Education Mohammed Tamim and Minister of Science and Technology Abd al-Karim al-Samarrai. In December 2013, Iraqi troops arrested another Sunni critic of Maliki, Ahmed al-Alwani, chairman of the Iraqi parliament's economics committee, killing five of his guards in the process.

Weakening of the Kurds

The second component in Maliki's strategy was the weakening of the Kurds, whose ambitions for independence he viewed as an existential threat to the survival of the post-2003 Iraqi state. Since 2008, in his attempt to project himself as the defender of the territorial integrity of Iraq, Maliki allied with the Sadrists, Arab Sunnis, and Turkomen in pushing to strengthen the power of the center in Baghdad vis-à-vis the Kurdistan Regional Government (KRG). In August 2008, the relationship between Baghdad and Erbil was so bad that violence was about to break out between Iraqi forces and Kurdish *peshmerga* fighters in Khanaqin, a Kurdish-majority town in Diyala Governorate.

The stand off over the status of Kirkuk and the failure to implement Article 140 of the 2005 Iraqi Constitution, which dealt with the final status of Kirkuk and the disputed territories, reached dangerous levels following the Khanaqin events.[13] Partly as a result, Kurdish leaders obstructed vital legislation dealing with elections and the hydrocarbons law.

The sidelining of Iraqi President Jalal Talabani from the political scene in Baghdad after he suffered a stroke in December 2012 removed an astute Kurdish political player who both put the brakes on Maliki's hegemonic ambitions and was an effective mediator in smoothing relations between Baghdad and Erbil, the capital of the KRG. In March 2014, Maliki cut the KRG's 17 percent share of the national budget, as part of a broader oil dispute between Erbil and Baghdad over the KRG's right to export oil to Turkey through a pipeline that was not controlled by the State Oil Marketing Organization (SOMO). KRG President Masoud Barzani called the action tantamount to "a declaration of war." For Maliki, economic independence moved the KRG one step closer to full independence.

Dismantling of the Sons of Iraq

Driven by his concern that the units created as part of the Awakening Movement, known as the Sons of Iraq, would morph into a non-state-controlled Sunni security force, Maliki proceeded to dismantle them in a three-step process: first, he denied the movement access to material and financial resources; second, he disbanded the tribal councils set up under the troop surge; and third, he established rival tribal structures and attempted to coopt the Awakening Movement's leaders.[14]

Despite promises of being integrated into the ISF, only 9,000 of the 42,000 strong force held security and public employment by 2010. Many Arab Sunnis perceived Maliki's policies as backsliding on the promises they thought they had won from the Americans.

Emergence of ISIS

It has already been argued that the 2007 surge weakened AQI but failed to defeat it. Maliki's targeting of Sunni leaders and protesters and his reneging on commitments made to the Sons of Iraq in 2010–11 created an environment conducive to the rebuilding of AQI, which began in 2011. In 2012, armed groups formerly affiliated with AQI were again mounting organized and coordinated attacks against military personnel and installations. Syria's civil uprising also gave AQI a new lease on life, allowing it to remobilize and recruit fighters from around the world and gain battlefield experience next door in Syria. The group saw an opportunity to participate in the fight against the regime of Bashar al-Assad. In 2013, after a split with al-Qaeda's leadership over control of Jabhat al-Nusra, its main franchise in Syria, AQI rebranded itself as ISIS, and in February 2014, formally separated from al-Qaeda. Prior to seizing Mosul on June 10, 2014, ISIS took control of Raqqa in northern Syria in 2013 and the cities of Fallujah and Ramadi in central Iraq in January 2014.

ISIS's takeover of Mosul is the fifth turning point in the conflict trajectory. It created a panic that Baghdad was going to fall next, prompting Grand Ayatollah Ali al-Sistani to issue a fatwa calling on Iraqi men to volunteer to fight against ISIS. As the ISF were in a state of disarray at the time, thousands of Iraqis started either forming their own units or joined existing non-state armed groups, giving rise to the PMFs.

The fall of Mosul to ISIS in 2014 once again pushed Iraq front and center onto the United States administration's agenda. Although his administration praised the April 2014 parliamentary elections in which Maliki's State of Law coalition won 92 of the 328 seats in the Council of Representatives as "another milestone in the democratic development of Iraq," President Obama soon abandoned his "let Maliki be Maliki" policies of the previous five years and questioned his leadership. On June 19, 2014, President Obama said, "It is clear, though, that only leaders that can govern with an inclusive agenda are going to be able to truly bring the Iraqi people together and help them through the crisis."[15] This statement was widely interpreted in Baghdad as an invitation to Iraqi politicians to push Maliki aside. However, it would not have sufficed to force Maliki to step aside if Grand Ayatollah Sistani had not followed up with an unusual public rebuke the next day, calling on Iraqi politicians not to cling to their posts, which was widely interpreted as a veiled reproach of Maliki.

In light of Grand Ayatollah Sistani's public stance, Tehran had no choice but to drop its support of Maliki's bid to return to the prime ministership. As a senior Iranian official told me in a conversation in Tehran months later, Iran's supreme leader had to accede to Sistani's wishes. Sistani's influence in Iraq and among Shi'a worldwide has always been a concern for Tehran. He is the most revered religious figure among Iraqi Shi'a and his influence among Iranian Shi'a increased post-2003. Furthermore, he does not support the interpretation of the concept of *vilayat-e faqih* (guardianship of the jurist) that underpins the Iranian constitution and political system, and his religious rulings and political statements impact not only Iraq's Shi'a and Iraqi politics, but can also influence Iranian politics as well. Since 2003, although Tehran has tried to cultivate influence inside religious circles in Najaf by funding religious schools, mosques, and paying stipends to students in religious seminaries with the objective of weakening Sistani's power base in Iraq and among Shi'a worldwide, the Iranian leadership has been careful not to oppose Sistani when he takes a public stand on an issue, as was the case in 2014 when Sistani opposed Maliki's candidacy for the prime ministership. Instead, Haider al-Abadi, another Da'wa official and at the time deputy speaker of the parliament, was asked to form the next Iraqi government.

Finally, the ISIS takeover of Mosul forced the Obama administration to agree to Iraqi and Kurdish leaders' requests to provide military and other support by sending weapons, humanitarian assistance, and troops and conducting airstrikes against ISIS positions in Iraq.

The Protest Movement

Beginning in mid-July 2015, one of the largest protest movements in modern Iraqi history erupted in Basra and spread to cities in central and southern Iraq, including Baghdad. The sixth turning point, this protest movement was the second of its kind after a similar wave of protests on February 25, 2011, called the "Iraqi Spring," was violently put down in Baghdad and Karbala. According to the late Iraqi political sociologist Faleh Jabar, "The 2011 protests were unprecedented in terms of magnitude and momentum. The 2015 protests, however, came as the number of towns with a population of a million or close to a million increased," following a pattern seen in social movements in the United States and Europe in the twentieth century that emerged in densely populated cities with widespread means of mass communication.[16]

The protest movements in both 2011 and 2015 involved demands to reform the political system, take action against corruption, and improve delivery of and access to government services. The 2015 movement started as a simple protest against power outages in Basra in mid-July and soon spread to Baghdad and cities in central Iraq. The movement was mostly led by Iraqi men and women under the age of thirty, who have come to see the ethno-sectarian quota system in place since 2003 as inextricably linked to corruption and bad governance. In the words of Jabar, the 2015 protest movement "displayed unmistakable signs of a popular shift from identity to issue politics."[17] Over time the protesters' attitudes changed and their focus shifted from a desire for improved services to demands for broader reforms and ultimately to a wider rejection of the state as an institution.

The first top-down attempt to transcend sectarian and ethnic fragmentation was tried in 2012 when a Shi'a-Sunni-Kurdish alliance led by Muqtada al-Sadr, Masoud Barzani, and the predominantly Sunni Iraqi National Movement of Ayad Allawi pursued a no-confidence motion in the Iraqi parliament to unseat then Prime Minister Maliki. Driven by different motivations but united by their desire to maintain the government in Baghdad, both American and Iranian diplomats worked assiduously to upend this move and succeeded in doing so.

The 2015 protest movement was strongly supported by the senior clerical establishment in Najaf. Sadr jumped on the bandwagon, calling on his supporters to join the protesters. Maliki and PMF leaders were strongly opposed to the protests, arguing that they detracted from the fight against ISIS. As Jabar writes, "They saw the protest movement as a threat to the Popular Movement's operations, commanders, and their political future."[18]

Prime Minister Abadi saw the protest movement as an opportunity to launch a reform program to fight corruption, improve services, and implement administrative changes, including the elimination of several high-ranking posts such as the multiple vice-presidents and deputy prime ministers. While the reform program met the protesters' demands, Abadi failed to implement it due to various obstacles including a worsening economic situation at a time when state funds needed to be prioritized for the fight against ISIS.

By early 2016, frustration at the lack of implementation of reforms and protest fatigue brought the movement to a slow end. The protest movement built momentum for political reform, changed the narrative of Iraqi governance, and solidified the shift from identity to issue politics that had been building since 2005. The results achieved in May 2018 by the electoral alliance between Sadr and the Iraqi Communist Party partly reflect the lingering impact of the 2015 protest movement on Iraqi society.

Moreover, the Iraqi protest movement would once again return in force in October 2019, as large-scale protests broke out in Baghdad and across southern Iraq in what became known as the *Tishreen* (October) movement. Centered on Baghdad's Tahrir Square, the protests echoed many of the same demands as in 2015, calling for the provision of basic services, including water, electricity, and gas, as well as jobs, freedom of speech, and an end to the *muhassasa* sectarian quota system and the rampant corruption prevalent in all sectors of government. Protesters also demanded an end to Iranian, Saudi, and American interference in Iraqi political, social, and religious affairs.

The Fight against ISIS

The seventh and final turning point is the removal of ISIS from its strongholds, which brought an end to any lingering hopes among some segments of the Iraqi population of restoring Sunni control of Iraqi state structures. In July 2017, three years after ISIS's takeover of Mosul, Iraqi Prime Minister Abadi declared the city liberated from the group. By spring 2019, all ISIS held territory in Iraq and Syria had been officially liberated. But as in 2007–8, this does not mean ISIS has been defeated. Sleeper cells are still active in Kirkuk and its outskirts, in areas between Kirkuk and Diyala, and in Anbar. ISIS members still kidnap and kill civilians and carry out random attacks.

The ongoing war in Syria provides a haven for ISIS fighters to regroup and move across the border into Iraq. More importantly, Iraq still suffers from the same political and socioeconomic problems that gave rise to AQI and ISIS. Iraqi security services will continue to require US help to fight what has once again turned into an underground insurgency.

Still, the political mood inside Iraq's Arab Sunni community is different than it was in 2010–11 when AQI regrouped after the surge. While in 2010–11 Arab Sunnis could rightly lay the blame for their political and socioeconomic marginalization at Maliki's doorstep, this time a Sunni force, not Shi'a politicians or the security services loyal to them, destroyed their cities and homes and forced them to flee their communities.

The suppression of the Syrian uprising has also dealt a blow to any lingering ambitions held by Iraqi Arab Sunni political and tribal parties of restoring the pre-2003 political order. Some of these ambitions partially contributed to ISIS's success and its ability to take over Sunni majority areas either through the collaboration of locals and/or without them putting up much of a fight. ISIS's brutality against its coreligionists and eventually its military defeat shattered these ambitions once and for all.

Grand Ayatollah Ali Al-Sistani

No analysis of post-2003 Iraqi politics is complete without unpacking the role Grand Ayatollah Sistani, a Shi'a *marja'* (source of emulation) and head of the Najaf *hawza* (a network of schools, learning centers, institutions, and charities), has played in Iraqi politics since the 2003 invasion. No other Iraqi figure, religious or secular, Shi'a or Sunni, Arab or Kurd, occupies the moral space he does or leverages their power as he does.

He has steered himself away from the minutiae of retail politics. Instead, his interventions have been mostly aimed at shepherding the democratic process in Iraq, demanding accountability of government officials, and stemming sectarian strife. According to a report of a conversation with the grand ayatollah, Sistani is most proud of four interventions he made since 2003.[19]

The first was when his office in Najaf issued an edict on June 26, 2003, demanding general elections be held for Iraqis to choose their representatives to a constitutional assembly, contravening a CPA plan to hold a complicated succession of caucuses to elect an assembly that would draft a constitution to be ratified in a national referendum. For Sistani, the CPA's caucus plan, which was to be controlled by an occupying force, would render the transition process illegitimate in the eyes of the majority of Iraqis. Eventually, the CPA acceded to Sistani's demand for popular elections and he agreed to a delay of general elections until December 2004.

The second was on August 27, 2004, when he negotiated a deal ending the three-week bloody standoff in Najaf between Sadr's armed followers and American and Iraqi government forces, helping to save lives on both sides and sparing the city of Najaf.[20] For Sistani, if Sadr had been killed in this confrontation, an intra-Shi'a civil war would have broken out, derailing the nascent political transition in Iraq that had brought the Shi'a majority control of the levers of power.

The third intervention was in 2006 in the aftermath of the bombing of the al-Askari mosque in Samarra, one of the holiest sites in Shi'a Islam. Sistani convened a meeting with the other Shi'a marja' in Najaf and issued a fatwa in the name of all four top Shi'a clerics in Iraq prohibiting attacks on Sunni mosques and the spilling of blood.

The fourth intervention Sistani is proud of is the June 13, 2014, fatwa calling on Shi'a men to volunteer and join the ISF to fight ISIS after the latter took over Mosul and began marching toward Baghdad. While Sistani never called on the volunteers to form their own brigades in what later became known as the PMFs, the implosion of the ISF forced the thousands of men who heeded Sistani's call to organize themselves into brigades and/or join pro-Iranian militias that were in operation in Iraq at the time including Kataeb Hizballah and Asa'ib Ahl al-Haq. As the conflict against ISIS dragged on, the Najaf hawza under Sistani's leadership and other Shi'a leaders including Sadr and Ammar al-Hakim formed their own militias under the PMF rubric.

While Sistani has tried to avoid wading into the fray of Iraqi politics, he did exercise his influence on politics directly on two occasions, when his decision to withhold support for a frontrunner for the prime ministership—Maliki in 2014 and Abadi in 2018—was enough to tip the balance against them.

A large question that looms over Iraq's path forward is who will succeed Sistani and what this means for Iraqi political dynamics and for Iraqi-Iranian relations in the future. Many have expressed fears over an Iranian religious takeover of Iraq. As Hayder al-Khoei argued, "These fears underestimate the resilience of the religious establishment in Iraq as well as the deep-rooted resistance to theocracy among the luminaries of Shi'a Islam in Najaf."[21] A period of uncertainty will follow Sistani's passing away as the process in Najaf to designate a successor evolves. After the passing of Mohammed Saeed al-Hakim in September 2021, there are two other grand ayatollahs in Najaf—Mohammed Ishaq al-Fayyad and Bashir Hussain al-Najafi—either of whom could make worthy successors to Sistani. The dynamics of the transition period will be influenced by opaque deliberations inside Najafi religious circles, and by "grassroots dynamics as tribes in southern Iraq, ordinary Shi'a laymen, and families across the region and wider world will begin to organically defer to one of the existing grand ayatollahs after Sistani."[22]

Why Attempts at National Reconciliation Failed

Since 2003, Iraqis and regional and international stakeholders in Iraq have talked about the need for national reconciliation. Official and unofficial national reconciliation initiatives were carried out. A number of plans for national reconciliation have been offered, starting as early as 2006. Nothing of substance has materialized from these initiatives, however.[23]

There have been three major impediments to national reconciliation: first, lack of political will; second, the absence of an honest broker; and third, the lack of a national reconciliation framework including a coordinating mechanism among multiple official and unofficial reconciliation initiatives at the national and local levels. We will explore each of these in detail.

Lack of Political Will

In June 2006, Nouri al-Maliki, then Iraq's prime minister, announced a 24-point national reconciliation plan that included amnesty for insurgents and opposition figures not involved in terrorist attacks, a reversal of de-Ba'athification laws that banned low-ranking former Ba'athists from reentering public service, a national conference with all warring parties, and a promise to purge key ministries, including the Ministry of Interior, of officials affiliated with Shiite militias, which at the time were involved in sectarian killings.

The plan did not succeed primarily because Maliki and other Shi'a and Kurdish leaders were not interested in national reconciliation with the Sunnis, whom they associated with an insurgency that was violently trying to upend the post-2003 political order. They felt they could win the fight militarily without having to make any political concessions to the Sunnis. Sunni insurgents saw the post-2003 political order as illegitimate and in need of overturning. Because they were ruled out from the amnesty offer, Sunni insurgents and Shi'a militia members had no incentive to give up their arms and sit at the negotiation table.[24] Maliki's plan was also conceived more in response to pressure exerted by American officials on him to work on national reconciliation and less because he believed it was needed.

In 2006–9, the Washington, DC based International Institute for Sustained Dialogue (IISD) convened a Track 2.0 initiative bringing together Iraqi parliamentarians, former Ba'athist officials living in exile, and Iraqi tribal leaders.[25] The agenda of this initiative was two-fold: to agree on, first, the elements of a political process to define a new governing partnership among Iraqi factions, including constitutional amendments, and, second, a legislative framework for reforming the de-Ba'athification law. After a three-year-long intensive effort of regular meetings held outside Iraq, the final draft documents generated by the group were rejected by Maliki, thus bringing the initiative to an end.

Absence of an Honest Broker

Both the Arab League and the UN attempted mediation between Iraqi factions; however, the Arab League failed and the UN met limited success.

In October 2005, the Arab League empowered its Secretary-General Amr Moussa to launch a mediation effort in Iraq. Sunnis welcomed the Arab League initiative, but Shi'a and Kurds viewed it with suspicion, arguing the Arab League failed over the years to raise objections to Saddam's treatment of Shi'a and Kurds. In November 2005, the Arab League organized a national conference in Cairo around mediation, but the effort proved fruitless and the whole initiative was brought to an end after the al-Askari shrine bombing in Samarra.

The divisions inside the UN Security Council (UNSC) in the lead-up to the US invasion of Iraq meant that the UN would not be able to play the role it played in other postwar settings such as Bosnia and Kosovo. Initially, the Bush administration did not want to cede any authority to the UN, yet eventually found it could not live without it.[26] However, UN officials were called upon to play a role in Iraq without having direct authority of their own. In 2004, Lakhdar Brahimi, the secretary-general's special representative for Iraq, helped mediate the transition from the US-controlled CPA to Iraqi sovereignty. The UN helped organize the 2005 elections and in 2007 the UN became a coleader with the Iraqi government of the International Compact for Iraq.[27] Pushed by the Bush administration, which was looking for ways to extricate itself from being the sole party responsible for Iraq, UNSCR 1770 was passed specifying, among other responsibilities, that the UN Assistance Mission for Iraq (UNAMI) "advise, support, and assist" the government of Iraq on national reconciliation. But the Maliki-led government did not welcome an expansion of the UN's role in national reconciliation and insisted that "UNAMI would act only as 'circumstances permit' and 'at the request of the government of Iraq.'"[28]

Despite their best efforts, successive representatives of the UN secretary-general have failed at bringing Iraqis to resolve a range of issues that divided them, including the sharing of oil revenues, the status of the disputed Kirkuk region, the demobilization of militias, and the protection of minority rights. In 2013–14, the fight against ISIS pushed these issues to the backburner, thus rendering the UN's efforts in promoting national reconciliation even more futile than in the past.

Lack of a National Reconciliation Framework

Since 2003, national reconciliation in Iraq suffered from the lack of a framework presenting a unified vision that includes a coordination mechanism among the different initiatives and plans to promote reconciliation at the national and local levels, and in the official and unofficial realms. During Maliki's stints as prime minister, the National Reconciliation Committee was neither politically independent nor empowered to shepherd the development of a national reconciliation framework and to coordinate among different reconciliation initiatives. During this period, national initiatives failed for the reasons outlined above. However, there were successful local reconciliation efforts that have endured. In 2007, a group of facilitators trained by the United States Institute of Peace brokered a reconciliation pact between Sunnis and Shi'a in Mahmoudiyah, an area south of Baghdad known then for heavy insurgent activity. This pact still endures while the tribal council established at the time still works on dispute resolution.

After ISIS took over Mosul in 2014 and Haider al-Abadi became prime minister, interest peaked again in the subject of national reconciliation. The problem at the time was that too many officials were put in charge of the national reconciliation file. Officially, it was in Vice President Ayad Allawi's hands. However, two committees were also working on national reconciliation: the National Reconciliation Committee, which answered to the prime minister's office, and a parliamentary committee on national reconciliation. The multiplicity of actors who considered themselves in charge of the file and the lack of a person or office to coordinate them meant nothing substantive was accomplished.

In August 2016, Abadi passed the General Amnesty Law, which allowed people convicted between 2003 and August 25, 2016, to apply for amnesty, except those convicted of thirteen crimes, including acts of terror resulting in death or permanent disability, human trafficking, rape, or theft of state funds.[29] On October 31, 2016, Ammar al-Hakim offered a plan, known as the "historic settlement," calling for the settlement of all conflicting issues among Iraq's societal components on a non-zero-sum basis with the help of UNAMI. In February 2017, Muqtada al-Sadr launched a competing plan advocating social reconciliation, the integration of the PMFs within the national forces, and an end to all foreign meddling in Iraqi affairs, also with UNAMI's support.[30] Simultaneously, Sunni political factions working with Sunni opposition figures living in exile were working on a document outlining a Sunni vision for the future of the political process in Iraq.

The parliamentary elections in 2018, which brought some of the Sunni expatriate opposition back into the political process and indicated a shift away from the old identity-politics framework that defined Iraqi politics since 2003, along with the defeat of ISIS's territorial caliphate, have shifted the priority in national reconciliation from the national to the local level.

A Path to Sustainable Peace in Iraq

This chapter has chronicled Iraq's spiral into conflict in the post-2003 period. At the time of writing, among all the civil war cases covered in this book, Iraq is on the most positive path. Sectarian competition seems to be becoming less relevant as a driver of political dynamics. In the May 2018 parliamentary elections, many of the major electoral lists campaigned across sectarian and ethnic lines. We witnessed a similar pattern in the government formation process, which led to the appointment of Adel Abdul-Mahdi as prime minister. The new political alliances brought together former sworn enemies like former Prime Minister Maliki, Badr militia commander Hadi al-Amiri, and Sunni opposition figure Khamis al-Khanjar. According to Fanar Haddad, "the fall of Mosul, the subsequent war against the Islamic State, the change of leadership in Iraq, and the reorientation of Iraq's regional politics" make sectarian civil war of the type seen in the post-2003 era less likely in the future.[31]

The October 2021 parliamentary elections further underscored this trend. While most of the media attention focused on the Sadrists' sizable gains and the equally sizable losses among candidates representing the Iranian-backed Iraqi militias, the election also witnessed the rise of new independent, civil society-based political parties, such as Imtidad and Ishraqat Kanun, that emerged out of the Tishreen protest movement. Benefitting from changes in the electoral law that made it easier for small parties and independents to win office, these parties successfully contested the election and won seats in parliament—despite not being able to promise jobs or money or rely on appeals to religion or ethnicity as drivers of voter mobilization.[32] It remains to be seen how these parties will affect Iraq's political dynamics going forward, but their representation in the legislature could lead to the development of a genuine parliamentary opposition that challenges the sectarian political system from within.

Nevertheless, the best we can say about Iraq at present is that it is in a state of unstable equilibrium, meaning that the current stability could be torn asunder by terrorist attacks by the still-present remnants of ISIS, or possibly by efforts by regional and international actors to use Iraq as a proxy theater for their own conflicts. For Iraq to move toward sustainable peace, it must address five key challenges: governance, marginalization, justice and accountability, reconciliation, and rebuilding the relationship between Baghdad and Erbil.

Governance

Ensuring effective governance at the national level and empowering local governance are key to stabilization and addressing the increasing gap between elected officials and their constituents. The focus should be on improving service delivery (especially in the water and electricity sectors), creating jobs (particularly among the youth), providing security, and rooting out corruption.

While the muhassasa system put in place post-2003 that contributes to poor governance is not going away any time soon, the government must prioritize measures that promote economic diversification beyond the oil sector, trim a bloated public sector that drains resources away from infrastructure investments, put in place a regulatory environment that is friendly to the private sector, and create jobs for the estimated 2.5 million unemployed Iraqis.

Regarding the security sector, there is a need for the Iraqi state to reclaim a monopoly over the use of force throughout its territories. While the Kurdish peshmerga and the PMFs are recognized as state actors, these groups have chains of command that are not directly accountable to the ministries of defense and interior and the prime minister's office. Neither the peshmerga nor the PMF leadership are about to give up their independent chains of command. Various political factions in the Shiite camp hold different views about the future of the PMFs, and this will depend partly on what role their leaders want to play in Iraq and partly on Iran's plans for this force.[33] The 2016 law that deemed the PMFs as a legitimate body within the country's security apparatus did not outline their future role in the Iraqi political process. There are serious concerns about their role in intra-Shiite politics and their potential hinderance to cross-sectarian accommodation. The question of the PMFs' future was once again thrust into the spotlight in late 2021 by two events. First, the October 2021 parliamentary elections saw the PMF-backed electoral list dealt a major blow, losing nearly two-thirds of its seats. Second, in early November, in the aftermath of this electoral loss, an assassination attempt was made on Prime Minister Mustafa al-Kadhimi using explosive-laden drones. The attack, widely thought to have been carried out by Iran-backed Iraqi militias, underscored the reality that these groups continue to operate outside state control and seem to feel sufficiently emboldened to try to get away with killing a sitting prime minister. Although the Iran-backed Iraqi militias are not a monolith, they continue to pose a threat to the authority and legitimacy of the Iraqi state.

Beyond security, good governance also means operating free and fair elections. The high election commission should be composed of independents and not representatives of political parties. Despite technical problems, Iraq's most recent election in October 2021 was considered an improvement over the previous one in 2018, which was marred by widespread irregularities and allegations of foul play.

At the local level, officials must be given the tools and means to develop and implement better plans from agricultural development to service delivery and to manage security, including community policing. Key to that is full implementation of Law 21 governing "provinces not incorporated in a region." A 2015 executive order by former Prime Minister Abadi to implement Law 21 has led to administrative but not fiscal decentralization, severely inhibiting the ability of local authorities to deliver on their mandate and provide public services.

The failure of the Iraqi state to provide adequate public services, sound governance, and transparency has been a key driver of recurring protests, including, most recently, those of the Tishreen movement that began in October 2019. While government forces and allied militias suppressed the protests violently, and a campaign of abductions, forced disappearances, and killings of protesters and activists, coupled with the impact of Covid-19, blunted their momentum, the underlying issues that brought Iraqis out to the streets, if unaddressed, are likely to reemerge again.

Marginalization

Rebuilding territories liberated from ISIS and bringing internally displaced people (IDPs) home to their communities will be critical to denying ISIS a path back to Sunni-majority communities, which in the past felt politically and economically marginalized and found in ISIS a means to reclaim their role in Iraqi political life. There are still close to 1.8 million internally displaced Iraqis, the majority of whom are from northern and central Iraq. The onerous security clearance system put in place at the federal and local levels to weed out former ISIS fighters and sympathizers that have taken refuge among IDP communities is being used as a tool by some militias to prevent IDPs from returning to their places of origin. Intra-communal and tribal vengeance remain a persistent issue in areas liberated from ISIS.

Justice and Accountability

Another critical component of weaving a new national tapestry will be the reform of the justice system to implement due process, including in trials of Sunni youth accused of belonging to ISIS and AQI. Iraqi prisons have long been breeding grounds for extremists. The 2005 anti-terrorism law, which allows individuals to be detained and imprisoned without charge or pretrial, remains a key issue.[34] Prime Minister Maliki used the law to target his political opponents and human rights organizations have spoken out against Iraq's handling of ISIS detainees and their families. It is crucial that the Iraqi judicial authorities install genuine systems of accountability for human rights abuses, including resolving cases of people who have disappeared. This accountability should not merely account for abuses carried out by ISIS, but rather, should also extend to people in government, state security services, and PMFs who are guilty of corruption and human rights abuses, including those responsible for killing hundreds of protesters and wounding thousands more during the Tishreen protests.

Reconciliation

Since 2003, many efforts aimed to promote national reconciliation focused mostly on political elites. Until 2014, national reconciliation centered on the Sunni-Shi'a divide. Since the parliamentary elections of 2018 and the decision by expatriate Sunni opposition figures to join the political process, reconciliation efforts have prioritized the local level. One specific issue is how to reintegrate families of former ISIS members, who may or may not have been complicit. These family members, as well as other innocent civilians who happened to live in ISIS controlled territory, are viewed suspiciously by state authorities and fellow Iraqis. These conflicts do not necessarily fall along the Sunni-Shi'a divide. They are also intra-communal. There have been stories about tribes in Anbar refusing to let their fellow tribesmen who collaborated with ISIS return and reclaim lands. These families will need to be reintegrated into Iraqi society if the current equilibrium is to be sustained and stabilized.

Rebuilding the Relationship between Baghdad and Erbil

The September 2017 independence referendum in the KRG and the subsequent capture of Kirkuk by Iraqi forces in October 2017, which stripped the KRG of half its crude exports, dealt a major blow to the Shi'a-Kurdish alliance. Formed prior to 2003 in opposition to the regime, this alliance was based on the ethno-sectarian power-sharing system put in place by the United States post-2003 political order and was later enshrined in the 2005 Iraqi constitution.

The two major points of contention between Baghdad and Erbil have consistently been oil policy and the status of disputed territories.[35] The prime ministerial appointment of Abdul-Mahdi, a long-time friend of KRG leadership, ushered in a new rapprochement between Baghdad and Erbil—a trend that has continued under Prime Minister Kadhimi and KRG Prime Minister Masrour Barzani. Unification of customs tariffs between the two sides, involvement of the peshmerga in the federal security apparatus, and the creation of a committee including representatives of both Baghdad and Erbil to supervise Kirkuk's security are all steps in the right direction.[36] As to the dispute over oil policy, Omar al-Nidawi argues that the key to finding a zero-sum solution lies in the downstream side of the oil industry, particularly the oil refineries.[37] A reset of the relationship between Baghdad and Erbil could help generate additional resources for reconstruction in ISIS-liberated areas, defuse potential flashpoints over disputed territories, and allow for better development of the country's oil resources. One positive sign at the end of 2021 is that Baghdad and Erbil are once again working together on the security front, following a rise in ISIS attacks in northern Iraq, to prevent the group's resurgence. ISIS has exploited the division between Baghdad and Erbil by focusing its attacks on disputed territories, but Iraqi forces and peshmerga are setting up joint coordination centers around the territories to improve security.[38]

Conclusion

The beginning of this chapter discussed how the civil war in Iraq represented a violent political renegotiation among various Iraqi factions. What was true at the beginning of the war is even more true in the current phase of Iraq's political history. Not only are reconciliation, renegotiation, and engagement necessary between political elites and citizens, but also between the Iraqi state and outside actors, namely Iran, Turkey, the United States, and Saudi Arabia, all of which are contending for political, and in some cases, religious and military, influence in the country.

The game for Iraq will be as treacherous coming out of the conflict as it was going in. Dealing with the future status of the PMFs and enhancing the capacity of the Iraqi military will be key to Iraq's long-term stability. Premature demilitarization of the country could lead to chaos, renewed attacks by ISIS, and possible Sunni–Shi'a and Baghdad–Erbil conflicts that could disrupt Iraq's current state of equilibrium. Waiting too long to demilitarize could jeopardize the legitimacy of the Iraqi government, leading to some of the same problems outlined above.

Balancing these realities will be even more difficult if the United States attempts to use the government in Baghdad as a spearhead to weaken Iran, as it did under the Trump administration. As part of its "maximum pressure" campaign against Iran, the Trump administration pushed Baghdad hard to attenuate its energy relationship with Iran and disband Iranian-supported militias. This forced Baghdad into an untenable position, possibly leading to more state fragility. For now, the Biden administration is taking a different approach toward Iran than its predecessor, focusing on efforts to revive the 2015 nuclear deal, but if the talks in Vienna fall apart and tensions escalate, Baghdad may once again be caught in the middle between Washington and Tehran.

Nonetheless, when it comes to Iraq's relations with its neighbors, it is not all bad news. After reestablishing relations with Saudi Arabia, Iraq has continued its reintegration into the Arab world, with Prime Minister Kadhimi pursuing closer economic, security, and political ties with Egypt and Jordan as part of the "New Levant" initiative. Iraq has also taken on a growing role as a regional mediator, hosting summits like the August 2021 Baghdad Conference as well as talks between Iran and Saudi Arabia. Such efforts should continue to help move Iraq's foreign policy into a more regionally focused and balanced direction.

The regional and international community must recognize the opportunities presented by Iraq's current position, as well as its precariousness. Rather than using Iraq as an instrument for advancing their individual agendas, they need to understand that the country can also be a contributor to much-needed regional stability. While all the cases presented in this book call for regional and international cooperation, Iraq, at this moment of both threat and opportunity, is in particular need of it now. Its future, and possibly that of the region, is hanging in the balance.

Notes

1 Fanar Haddad, "Shi'a-centric State Building and Sunni Rejection in Post-2003 Iraq," in *Beyond Sunni and Shi'a—The Roots of Sectarianism in a Changing Middle East*, ed. Frederic Wehrey (Oxford: Oxford University Press), 115–34.
2 Harith Hasan Al-Qarawee, "The 'Formal' Marja': Shi'i Clerical Authority and the State in Post-2003 Iraq," *British Journal of Middle East Studies* (February 2018). Available online: https://doi.org/10.1080/13530 194.2018.1429988 (accessed June 4, 2018).
3 Amatzia Baram, *Saddam Husayn and Islam, 1968–2003: Ba'thi Iraq from Secularism to Faith* (Baltimore: Johns Hopkins University Press, 2014).
4 This ethno-sectarian political system was a pre-2003 invention of the Iraqi opposition dating as far back as 1992, when several conferences of the Iraqi opposition in exile were organized on the basis of a similar quota system, starting with the 1992 conference in Vienna, which led to the creation of the Iraqi National Congress (INC). At a meeting of the INC held in Erbil, Kurdistan in February 1993, a consultative committee set up led by the late Ahmad Chalabi was divided on the basis of an ethno-sectarian quota system: 33 percent of seats were given to Shi'a, 25 percent to Kurds, 7 percent to Sunnis, 6 percent each to Turkmen and Assyrians, and 3 percent to secular and liberal parties.

5   Renad Mansour, "The Sunni Predicament in Iraq," *Carnegie Endowment for International Peace*, March 2016, 4.

6   Muhanad Seloom, "An Unhappy Return: What the Iraqi Islamic Party Gave Up to Gain Power," Carnegie Middle East Center (November 2018).

7   Nathaniel Rabkin, "The Sunni Religious Leadership in Iraq," *Current Trends in Islamist Ideology*, 23 (June 2018): 45–65.

8   George Packer, "Betrayed," *New Yorker*, March 19, 2007.

9   Hannah Fischer, "Iraq Casualties: US Military Forces and Iraqi Civilians, Police and Security Forces," R40824, Congressional Research Service, December 6, 2011.

10 This particular reading was relayed to the author during a conversation with a leader of one of the Sunni insurgent groups conducted in 2007 on the margins of a meeting in Amman, Jordan as part of a three-year Track 2.0 dialogue initiative on national reconciliation in Iraq organized by the International Institute for Sustained Dialogue.

11 Leon E. Panetta, " 'Surge' Not Working as Hoped," *Monterey County Herald*, September 9, 2007.

12 Kevin Charles Redmon, "The New Abu Ghraib," *The Atlantic*, May 3, 2010.

13 While Article 140 of the Iraqi Constitution places the disputed territories in northern Iraq, including Kirkuk, under federal authority, it makes the Iraqi government responsible for putting in place policies to unwind the effects of Arabization policies implemented by the regime pre-2003, to be followed by a census and a referendum to determine the will of the citizens in these regions in resolving the territories' final status. Article 140 sets a deadline of December 31, 2007, for implementing these measures, without providing a roadmap of what would happen if this deadline was not met.

14 Sons of Iraq are Sunni volunteers working in local security forces created by Sunni sheikhs, tribal leaders, and other local power brokers entering into security contracts with US coalition forces. By spring 2008, these local security forces were established in two-thirds of the country's provinces, including Nineveh, Diyala, Babil, Salahuddin, and Baghdad.

15 "Transcript: President Obama's June 19 remarks on Iraq" *Washington Post*, June 19, 2014.

16 Faleh A. Jabar, "The Iraqi Protest Movement: From Identity Politics to Issue Politics," *LSE Middle East Center Paper Series* 25 (June 2018): 12.

17 Ibid., 9.

18 Ibid., 22.

19 Abbas Kadhim, "Revisiting the History of the Shi'a Marja'yah Under the Ba'ath Regime in Iraq," Middle East Institute (September 12, 2018). Available online: https://www.mei.edu/events/revisiting-history-shia-marja yah-under-baath-regime-iraq (accessed October 5, 2018).

20 Abbas Kadhim, "The Hawza Under Siege—A Study in the Ba'th Party Archive," Institute for Iraq Studies, occasional paper no. 1 (Boston: Boston University, June 11, 2013).

21 Hayder al-Khoei, "Post-Sistani Iraq, Iran, and the Future of Shi'a Islam," *War on the Rocks*, September 8, 2016.

22 Ibid.

23 Omer Kassim and Randa Slim, "Iraq After ISIS: Three Major Flashpoints," Middle East Institute (April 6, 2017).

24 Lionel Beehner, "Impediments to National Reconciliation in Iraq," Council on Foreign Relations (January 5, 2007).

25 This initiative was co-led by the late Harold Saunders and the author who at the time was the vice president of the International Institute for Sustained Dialogue.

26 James Traub, "The UN and Iraq: Moving Forward?" *Policy Analysis Brief* (October 2017). Available online: https://www.stanleyfoundation.org/publi cations/pab/Traub_PAB_1007.pdf (accessed October 8, 2018).

27 The International Compact for Iraq, launched in 2007, is a joint initiative of the Government of Iraq and the UN that committed Iraq's leaders to key political steps and policy reforms in exchange for economic and other forms of support from the international community.

28 Traub, "The UN and Iraq: Moving Forward?" 4.

29 Matthew Schweitzer, "Pursuing National Reconciliation in Iraq," *EPIC*, November 11, 2016.

30 Kassim and Slim, "Iraq After ISIS."

31 Fanar Haddad, "The Waning Relevance of the Sunni-Shi'a Divide," The Century Foundation (April 10, 2019).

32 Paul Salem and Randa Slim, "The United States Will Need a 'Diplomatic Surge' in Iraq," *Omphalos Lawfare*, April 10, 2017.

33 Renad Mansour, "Rebuilding the Iraqi State: Stabilisation, Governance, and Reconciliation," *European Parliament Directorate-General for External Policies* (February 2018).

34 Omar al-Nidawi, "While Iraq's Next Government May be 'Business As Usual,' the Election has Planted the Seeds for Change," Middle East Institute (November 1, 2021).

35 Omar al-Nidawi, "Finding a Way Forward in the Baghdad-Erbil Oil Dispute," Middle East Institute (March 6, 2019).

36 Diyari Salih, "The Kirkuk Case and Baghdad-Erbil Relations," *LSE Middle East Centre Blog*, February 27, 2019.

37 Nidawi, "Finding a Way Forward."

38 Samya Kullab, "A Fragile Partnership in Iraq Tries to Prevent Is Revival," *AP*, December 17, 2021.

9 THE DIPLOMACY OF ENGAGEMENT

Ending Civil Wars in Transitional Middle Eastern States

Chester A. Crocker

Introduction

Engagement strategy can be applied in a range of contexts: for example, to shape relations with a rival or adversary, to move a recalcitrant pariah state, to press for an end to acts of terrorism or war crimes, and to support a strategy of mediation in violent conflicts. This chapter looks at the challenges and trade-offs that arise when external powers seek to shape political crises and bring civil wars under control. The turmoil sweeping the Middle East since the start of this century offers eloquent examples of such transitional struggle. In just one example, Algerian diplomat Lakhdar Brahimi, operating under a joint UN–Arab League mandate starting in 2011, sought to engage the Syrian regime and opposition groups in a mediation effort with the support of states in the Friends of Syria group. These challenges are not confined to the Middle East. American mediators worked to dampen down regional violence and promote political solutions in southern Africa in the 1980s.[1] Former Finnish President Martti Ahtisaari engaged in mediation with the

Indonesian government and an Acehnese rebel movement to negotiate an autonomy deal in 2005 ending decades of violence in Aceh.[2]

People use the term diplomatic "engagement" to mean very different things. Some use it as foreign policy shorthand for simply talking to another government or as another word for "normal" diplomacy. Others use it as a weapon of advocacy or rhetorical attack: "We've tried military intervention, it's time for a policy of engagement," or "we tried engagement with Iran and it failed so we need to keep all options on the table." Properly understood, the purpose of an engagement strategy is to change the target's perception of its own interests and, hence, to modify its policies and its behavior.

Engagement is not about sweet talk. Nor is it based on the illusion that problems can be solved if only people would talk to each other. While talk is required, the purpose of engagement is not simply "getting involved," "showing concern," or "reaching out" to another party. The purpose of engagement is not improved relations, although better relations might be the ultimate result. The engager's purpose is to change the target's behavior toward more cooperative and constructive policies. Engagement is a process that involves exerting pressure, by raising questions, probing assumptions, and exploring hypothetical possibilities. Above all, it involves testing how far the target might be willing to go. Properly understood, the diplomacy of engagement places the ball in the target's court.

Clearly, different types and amounts of power or leverage are called for depending on the context and the targets. But engagement is generally about exploring the possibility of an understanding and defining a roadmap for future relations. At times, engagement diplomacy can be based on "pure" negotiated procedures but it can also be backed by raw (if diplomatically worded) exercises of coercive influence (deterrence, compellence, sanctions, vetoes or offers of assistance, the promise or denial of membership in an institution or formal relations).[3]

Even the most creative and powerful outsiders cannot impose durable political order on transitional societies unless they are prepared indefinitely to occupy and administer them, a lesson brought home dramatically in Afghanistan in 2021. In a world where the norm of self-determination prevails, the citizens of these places are not likely to accept such a notion. This principle will also likely be tested with Russia and Iran's involvement in Syria. Citizens are the ones who pay the price of violent civil conflicts and it is they who will ultimately shape their course in this age of awakening. On the other hand, however, the decisions taken by the United States and other powerful actors can make a significant difference, especially at critical junctures in the life of a violent transition process. This places a special onus on the shoulders of powerful actors: their interventions (political as well as military) may shape who comes out on top; but, by the same token, a decision not to intervene or to terminate an intervention may also shape the outcome by standing aside and letting the contest go to the best armed local protagonist.

A Universe of Transitions

How do civil war transitions end? At least seven possible outcomes can be identified. These include: (1) a "revolution" in which a more or less coherent new order sweeps away the old as a result of violent struggle (Ethiopia, 1974; Uganda, 1986; Russia, 1917; Afghanistan, 2021); (2) a velvet "revolution" in which the regime collapses amid a mixture of street power, external pressure, and leadership splits (Iran, 1979; the Philippines, 1986; Egypt and Tunisia, 2011; the Soviet Union, 1991); (3) bloody, broken-back regime change following prolonged strife as regime elements defect and leaders arrange their exit or are killed (Yemen, 2011; Libya, 2011; Ethiopia, 1991); (4) effective repression using scorched earth tactics so that the opposition is defeated (Peru, 1992–2012; Syria, 2011–18; Sri Lanka, 2009; Zimbabwe, 2000–); (5) drawn-out political stalemate followed by "negotiated revolution" (South Africa, 1992–4; Algeria-France, 1962; Burma, 2010–); (6) prolonged, bloody strife that prompts coercive external intervention and an imposed peace (Bosnia, 1995); (7) prolonged strife that prompts powerfully backed, externally led negotiations leading to an internationally monitored transition period and elections (Namibia 1966–90; Liberia, 1989–2005; Mozambique 1976–94; El Salvador, 1979–94).

These outcomes may only be stage one of a longer transition process whose next stage is unclear. Prolonged stalemate could evolve into a de facto partition of the state into ethnic, regional, or confessional rump enclaves as the regime arms its core supporters and the central state loses control of much of the territory (Somalia, Democratic Republic of the Congo). The Egyptian example suggests that velvet revolutions can morph into directions that remain unpredictable for some time. Bloody regime change after externally assisted civil strife in Libya has been followed by new phases of polarized conflict among militia factions as well as fragile steps toward a political settlement, amid political and military initiatives by interested outsiders. Successful negotiation can sometimes produce autonomy arrangements that partially decentralize power while the now-more-constrained state remains intact (Indonesia–Aceh, Philippines–Mindanao).

If outside states attempt to freeze power relations or entrench political-military groups in open-ended power-sharing structures, they will likely sow the seeds of future conflict and distort the chances for organic political development (Lebanon and Bosnia). Powerful local actors—the men with the guns—will often try to game the arrangements that flow from negotiated peace deals and use the trappings of democracy to seize and hold onto power, as in Cambodia, Sudan/South Sudan, and Angola. Too often, such negotiations will simply reflect the balance of coercive forces on the ground at the moment they take place and lead to the marginalization of unarmed civilians. Avoiding this outcome requires that outside interveners maintain a high level of commitment to peace building during and beyond the immediate transition period. The Iraq experience suggests that premature withdrawal of outside coercive power can be as destabilizing as the initial, poorly managed intervention.

The Challenges of Engagement

Engagement in civil war transitions is fraught with strategic challenges. Outside powers need to navigate between competing priorities as they consider whether, when, and how to bring their influence to bear. A "peace at any price" approach might respond to immediate humanitarian imperatives, but it also could entrench the wrong actors, prolonging rather than resolving the society's problems. Thus, a central issue is the timing of cease-fires and the extent to which the act of engagement is motivated primarily by a concern to preempt or stop the violence.[4] In Syria, outside actors as well as armed Syrian parties have displayed a wide range of motives in proposing or opposing cease-fires, often with little regard for their impact on civilians. Humanitarian agencies have struggled to prioritize the goal of saving lives and bringing relief to desperate local populations, while armed actors frequently gamed the whole discussion: rebels to achieve relief from military pressure by the regime and its allies, while the latter used cease-fire offers as a technique to force rebel units to relocate. It has not been clear how local military pauses could be effectively linked to national-level political dialogue, in part due to divisions among anti-regime forces.

The timing of third-party engagement has far-reaching implications. It affects the central question of deciding how much of the existing state apparatus can serve as the institutional base for the transition and future governance. A related question concerns the fate of people associated with the current government during the previous decades of misrule. The task here is to mesh the quest for as much of the right kind of change as possible with the necessity of achieving some measure of continuity—both to reassure the incumbents' core constituencies and their allies and to avoid a descent into chaos. Timing and sequencing are of critical importance in order to avoid "wasting" finite leverage by premature action, on the one hand, and delaying so long that the "ripe" moment for intervention is lost, on the other. The United States and other "friends of Syria" wrestled with this challenge during the first three years of that country's civil war (2011–13), and the policy dilemmas only escalated further when the Russians—in parallel with Turkey's and Iran's own actions—decided to move into the vacuum created by US hesitation.

The greatest challenge facing outsiders is their overarching responsibility to avoid making an already troubled society (and region) even worse. The test of statesmanship in such violent transitions is to define the least bad outcome. This requires a very careful assessment of local and regional players. The "bad guys" may be evident, but "good guys" could be hard to find. If so, it will be best to help foster a credible transition process rather than trying to select winners. It must be acknowledged, however, that outsiders typically have a preference for one side in a civil war and may find themselves almost "forced" by circumstances to pick winners — especially when other outsiders back the "other side." This was the awful dilemma faced by George Marshall, President Harry Truman's envoy, when he sought to stop the Chinese civil war in the immediate aftermath of Japan's defeat in the Second World War.[5] UN-backed mediators have had a different challenge when working for political settlement of the civil wars in Yemen, Libya, and Syria: as representatives of a divided Security Council, these envoys were often faced with the additional problem of Middle East political fragmentation. Such diplomatic incoherence has reduced the prospects for building leverage for effective mediation.

It is important to underscore the division between external powers over engagement in the Middle East cases: on one side there is a group of major states that increasingly opt for some form of retrenchment, the disengagers include the United States, France, Britain, and their Western allies. Other states see merit in getting engaged in order to pursue national interests and take advantage of the reticence of the first group. Turkey, Russia, the UAE, Egypt, Qatar, Saudi Arabia, and China are among those with an appetite for engagement, even if only to experiment with the use of available tools and the absence of effective "discipline" from a rules-based international or regional order. Prime examples include Yemen, Syria, and Libya (discussed in detail in Chapters 4, 5, and 7) and the more recently emerging case of the Red Sea/Horn of Africa region. In addition to the cases of Yemen, Syria, and Libya, the civil wars in Somalia, Ethiopia, and South Sudan have become magnets for competing forms of engagement by this second group.[6] These cases demonstrate the multiregional character of contemporary engagements as African conflict parties export their divisions to external states, which then reciprocate by injecting their own divisions into African cases.

The Tools of Engagement

The first step in devising a strategy of engagement in civil wars—in the Middle East as elsewhere—is to identify the purposes and interests at stake. Are the external actors motivated primarily by strategic interests and rivalries, by the perceived need to "drain the swamp" and degrade terrorist movements, by a concern to resolve conflicts and prevent state failure, or by basic humanitarian reflexes? The active Middle East conflicts discussed in this volume raise most of these issues in one form or another. But specific external actors will each have its own lens for setting priorities. The UN Security Council will have a messy mélange of P-5 and other motivations reflecting their relations with the major regional powers—that is, Iran, Saudi Arabia, Israel, Egypt, and Turkey.

Once purposes and interests are clarified, the external party needs to select a mixture of tools appropriate to the specific case. The main requirement is leverage, and leverage comes from power, actual and potential, in one of its many forms. Direct military intervention may be the most compelling but also the least flexible form of power for use in support of engagement in violent transitions. To paraphrase Colin Powell in the Iraq context, if we break the target state and disrupt its social fabric we may end up owning the result. In the case of Libya, the Western powers have tried to *disown* the result, without success. Another problem, as Samuel Huntington observed in commenting on the poor record of most small, incremental interventions, is that military forces are "not primarily instruments of communication to convey signals to an enemy, they are instead instruments of coercion to compel him to alter his behavior."[7] They are a blunt instrument, difficult to calibrate. Furthermore, military intervention, even if justified on largely humanitarian grounds, involves taking sides, as previously noted.

Analyzing the so-called values cases of the 1990s where US national security interests were not directly involved—Haiti, Somalia, Bosnia, Rwanda—Richard Betts made a persuasive case that "impartial" intervention is a delusion. As he put it, to intervene militarily is to decide who rules the target state—a reality both when outsiders arrive and when they leave.[8] But nonintervention by a powerful actor such as the United States raises another dilemma because the option to do so existed: as we have seen in Syria, inaction by one powerful actor can simply deliver the society to those who are best armed and organized, in other words, it is another way to decide who rules. We have seen the first principle at work in Afghanistan from 2001 to the chaotic departure of the United States and allied forces in 2021 and the second principle in the Great Lakes region of Africa since 1994. These examples of the use and the nonuse of direct military instruments by powerful states only underscore the importance of an integrated analytic approach by policy makers so that the relevant instruments of power can be understood in a realistic context.[9]

The United States and its allies hold many tools of leverage and influence. One is economic sanctions designed to wear down and isolate the target regime. But broad trade and investment sanctions are another blunt instrument that tends to hurt civilians first and foremost. This explains the increased recourse to targeted financial, travel, and other sanctions tools focused on the regime itself and on those who do business with it.[10] Another tool is humanitarian aid to mitigate the suffering of affected populations. Such assistance will seldom be viewed as impartial and will almost always be perceived as "intervention" by the incumbent regime, which will seek to control distribution channels—as the Assad regime has done with UN aid in Syria[11]—though best efforts can be made to bring relief to all sides. Alternatively, humanitarian assistance can be employed as an openly acknowledged act of solidarity with opposition elements, as was the case with relief and humanitarian assistance programs employed by the United States from Pakistan into Afghanistan before the Soviet withdrawal and the cross-border feeding program from Sudan into the Tigray and Eritrea areas of Ethiopia, both during the 1980s. In cases such as these, humanitarian and strategic purposes were joined and the goals included creating pressure for negotiations. The pressure can take the form of conditional offers of support with the international financial institutions or commitments to sponsor roundtable meetings on future reconstruction efforts in cases such as Yemen and Syria.

Another tool in an engagement strategy could be the provision of lethal assistance to opposition forces in hopes of leveling the playing field, accelerating the arrival of a ripe moment for negotiation. Whether supplied through proxies or directly, overtly or covertly, such external aid serves multiple purposes: it can give the provider a seat at the table in future talks; it sends a signal to the regime's backers that they face competition and their actions will not be cost free; if successfully employed, such aid could create or strengthen a stalemate. Over time, these tools are part of a strategy of "ripening" the transitional civil conflict by bleeding the regime. This approach could have been employed robustly in the case of Syria. Of course, there are also downsides. The ultimate destination of weapons is hard to control in a civil war. Lethal intervention of this type could become a slippery slope leading to pressure for additional decisions. The provision of such support requires a choice to be made about recipients or "good guys" when, in reality, the "good guys" may be a mixed bag. Above all, the external intervenor needs to keep eyes fixed on the broader—and most important—goal of backing a successful transition process.

The protracted Syrian civil war sadly illustrates all of these points. Backing "the opposition" in order to level the playing field in support of a negotiated settlement becomes much more complex when the opposition is deeply fragmented and includes undesirable elements. Using military tools to support a negotiated outcome raises serious geopolitical issues when other powerful states are backing the current regime. Yet, such tools may be the only way to get their attention and neutralize their coercive tools. A further policy conundrum underscored by the Syrian case is that once an external power such as the United States engages in an effort to shape a civil war outcome on acceptable terms, the domestic political stakes get higher. After months of mounting political pressure to take a clear stand against the regime, President Barack Obama used the occasion of an August 2011 visit by Turkish Prime Minister Recep Tayyip Erdoğan to declare that "the time has come for President Assad to step aside." But such a statement is not a policy and it only accentuated further pressure for decisions to back up the words with action. The diplomacy of engagement in the Syrian conflict raised three domestic political dilemmas: the slippery slope problem in providing lethal aid, the question of how to select and characterize opposition elements worthy of support, and the ever-present need to explain why it may be necessary to work with elements of the very regime that "must go" in order to achieve a negotiated outcome.

Where Possible, Create Coherence and Borrow Leverage

In many cases, the tools discussed above—by themselves—will be unlikely to produce a successful outcome. They are too narrowly conceived and too unilateral in scope. The remedy lies partly in finding sources of borrowed leverage and credibility. Neighboring states, regional hegemons, and major powers associated with the regime or its opponents are the most obvious sources of the leverage needed. Close behind them are regional organizations, alliances, and the UN. Examples where these techniques were applied include: the complex Cambodia diplomacy of the early 1990s, exploiting broader geopolitical dynamics; Russia's efforts to convene regional partners in the Astana talks on Syria; standing up the transitional regime in Liberia in 2003 with the help of the UN and African partners; partnering with UN mediators and Central American leaders to produce the 1992 El Salvador settlement; borrowing leverage from African neighbors, Western allies, the UN secretariat, the Cubans, and the Soviets to produce the 1988 Namibia–Angola peace accords; and below-the-radar cooperation by French, UN, African Union, and US officials that stopped a civil war and removed a stubborn tyrant from power in Cote d'Ivoire in 2011.

The practice of recruiting groups of "friends" or "contact groups" around the leading conflict managers is another example of the search for leverage.[12] Practitioners need to be aware, however, that borrowed leverage is often accompanied by complexity and even confusion, adding substantial burdens of coordination and lateral diplomatic legwork, as illustrated by the fate of the International Syria Support Group. The balance sheet of multilateral conflict management requires careful accounting because the motives and interests of those who are recruited need to be taken into account.[13]

The Syrian case by Robert Ford in this volume makes abundantly clear why the efforts to promote a negotiated settlement were bound to fail. Efforts by UN envoys, the United States, and other Western diplomats to borrow leverage and corral the Syrian parties into a unified approach were doomed because Moscow and Tehran were unwilling to impose compromise on the Assad regime and because Washington and its diverse allies were not prepared to raise the ante and effectively pressure them to do so. The painful result was an absence of the coherence essential to Western/Arab diplomatic progress. By contrast, the Russians, in loose parallel with Iran, did have an effective strategy for ending the Syrian Civil War, albeit at an atrocious cost to the Syrian people, a cost substantially increased by feckless American, European, and Sunni Arab diplomacy.[14]

Diplomacy with Regimes and Rebels

Borrowing leverage is the essence of good diplomacy in conflict environments. But it is not the only diplomatic tool in the arsenal. If the troubled regime is a friendly one at some level—for example, Egypt under Hosni Mubarak, the Philippines under Ferdinand Marcos—Washington has the option of withdrawing or reducing its support. If the target is a rogue, warlord, or an unfriendly regime, US diplomacy can facilitate a leader's exile by speaking to those who might accept him, as Washington did successfully in Liberia (2003). An unheralded but brilliant example of arranging a soft landing occurred in Ethiopia in 1991 when rebel forces were on the outskirts of Addis Ababa. The Soviet-backed tyrant Mengistu Haile Mariam and his immediate coterie escaped to Zimbabwean exile in a carefully orchestrated exit just before the Tigrayan rebel chieftain Meles Zenawi and his forces entered the city. That diplomacy was conducted by US officials using one of the most powerful modern diplomatic weapons, a cell phone.

Calibrating relations with regimes and rebels or civilian-led opposition groups requires clear thinking about basic objectives as a transition unfolds. Engaging effectively in civil war diplomacy requires choices on issues such as public distancing and pressures, channels and levels for engaging oppositionists, and what forms of tangible support to withdraw or provide. As argued earlier, the choices depend on the engager's purpose: is the goal to help insurgents replace the regime? To warn them against unacceptable behavior? To curry favor with them in case they come out on top? To send a message to the regime's backers? Or, simply to have a seat at the table and keep options open as events unfold? Even more basic issues lie behind these questions. Is the goal a negotiated transition in which there are elements of continuity as well as change? In the case of Syria, few of these questions had a credible and coherent answer from the United States and its partners. A similar judgment can be reached on the Libya case.

The most important choices involve (1) when to reach out to local opposition parties as a regime begins to run into trouble; (2) whether and how to engage with armed actors, including those that may engage in acts of terror or other forms of criminal activity; and, (3) what roles armed opposition movements and their civilian-led counterparts will play in negotiating the transition. The political context shapes the answer. In the case of a previously friendly regime which finds itself sliding into political crisis—Iran under the Shah, the Philippines under Marcos, Egypt under Mubarak—the act of engaging opposition groups sends a powerful signal of distancing and hedging. That, in fact, may be its primary initial purpose. Diplomatic support and institution-building aid may follow. (Lethal assistance to rebels confronting a friendly regime would not make strategic sense.) Even in relatively peaceful settings where the goal is to hedge and broaden contacts in the society, engaging with opposition movements should not be viewed as a gift to them. Once again, engagement is not making nice, it is a test that could open the door to a possible roadmap for relations. It may also be undertaken to protect future equities and avoid estrangement from a future leadership. In any event, it should be done early in the process, ideally before political conflict ripens into crisis.

What to Do as Civil Strife Heats Up?

The picture gets more complicated once the crisis facing a previously friendly regime crosses the line toward violence. One reason is that state institutions, and the people running them, may be at risk. This makes it important to assess the pros and cons of working toward a relatively soft landing versus sweeping away the old order. As regime brutality converts protesters into rebels (often due to provocation aimed at precisely this result), it becomes important to know more about the armed groups that emerge. They may be led by patriots or warlords, the leadership may be pragmatic or ideologically rigid, its agenda may be homegrown or shaped by those who arm and fund it, the agenda may be driven by principle or by the raw quest for power, the armed opposition may be cohesive or fragmented and doomed to a future of fratricidal strife as the old order crumbles. Armed groups may or may not respect the rights of innocent civilians.

In sum, a deep dive into the granular details of a specific scenario is required in order to get some answers. Early engagement will be called for, not as an act of solidarity with future "good guys," but to send warnings, clarify positions and interests, ask tough questions, and obtain information. As the old regime goes down, it becomes increasingly important to avoid rose-colored glasses in viewing likely successors: there are no Nelson Mandelas in most scenarios in the Middle East.

Engagement with armed opposition groups has become an increasingly fraught undertaking. If a group has managed to get itself on the United States, UN, or EU lists of proscribed entities because of terrorist acts, officials may be deterred by the risk of political controversy or legally prohibited from contact with them in the absence of special waivers—a relatively recent development that severely complicates peacemaking in conflict zones. Since the June 2010 US Supreme Court decision in *Holder v. Humanitarian Law Project*, nonofficial organizations have also been directly constrained in their dealings with armed groups that are on US terrorism lists. This prohibition can be interpreted as criminalizing mere training, advising on political solutions, and providing humanitarian aid. The US legislation, court decisions, and executive branch regulations represent a form of unilateral diplomatic disarmament. The net effect is to require that communication with such armed groups take place through private, non-US intermediaries and to place excessive reliance on intelligence channels or on other friendly third parties that are free from such self-defeating inhibitions.[15]

These legal and legislative developments compound an already complex environment for engaging armed actors. Contact with armed groups operating in friendly states (e.g., Spain, Colombia, the Philippines, Yemen, or Northern Ireland) is highly sensitive politically. Key exchanges typically take place in the utmost secrecy, often conducted by nonofficial bodies. If external actors are to engage successfully in conflict-torn polities, they will need sufficient flexibility to deal with the major political forces emerging during violent transitions, and the earlier the better. After all, in places as diverse as South Africa, El Salvador, Kashmir, the Palestinian territories, Nepal, and Afghanistan it is hard to imagine how outside powers could have exerted influence for constructive change without being able to engage these emerging forces, challenging them to operate as *political* rather than violent actors.

The purposes of engaging armed actors must be stated as clearly as possible. First, engagers will want to support moderate voices and undercut the rabid extremists and greediest warlords. They will also wish to make clear the limits of what can be achieved by the gun and to encourage a return to politics. By debating, arguing from experience elsewhere, and opening the eyes of blinkered militants, the goal is to raise doubts by asking awkward questions—a classic tool of good diplomacy. A third purpose may be to split the leadership or entice it to think and act politically so that a negotiated transition can have a chance. The most basic message is this: terrorism and armed struggle cannot get you what you say you want, but politics can.[16] It is this approach that has eventually prevailed as successive British governments and international mediators grasped the Northern Ireland nettle. This is also the approach pursued almost invisibly by various third parties that have successfully pushed Euskadi Ta Askatasuna (ETA) to abandon the violent pursuit of Basque national aspirations.[17] This line of reasoning has motivated third-party peacemaking efforts between Israel and the Palestinians, both before Oslo and more recently in diplomatic efforts to isolate and pressure Hamas. However, as the Afghanistan case so clearly demonstrates, this approach to engaging armed militants only works if they can be persuaded that they do not have the option to go for outright military victory. This will not work if the engaging party is vital to stability yet is heading out the door.

This logic applies equally to violent transitions that threaten *unfriendly* regimes. Policy toward such places as Cambodia, Zimbabwe, Burma, Angola, Sudan, and Kosovo required a similar calculus about how much and what kinds of support to offer opposition groups. In Cambodia and Angola, US officials had few illusions about the character and conduct of the Khmer Rouge and União Nacional para a Independência Total de Angola (UNITA), respectively, and they did not entertain ideas of their achieving an outright military "win." Where they faced both armed and nonviolent groups, as in Kosovo, an effort was made to walk a balanced line—recognizing the critical role played by the men with the guns but taking steps to include those relying on nonviolent methods. Trying to exclude relations with armed groups actually marginalizes the conflict manager more than them, a point that applies even to the more radical among them. The cost of allowing armed groups to dominate transitional diplomacy was essentially ignored in the case of Sudan, which culminated in a negotiated pact between Khartoum and the Sudanese People's Liberation Army in the 2005 Comprehensive Peace Agreement.

The role armed groups are permitted to play in an eventual negotiation process matters very much. Unless they are somehow defeated or marginalized by civilian leadership, armed groups will assert the right to be at the table on matters affecting security, cease-fires, external military monitoring, future force configurations, and disarmament. These are the topics on which armed groups have a direct, "professional" stake and on which their buy-in is essential. Furthermore, they are most unlikely to cooperate unless they get credible answers to their priority security concerns: who will guarantee an agreement and assure that others respect their commitments? What remedies will be available to one faction if others cheat?

Having recognized their role in the negotiation of security issues, however, it is imperative that armed groups *not* be given carte blanche to dominate other items on the agenda of a negotiated transition. Issues such as election monitoring, refugee return, freedom of assembly and speech, economic reconstruction, and the administration of justice and post-conflict accountability mechanisms are rightly in the purview of civil society actors and political parties at the negotiating table. Again, Afghanistan sadly illustrates what can happen if armed groups have a monopoly of real power.

The case of post-Gaddafi Libya illustrates what can happen when there is no authoritative, binding understanding about the intricate process by which a successor regime achieves a monopoly on the use of armed force. It further underscores what happens when outsiders intervene for the narrow, short-term purpose of getting rid of an odious regime but make no serious, sustained effort to help the "liberated" citizenry establish a constitutional order. Creating vacuums—as in Libya and Iraq—does not help to end civil war. Rather, it increases the likelihood of new wars. Unless external powers are prepared to establish "post-war" security in a place they have "liberated," they should not engage in coercive regime change in troubled countries.

Negotiating a political transition in such an environment is a process in which issues need to be sequenced. Giving armed militias—especially ones organized on regional or sectarian lines—a direct role in shaping the terms of political change and writing a new constitution poses dangers for the future. It encourages armed actors to permanently entrench their positions and block the emergence of a civil order. The experience of Bosnia after Dayton illustrates the pitfalls of guaranteeing sectarian or nationalist militants a power base from which to make political demands. The lesson here is to detach the immediate transition arrangements in which power is inevitably shared from the next phase in which political roles are defined constitutionally. That requires accepting the responsibility for some form of transitional international authority.

What to Do with the State?

It may be, as Dirk Vandewalle has argued, that Libya's is an extreme case because Muammar Gaddafi destroyed any institutions he inherited and left few behind when he was murdered.[18] In most cases, however, the transitional polity will feature a range of still operative administrative institutions as well as an inevitably politicized security cluster of agencies, forces, and services. Their fate and the fate of the personnel who staff them will be important subjects of transitional negotiation. If a chaotic, Iraq-style vacuum is to be avoided, those issues will need to be negotiated with representatives of the existing state. Thus, the role of externally led diplomacy is to seize the window of opportunity created by the changing balance of military forces and to support a negotiated transition. Diplomacy and military power must work hand in glove— they are not opposites or alternatives.

When contested transitions reach their culminating point, incumbent leaders make their choices. Scorched-earth leaders meet Gaddafi's fate or face the prospect of trials at the International Criminal Court. When the walls close in and power shifts toward the challengers, some leaders opt to flee and accept the uncertainties of exile, as in Haiti, Ethiopia, Iran, Liberia, or the Philippines. This is one end of the spectrum of regime transitions. At the other end of the spectrum, there is South Africa, where open warfare was preempted by farsighted leaders capable of negotiating and managing change. However, just as there are no Mandelas in the truly violent scenarios such as Libya or Yemen, there are also no F. W. de Klerks capable of seeing what is best for their country and what serves the long-term interests of their core constituency.

To be sure, transitional negotiations do not always succeed and their successes are often short lived. External parties are always hard pressed to keep things on track and to sustain the conflict parties' interest in some form of coexistence. It is ambitious to devise credible external guarantees, to sustain outsiders' interest and commitment to providing peacekeepers and political support so that the parties receive necessary assurances as the transition unfolds. Each political settlement may be nothing more than another chapter in a continuing narrative of instability.

Engagement in transitional polities is not without risks. Decision-makers who seek to help manage and end such conflicts can expect to face criticism for arranging soft landings and power-sharing compromises. Purists identified with one side or another will demand a clear alignment with the "good guys" (even where these are in short supply), and will decry any evidence that diplomats are attributing "moral equivalence" to the conflict parties. Engagement with odious political actors (in the regime or the opposition, or both) will be attacked as conferring legitimacy on them. If an emerging political settlement leaves elements of the old regime and its administrative apparatus in place, voices will be raised demanding regime change and a complete overthrow of the old order. An authoritarian state such as Russia under Vladimir Putin may have few qualms about the ethical consequences of its strategic calculations; Western officials squirmed when acknowledging the possibility of dropping the demand that "Assad must go."

The conflict parties will test each other and the peacemaker by pronouncing a series of nonnegotiable preconditions that the other side must meet before talks can begin. Such demands will need to be answered or—better yet—set aside so that serious talks can begin. Sometimes, the most difficult risks arise later, after relationships have evolved to the point that the parties respond seriously to the tests and probes of an engagement strategy. At this point, external actors need to reflect on what to do if the parties "bite": what does the target party get if it says "yes" to the challenge of a compromise deal? The greatest risk of engagement diplomacy, in sum, is that it will work and thereby force the engager to make decisions as well.

Due to its geopolitical salience, the Middle East attracts a confusing mixture of commercial engagement, counterterrorism programs, direct military support and intervention, and peacemaking initiatives. Peacemaking aimed at ending or managing civil wars typically competes directly with the strategic motivations of external states and major regional powers. The result of this competition is the internationalization of such conflicts as those in Yemen, Libya, Syria, Afghanistan, and Iraq. Under the guise of working to end a civil war, the actions of outsiders are often aimed at assuring that the war has the "right" ending. But when states get tired of their engagements, they prioritize winding down their commitments and getting out.

Notes

1 Chester A. Crocker, "Peacemaking in Southern Africa: The Namibia-Angola Settlement of 1988," in *Herding Cats: Multiparty Mediation in a Complex World*, ed. Chester A. Crocker, Fen Osler Hampson, and Pamela Aall (Washington, DC: US Institute of Peace, 1999).
2 Martti Ahtisaari with Kriistina Rintakoski, "Mediation," in *The Oxford Handbook of Modern Diplomacy*, ed. Andrew Cooper, Jorge Heine, and Ramesh Thakur (Oxford: Oxford University Press, 2013).
3 Robert Jervis, "Getting to Yes with Iran: The Challenges of Coercive Diplomacy," *Foreign Affairs* (January–February 2013).
4 Silvie Mahieu, "When Should Mediators Interrupt a Civil War? The Best Timing for a Cease-Fire," *International Negotiation* 12, no. 2 (2007): 207–28.
5 Daniel Kurtz-Phelan, *The China Mission: George Marshall's Unfinished War, 1945–1947* (New York: W.W. Norton, 2018).
6 See "Final Report and Recommendations of the Senior Study Group on Peace and Security in the Red Sea Arena," Washington, DC USIP, 2020. Available online: https://www.usip.org/publications/2020/10/final-report-and-reco mmendations-senior-study-group-peace-and-security-red-sea (accessed September 17, 2021).
7 The writer is indebted to Fen Hampson for bringing this argument to his notice (referred to in Fareed Zakaria, "Chances are Small the US will Achieve Its Aims in Syria," *The Daily Star*, June 24, 2013). This argument first appeared in Samuel P. Huntington, *American Military Strategy* (Berkeley: Institute of International Studies, University of California, 1986), 15. See also Karin von Hippel, *Democracy by Force: U.S. Military Intervention in the Post-Cold War World* (Cambridge: Cambridge University Press, 2000).
8 Richard K. Betts, "The Delusion of Impartial Intervention," *Foreign Affairs* 73, no. 6 (November–December 1994).

9   To be sure, there has been major intervention by "blue helmet" UN
    peacekeepers in the Democratic Republic of the Congo, but seldom has
    peace enforcement been attempted in this vast country, leaving the civilian
    population frequently at the mercy of rival armies and armed militias
    jockeying for control of territory and resources.

10 David L. Asher, Victor D. Comras, and Patrick M. Cronin,
    Pressure: Coercive Economic Statecraft and US National Security
    (Washington, DC: Center for a New American Security, 2011).

11 Annie Sparrow, "How UN Humanitarian Aid Has Propped Up Assad,"
    Foreign Affairs, September 20, 2018. Available online: https://www.foreign
    affairs.com/articles/syria/2018-09-20/how-un-humanitarian-aid-has-prop
    ped-assad. (accessed March 31, 2022).

12 For a comprehensive treatment of this practice including case studies,
    see Teresa Whitfield, *Friends Indeed?: The United Nations, Groups of
    Friends and the Resolution of Conflict* (Washington, DC: US Institute of
    Peace, 2007).

13 Chester A. Crocker, Fen Osler Hampson, and Pamela Aall, "Conclusion"
    in *Herding Cats: Multiparty Mediation in a Complex World*, eds. Chester
    A. Crocker, Fen Osler Hampson, and Pamela Aall (Washington, DC: US
    Institute of Peace, 1999).

14 The UN-led phase of this diplomacy through 2013 is discussed in Chester
    A. Crocker, Fen Osler Hampson and Pamela Aall, "Why Is Mediation so
    Hard? The Case of Syria" in *Handbook of International Negotiation*, ed.
    Mauro Gallucio (New York: Springer, 2014).

15 For discussion of the pros and cons of these developments in the American
    legal and regulatory context, see Veronique Dudouet, "Mediating Peace
    with Proscribed Armed Groups" *US Institute of Peace Special Report* 239
    (May 2010). Teresa Whitfield, "Engaging with Armed Groups," *Center for
    Humanitarian Dialogue Mediation Practice Series* (October 2010). Available
    online: http://www.hdcentre.org/wp-content/uploads/2016/08/34Engaging
    witharmedgroups-MPS-October-2010.pdf (accessed March 21, 2022).

16 I. William Zartman and Guy Olivier Faure, "Introduction: Why Engage,
    and Why Not?" in *Engaging Extremists: Trade-offs, Timing and Diplomacy*,
    ed. William Zartman and Guy Olivier Faure (Washington, DC: US Institute
    of Peace, 2011).

17 On the Northern Ireland process, see Jonathan Powell, *Great Hatred, Little
    Room: Making Peace in Northern Ireland* (London: The Bodley Head,
    2008). On the Basque case, see Teresa Whitfield, *Endgame for ETA: Elusive
    Peace in the Basque Country* (Oxford: Oxford University Press, 2014).

18 Dirk Vandewalle, "After Qaddafi: The Surprising Success of the New Libya,"
    Foreign Affairs 91, no. 6 (November/December 2012).

CONCLUDING THOUGHTS AND POLICY TAKEAWAYS

Paul Salem and Ross Harrison

We hope that this volume has helped readers gain a deeper understanding of the complex roots and dynamics of civil wars in the Middle East. Our intention has been that it will also aid policymakers and practitioners to develop more effective ways to end these conflicts so that civilians can once again live in peace. Mitigating civil wars will also go a long way toward returning this most tumultuous of regions to a more stable equilibrium.

Given the intensity of the wars of the past decade, and how interwoven they are with regional and global politics, ending them in a sustainable way will be particularly difficult. Civil war is not new to the Middle East, nor is it peculiar to this part of the world. But the number of countries simultaneously at war in this past decade makes this region in many ways sui generis and speaks to a broader regional dysfunction that will complicate efforts to transition to peace.

In this second edition, we have tried to dig deep into the five cases of Libya, Yemen, Syria, Iraq, and Afghanistan, while also providing the broader historical and global contexts. But we acknowledge that these cases will continue to evolve significantly in unpredictable and unfathomable ways. What we can say with a high degree of surety is that while one tends to think of war as discrete from peace, civil wars in the Middle East are likely to remain a messier reality. As the chapters in this book make clear, the lines between civil war and civil peace are likely to remain blurred. And if, as Carl von Clausewitz observed, "war is the continuation of politics by other means,"[1] it follows, then, that unless the politics of countries mired in conflict can be expressed constructively through lasting settlements or accommodations, and functioning political systems, the specter of further instability and recurring civil war will persist.

Grappling with this question of the lines between war and peace, Jessica Maves Braithwaite in her chapter notes that academics have typically described civil wars as ending either through outright victory by one side, or through a negotiated settlement. While some of the cases that we examined have seen a conclusion or at least suspension of conflict—for example, the Taliban victory in Afghanistan and the peace process in Libya—several of the ongoing civil wars in the Middle East, such as Syria and Yemen, might not see similar conclusions anytime soon. It is quite possible that civil war might become more of a chronic condition in these countries, with conflicts transitioning from a higher to a lower level of intensity, but nevertheless continuing and remaining unresolved for a prolonged period.

This chronic condition of civil war, with vacillations in the intensity of conflict, could be thought of as a type of ongoing, albeit sometimes violent, negotiation between the contending parties over governance and societal issues. The phenomenon of organizations, like al-Qaeda and ISIS, using terrorism to advance their own ideological agendas is also likely to increase the probability that civil war will be more of a chronic condition.

None of the authors in this book paint a particularly optimistic picture of the balance between governance and conflict in their country-specific accounts, though there is considerable variance across the countries covered. Iraq has emerged from civil war and is in a state of what can best be described as unstable equilibrium; an inclusive, if often dysfunctional, political system struggles to manage and contain potential conflict. The Afghan Civil War has ended—at least temporarily—with a victory by one side, the Taliban, over the central Afghan government, which had been shored up by the United States and much of the international community. But it is unclear as of this writing whether the Taliban can or will try to govern in a way that considers the interests of large swaths of the Afghan population, and whether future civil conflict can be avoided. The Libyan civil war seems to be (at least temporarily) in abeyance as a negotiated political process, achieved in late 2020 and backed by the international community, moves tentatively forward. In Syria, the conflict is effectively frozen, with the Assad government controlling the capital and other key parts of the country, but unable to fully defeat its rivals and regain complete control of Syria. While there are few major military confrontations taking place, there is also no political process to bring the conflict to an end, reunify the divided parts of the country, and resume some form of unified national political and economic life. In Yemen, the conflict continues despite attempts at a negotiated ending: so far the Houthis have refused numerous overtures by the international community and Saudi Arabia to negotiate, choosing instead to push for more military advantage on the ground, particularly through the attempt to conquer the strategic city of Marib. Whether they will choose to negotiate peace if and when they take Marib or instead continue with military campaigns in other parts of the country is difficult to ascertain at this time.

And sadly, as we go to press with this second edition, civil war has erupted in a sixth regional country, Ethiopia, with government forces arrayed against Tigray groups. This conflict has already drawn in regional actors and has defied regional and international diplomatic efforts to stop it.

Conflict Reduction: A Glass Half Full or Half Empty?

Several of the countries experiencing wars that seem impervious to full resolution have nonetheless seen reductions in the intensity of fighting, such as Iraq, Libya, and Syria. Managed and monitored properly, conflict reduction can serve as a platform for reducing violence further, or at least for preventing a slippage backwards into extreme violence. Lower levels of conflict are also an opportunity for ordinary citizens to return to a semblance of normalcy in their lives. They may allow for reconstruction efforts to begin, for some refugees to return, for transport services to be restored, and for distribution of essential goods and services to take place as well.

Lower levels of conflict also at least hold open the possibility of constructive engagement as analyzed in the chapter by Chester Crocker. Negotiating peace between combatants while a civil war is raging can be the equivalent of trying to change the tires on a car while it is still barreling down the highway. In contrast, lower intensity conflict, even if it reflects a stalemate between the protagonists, may in fact ultimately slow things down such that conditions become more conducive to positive engagement.

But there are significant problems that chronic conditions of conflict could create for all the states and populations entangled in these wars. International and regional powers and investors will likely be reluctant to invest significant political and financial capital in reconstruction efforts when the specter of renewed violence looms. The United States has shown scant interest in reconstruction in Syria, and continued violence, even if sporadic, would make any change in this position extremely unlikely, regardless of who sits in the Oval Office. Reconstruction in and aid for Afghanistan will be a particularly nettlesome problem for global and regional actors, given the Taliban's history of association with terrorist groups and poor capacity to govern.

Moreover, ongoing civil wars, even at lower levels of violence, function as conflict traps which draw in regional and international powers and increase the levels of tension between them. In doing so, chronic violence doesn't just make life difficult within the states in civil war, but it also perpetuates conflict and dysfunction in the broader region. The region-wide contestation between the main regional states of Iran, Saudi Arabia, Turkey, and Israel, in addition to Egypt, the UAE, and Qatar, as examples, has been exacerbated by the continuation of civil wars in the weaker states of the Middle East. While the rivalry between various coalitions of these powers for regional influence predated the civil wars in Syria, Iraq, Libya, and Yemen, the competition became more hostile, intense, and direct after these countries descended into civil war. In a way, this rivalry between the major regional powers represents a regional civil war, sitting atop the country-specific civil wars. As local civil wars continue to export tensions up the food chain to the regional powers, a negative feedback loop is created, sustaining and even perpetuating the violence of the civil wars and stoking animosities between the regional powers. This negative feedback increases the risk of the prolongation or recurrence of civil war.

On a positive note, we have seen some progress toward de-escalation among the major regional powers that could improve the prospects for trying to bring the phenomenon of multiple, simultaneous civil wars to a close in the Middle East. In 2021 the rift with Qatar within the Gulf Cooperation Council (GCC) was patched up, Saudi Arabia and Iran engaged in talks in Baghdad, and the UAE renewed high-level ties with Turkey and sent diplomatic missions to Iran and Syria. And this comes after the Abraham Accords of 2020, which ushered in new levels of potential cooperation between Israel and key Arab states in the Gulf and North Africa. Leveraged properly, all these diplomatic steps will be important in maintaining the precarious stability in countries such as Iraq—or Lebanon and they could also continue to play an indirect role in encouraging conflict resolution in Libya. While so far these initiatives have not managed to de-escalate the civil war in Yemen, or find a way forward for the painful stalemate in Syria, attempts to mitigate conflict among the major regional powers will be critical to improving conditions even in these dire cases.

Pathways Toward Resolution

As you might have already gleaned from the above analysis, there are no silver bullet policy solutions for transitioning numerous failed or failing Middle Eastern states from civil conflict to peace and stability. But notwithstanding the constraints, there are some insights that policymakers at the national, regional, and international levels should bear in mind as they plan their actions and formulate their strategies.

Albert Einstein famously said that "no problem can be solved from the same level of consciousness that created it." While he was referring to problems of science and physics, his dictum also applies to the current civil wars in the Middle East. The problems and grievances that dragged countries into civil war will likely not be the same drivers and dynamics required to resolve the conflicts. Civil wars have a transformative effect on societies, meaning that the country coming out of civil war isn't the same one that entered. The implication of this is that resolving the grievances that tipped a country into war may be a necessary but insufficient part of what it takes to shepherd a country out of war. In other words, while local-level grievances and dynamics were the root causes of the wars, the entry of regional and international actors has since become a complicating factor. Resolution of the conflicts now requires coping with the issues at the national level that sparked the civil war, but also necessitates bringing into alignment the regional and international actors that have further entangled the conflicts.

Each of the civil wars covered in this book entails a complex web of local, regional, and international drivers. And each of these wars will likely require a different cocktail of national, regional, and international interventions to move to a more positive future.

National Level

While each country-chapter author cites unique reasons for the eruption of civil war, there are threads of commonality that emerge. They all point to deficits of political will, political dislocations, deep societal divisions, and a lack of institutional capacity and legitimacy, as the key drivers that perpetuate conflict. The authors also point to continuing divisions and proxy conflicts at the broader regional level among rival countries in the Middle East, as well as renewed competition among global great powers, as conditions that make permanently ending these civil wars even harder.

There are some general recommendations for national-level actors operating amid civil war and post-civil war environments that pertain to all the cases in this book. Leaders need to work equally hard in winning the peace as they did in prosecuting their wars. That will involve creating new social contracts that won't necessarily allay all pre-civil war grievances among opposition groups, but it may at least create a modicum of political will to cooperate on rebuilding their countries. Incorporating losers and making leaders from the various regions of the country stakeholders in the peace are part of this as well. While this may be an insuperable task in an age of emboldened and technologically empowered citizenries, transitioning from war to peace will require better integration of conflicting groups into the new sociopolitical order rather than renewing an imposed order based on large-scale exclusion.

Syria is one of the more intractable cases, largely because of the utter intransigence of the regime, but also because of the fragmentation and polarization of the opposition, the degree of entrenchment of outside actors, such as Iran and its Shi'i proxy militias including Hezbollah, the presence of extreme radical groups such as ISIS and al-Qaeda, as well as the major roles played by Turkey and Israel.[2] Russia remains the main extra-regional power in Syria, notwithstanding the fact that the United States still has a small force mainly in the northeast of the country. As of this writing, the conflict is temporarily frozen, with no major ongoing military operations. There is neither a credible ongoing political process that could lead to a final settlement, nor does there appear a viable near-term pathway for the Assad regime to reconquer all the parts of the country outside of its direct control. For Syria to move beyond conflict, and toward a stable and integrated national life, the country would have to transition from a praetorian regime to a more inclusive and responsive national political system. Serious reconstruction efforts will also depend on this, and possibly on how far efforts by the UAE and other Arab states to reconcile with the Assad regime will go. Ironically, Syria is a case where regional and international involvement in the civil war has been the greatest, but where resolution will depend as much or more on changes at the national level with the Assad government than on the role of outside actors.

Yemen is in a worse state than Syria, as conflict is still ongoing and an intense socioeconomic and humanitarian crisis grips the country. There have been several attempts at negotiating peace in Yemen, and some have made fleeting progress. Saudi Arabia has also become convinced of the need for a negotiated settlement and has engaged the Houthis in talks. As of this writing, however, the Houthis, with backing from Iran, continue to pursue the military option. As mentioned earlier in this conclusion, it is not clear whether if and when they seize Marib they would pivot to negotiations to secure their writ over what was formerly North Yemen, or whether they would push their advantage and seek a broader military victory as well in the former South Yemen. The challenge for the country is twofold: first, how to get to at least a precarious peace that will end the current fighting and alleviate the dire humanitarian conditions; second, how to turn even a temporary peace into a more sustainable political and institutional reality. None of this will be easy. Yemen has suffered from bouts of civil war since the 1960s, and the country was only unified—precariously—in 1990. For almost all its modern history, the state never had full and effective sovereignty over the whole country. But it's not all bad news, unlike Libya, Yemen has always had a rich vein of politics and negotiation that has persisted alongside bouts of armed conflict. During previous periods of civil war over the past decades, it has found mechanisms to transition from war to a tenuous peace. This time, intra-Yemeni negotiations must remain the main avenue for finding a negotiated end to the Yemeni conflict. This is not to ignore the important external and proxy aspect of the conflict. Although the latest bout of civil war in Yemen erupted for internal reasons, key regional powers—Saudi Arabia and Iran—ended up on opposing sides. If there is no de-escalation between Iran and Saudi Arabia in Yemen, or no agreement to forego Yemen as a regional battleground, it is hard to imagine that local parties will be encouraged—or even allowed—to come to a final agreement.

Libya is in a better condition than Syria and Yemen. There is no entrenched regime to deal with, no major ongoing fighting as of this writing, and the international community has encouraged the warring factions to move forward in a tentative peace process. The challenge in Libya is to keep the international community, including key players in the Middle East such as Turkey, Egypt, and the UAE, focused on encouraging negotiation over military action and to encourage domestic players to see through the peace process to fresh elections and a new inclusive political arrangement. The risk of backsliding into civil war always exists. The challenge, if and when the peace process sets in and elections take place, is to move quickly to build viable state institutions and the pillars of a functioning economy. The country does not lack for resources—it can pay for its development through the sale of its oil—but it will need agreement among external actors as well as technical and political assistance to build the institutions of a functioning state.

Afghanistan has seen an abrupt—if perhaps temporary—end to its civil war, with an American retreat and a swift Taliban victory; but the challenges to the country's near future remain formidable: will the Taliban be able to maintain their hold on the country or will rival groups challenge their rule in various parts of the country, leading to a new round of civil war? Will the Taliban's poor governance and international isolation lead to a deepening of an already acute socioeconomic crisis, creating further famine and other forms of political and societal collapse? And will Afghanistan—through the decisions of the Taliban, or despite them—become a center of international terror by hosting groups such as al-Qaeda and ISIS, thus drawing in international military action once again? The international community also has important decisions to make: will it hold fast to its boycott and sanctions against the Taliban-led order in Kabul, or will it engage the Taliban to help alleviate humanitarian suffering and stabilize the country? And how will key regional actors, such as Pakistan, Saudi Arabia, and Iran, deal with the new realities in Afghanistan? Typically, the end of civil wars is cause for general celebration, but the ending of the war through a victory by the Taliban has left wide cross-sections of the Afghan population, and many players around the world, deeply distressed. Can the lopsided peace in Afghanistan be evolved into a more inclusive political arrangement and a peace that a wider swath of Afghans can buy into and celebrate? Working to evolve the peace in Afghanistan and prevent that country from descending into another round of state failure and civil conflict will be a necessary challenge in the years to come.

Iraq, from where things stand today, deserves the most optimistic outlook of all the cases covered in this book. Almost all the territory that was captured by ISIS in 2014 has been retaken by the Iraqi military and the Kurdish *peshmerga*. This was achieved with the help of US air power and the *Hashd al-Shaabi* or Popular Mobilization Forces, many of which are supported by Iran. Moreover, with all the elections since then, including the parliamentary elections of 2021, there has been some hope that Iraq will be able to move toward a more inclusive and sovereign future. In addition to endeavoring to consolidate a conciliatory pathway with the Sunni and Kurdish communities—a process that had started under former Prime Minister Haidar al-Abadi during his 2014–18 tenure—the government of Prime Minister Mustafa al-Kadhimi also seems intent on reorienting its foreign policy to a more balanced position between the United States and Iran, and between Saudi Arabia and Iran.

But there are several wildcards that could upset the unstable equilibrium that best describes conditions in Iraq and that policymakers at all levels must consider when formulating strategies for the country. Corruption has been rampant both in Baghdad and the Kurdish capital of Erbil, something that will likely prove a scourge when trying to forge a new social contract between rulers and ruled. ISIS, which has been deprived of its territory, could still act as a major spoiler of any reconciliation process. For its part, the United States under President Joe Biden must continue to resist enlisting Iraq in its battle with Iran, as the Trump administration did. Failure to do this could give Tehran an incentive to push back against the United States presence in Iraq and make the country once again a proxy arena for US–Iranian contestation. A balanced non-escalatory US role could also encourage Baghdad's new nationalist path toward reintegration into the Arab world and aid a transition to a less dependent, more healthy relationship with Tehran. Moreover, US policymakers need to acknowledge the fragility of the current situation, and support efforts toward reconstruction of the areas hardest hit by ISIS, such as Mosul and Anbar.

Regional Level

There are three major regional conflicts that impact the context of civil wars in the Middle East. The first is between Iran and Israel. These two antagonists are locked in what they both view as an existential struggle. The leaders of the Islamic Republic are convinced that Israel—and behind it the United States—is committed to regime change in Iran. Israel in turn takes Iran at its word that the Islamic Republic wants to "wipe Israel off the map." This regional conflict is behind Iran's building up of Lebanese Hezbollah on Israel's northern border. It is also behind Iran's all-in effort to save the Assad regime in Syria, and the heavy presence of the much-vaunted Quds Force and its network of allied militias deployed in Syria. This conflict is currently being heightened by the potential unraveling of the nuclear deal that had held Iran's enrichment program in check, Iran's steady progress toward nuclear weapon breakout capacity, and the increase in the quantity and quality of Iran's missile arsenal, which it shares with Hezbollah and other proxy clients. This puts the two countries on the risky path of sudden major escalation. This tension not only prolongs civil war in Syria, and state failure in Lebanon, but also risks a region-wide war. The Biden administration is trying to return to the 2015 nuclear deal, but so far without success. If that effort fails, the region might be set on a new escalatory spiral that could make ending the civil wars in the region even more difficult.

The second regional conflict is that between Iran and Saudi Arabia. These countries have been at loggerheads at least since 1979 when the Islamic Republic in Tehran vowed to export its revolution to the monarchies in the region and picked up the mantle of revolutionary political Islam, particularly for the Shiite communities around the Muslim world, and Saudi Arabia responded by picking up the mantle of Sunni Islam, thus pitting the two petrostates as drivers of a sectarian conflict throughout the Muslim world. The civil war in Yemen is the most obvious reflection of this regional struggle. Although the civil war in this country was and is mainly driven by domestic Yemeni divisions and disputes, the rival regional powers have exacerbated the conflict. Iran found the Houthi rebellion a handy entry point to project its power into the Arabian Peninsula and saw the international maritime chokepoint of the Bab al-Mandeb strait as an opportunity for pressuring both regional and international powers. Saudi Arabia, under Crown Prince Mohammed bin Salman, first led Saudi Arabia into war in Yemen—expecting the conflict to be brief and victorious—but has since pivoted to wanting to end the war and reestablish constructive ties with Tehran. While Saudi Arabia seems willing to turn away from grand regional ambitions and focus on economic development at home, Iran—perhaps out of a mixture of paranoia, geopolitical opportunism, and ideological ambition—seems committed to maintaining a grand regional footprint, including in Yemen, something that the Saudis will bridle at in any negotiation. While there are many common interests between Iran and Saudi Arabia, and one could easily imagine a pathway of cooperation between the two, the renewed radical tilt in Iranian political leadership since the 2021 election of President Ebrahim Raisi is pointing in a different direction, which bodes ill for Iranian–Saudi détente and for the future of the conflicts in Yemen, Syria, Lebanon, and Iraq.

The third regional conflict is that between rival Sunni powers, pitting Turkey—and Qatar—which have backed the Muslim Brotherhood and maintained relations with Iran, against the UAE, Egypt, Bahrain, and Saudi Arabia, which have regarded the Brotherhood (and Iran) as mortal threats to their political systems. This rivalry played itself out in the events in Egypt between the Brotherhood's rise to power in 2012 and the coup that unseated President Mohammed Morsi in 2013. It has also persisted in the civil war in Libya, where Turkey backed the Islamist-leaning government in Tripoli, and Egypt and the UAE (and Russia) backed General Khalifa Hifter and his forces against them. This regional rivalry has shown signs of ebbing: the Saudi crown prince has led a reconciliation with Qatar within the GCC, and the UAE crown prince has visited Ankara to repair ties with Turkey's president, Recep Tayyip Erdoğan. This easing of intra-Sunni tensions has been a factor in moving the Libyan conflict away from armed conflict and toward a peace process. This de-escalation and reconciliation will likely remain at risk of backsliding, but there are encouraging signs that both sides of this regional divide have recognized that the benefits of de-escalation and cooperation outweigh those of fueling conflict between them.

But it is important to note that in addition to early signs of de-escalation between Saudi Arabia and Iran, and the healing of divisions between Turkey, Qatar, the UAE, and Saudi Arabia, there have been other positive signs at the regional level as well. While the Abraham Accords between Israel and a number of Arab states, including the UAE, Bahrain, Sudan, and Morocco, don't directly weigh on the civil wars, they do demonstrate that even age-old hostilities can be overcome. These accords are an important example of regional actors moving beyond hostility and toward de-escalation, normalization, and even cooperation. But optimism needs to be tempered by the fact that the Abraham Accords have exacerbated some other regional fault lines and tensions. The Israeli–Palestinian conflict has persisted for seven decades. The consensus Arab position, at least since 2002, has been that the Arabs would normalize relations with Israel on condition that Israel reach agreement with the

Palestinians on a two-state solution. This had given the Palestinians some leverage with the dominant Israelis in potential peace talks. But the signatory states' decision to normalize relations with Israel without any major concessions from Israel toward the Palestinians—except a pledge by Israel to "suspend" annexation of Jewish settlements on the West Bank—meant the Palestinians lost one of their few points of leverage with the Israelis. If a negotiated and sustainable resolution to one of the longest running conflicts in the Middle East, that between the Israelis and Palestinians, seemed remote before the Abraham Accords, it seems even more so today. This means that the Israeli–Palestinian conflict—in some senses a long-running civil war—will likely be with us for decades to come. A second possible negative outcome of the Abraham Accords is that as Israel and key Arab states draw closer together, this will escalate threat perceptions and potentially lead to further conflicts with Iran. This could exacerbate regional tensions and even prolong the civil wars covered in this book.

International Level

Because of the regional tensions covered in the previous section that prevent resolution of several of the civil wars, global actors like the United States, Russia, China, and the Europeans also need to encourage regional actors like Iran, Saudi Arabia, as well as Turkey and Israel, to move toward some kind of cooperative framework for the Middle East. In this vein, there needs to be a focus on creating a security architecture for the region.[3] Other regions, such as Europe, Africa, and Southeast Asia, have all developed institutional means for managing conflict and avoiding all-out or proxy war. While this is unlikely to emerge in the current regional and global political climate, policy should be moving in the direction of working toward such a security architecture for the Middle East.

In addition, the more that the United States, Russia, and China act at cross purposes, pursuing their competition in the region, rather than agreeing on paths forward, the more difficult it will be to bring the civil wars to an end—and indeed, to prevent the collapse of other states into civil wars.

If the great powers align on Yemen, Syria, Iraq, Libya, and Afghanistan, this will put enormous pressure on regional actors to fall in line, which in turn puts strong pressure on national-level actors as well. While solutions can't come from the top, they can be encouraged by global actors. Great power cooperation bore fruit in the international effort to get Tehran to the negotiating table during the Obama administration to secure the nuclear deal between Iran and the P5+1. But since then, and particularly since the Trump administration withdrew from the Iran nuclear deal, international cooperation on the issues facing the Middle East has been on the decline. The UN Security Council has ceased to find consensus on critical issues, particularly since the fallout over its decision on NATO's intervention in Libya. While former US President Barack Obama continued to try to work multilaterally, President Donald Trump rejected multilateralism and UN institutions in favor of a nationalist, US-alone approach. Although President Biden has eschewed the unilateralist approach taken by Trump, it is unclear whether hostilities with China on trade matters and on Taiwan, and acrimony with Russia on Ukraine, will allow for any constructive great power dialogue on the Middle East.

Multilateral diplomacy between the global actors, when and if it emerges, needs to reflect an understanding that there are sins of commission and omission. While completely eschewing involvement by regional and international actors is neither possible nor desirable, what matters is the *kind* of intervention. Borrowing the Hippocratic Oath from the medical profession, the political equivalent would be "do no harm." This means that at all costs, actions by global actors that create political and security vacuums, as was the case in Libya, Afghanistan, and Iraq, should be avoided.

There also needs to be an understanding among policymakers that the civil wars have become a Gordian knot of national, regional, and international actors. International actors conscious of this fact need to develop policies consistent with becoming stakeholders in winning the peace just as they were protagonists in trying to win the wars.

This looks unlikely in the near future. Despite efforts by the Biden administration, the level of international disorder and destructive contestation created by the Trump administration—and Russia—now rivals that which exists regionally in the Middle East. This does not bode well for future conflict de-escalation or lasting resolution of the civil wars. Suffice it to say that rebuilding multilateralism and international cooperation and working toward finding common approaches to regional challenges—particularly the challenges of ending the civil wars—would be tremendously valuable in an otherwise very divided and diplomacy-poor Middle East environment.

Final Thoughts

At the end of the day, the future of the states in civil war covered in this book, and the broader region, will be shaped by the ebb and flow of power across the national, regional, and international levels. While national-level actors have tremendous agency and can defy the efforts of regional and international powers, it is important to recognize that regional and international forces can either be agents or spoilers of peace.

Also, pathways toward peace will require intensive reconstruction efforts, which necessitate a confluence of national, regional, and international actors, all pulling in the same direction. Reconstruction efforts in all the civil wars covered in this book, in addition to repairing damaged hard infrastructure, will need to painstakingly repair broken social contracts torn asunder by civil war and conditions leading up to the collapse into war. This will have to involve a weaving back together of social, political, and economic systems. Addressing how macro and micro economic factors interact with politics and social forces should be a central part of this. A focus on the political-economy, past, present, and future, will be necessary to start rebuilding a functioning system that addresses the issue of broken social contracts and failed legitimacy formulas between states and societies. Turning profiteering-driven war economies into functioning national economies will require extensive expertise and coordination between national, regional, and international actors.

As we conclude this second edition of this book, we want to reinforce that some progress in the de-escalation of tensions among key regional powers has been made. Moreover, we can point to a tentative but potentially promising peace process in Libya and continued precarious stability in Iraq. But notwithstanding these hopeful signs, the conflict in Yemen rages on, and the conflict in Syria is frozen but without a real resolution in sight. Also the Taliban victory in Afghanistan might have ended that civil war for now, but it raises a whole new set of concerns and challenges.

But history has its ebbs and flows, and policymakers should be aware of the need to create—or take advantage of—the moments of international and regional alignment mentioned above, to bring more of these civil wars to a final and sustainable end. Our hope is that this volume contributes, if not precise roadmaps for resolving these conflicts, at least critical insights about their causes, drivers, and dynamics that can be useful in finding and forging transitions from civil war to a sustainable peace. The combination of academic, analytic, and practitioner perspectives should help policymakers step back from the immediacy of today to consider the various elements of a broader sustained strategy. We hope that they find useful insights in this volume that can help them forge pathways toward resolution of the civil wars in the Middle East, and help bring about a more stable regional environment.

Notes

1 Carl von Clausewitz, *On War*, trans. Col. J. J. Graham, new and revised edition with introduction and notes by Col. F. N. Maude, in three volumes, vol. 1 (London: Kegan Paul, Trench, Trubner, 1918), Chapter 1.
2 See Nadar Hashemi and Danny Postel, *Sectarianization: Mapping the New Politics of the Middle East* (Oxford: Oxford University Press, 2017) for an analysis of this phenomenon of sectarianization of populations amid civil war.
3 See Ross Harrison and Paul Salem, *From Chaos to Cooperation: Toward Regional Order in the Middle East* (Washington, DC: Middle East Institute, 2017), particularly Chapter 11, by Ross Harrison for both the constraints and opportunities for establishing a regional security architecture for the Middle East.

INDEX

role in domestic settlements 186
in Syria 141–2
Taliban and 173
in Yemen 103, 112–13
al-Qaeda in Iraq (AQI)
Ba'athists collaboration with 76, 212
emergence of 210, 213, 216
sectarian violence 213, 214
Sunni disillusionment with 215
weakening and rebranding 219–20, 223
See also ISIS (Islamic State in Iraq and Syria)
al-Alwani, Ahmed 218
al-Amiri, Hadi 229
AMSI (Association of Muslim Scholars in Iraq) 212–13
Arab-Israeli conflict 1, 11, 21–2, 267–8
Arab-Israeli War (1967) 18, 21–2, 27, 64, 78, 121 n.3
Arab League 56 n.42, 57 n.50, 128, 140, 227, 239
Arab nationalism. *See* nationalism
Arab Spring uprisings
effects on regional order 14
in Libya 77–8
in Syria 126–8
underlying causes of 60–1
in Yemen 91, 96, 99–101
al-Assad, Bashar
need for manpower 129, 136
rejection of negotiation terms 128, 130, 136–7
use of chemical weapons 128
al-Assad, Hafez 30–1, 63
Association of Muslim Scholars in Iraq (AMSI) 212–13

Astana Process
call for cease-fire zones 130
as effort for political resolution 138
Iran-Turkey mediation efforts 82
mediation effort 82
as resource for leverage 247
See also Syrian Civil War (2011–)
Autonomous Administration of North and East Syria (AANES) 126, 142–3. *See also* Syrian Civil War (2011–)
Awakening Movement (Sons of Iraq) 213, 215, 216, 219, 236 n.14

Ba'ath Party (Iraq). *See* Iraq Conflict (2003–)
al-Bahah, Khaled 107
Balfour Declaration 11, 21
Barre, Siad 28
Barzani, Masoud 219, 222, 233
al-Bashir, Omar 24
al-Beidh, Ali Salem 94, 105, 121 n.9
Beirut Port blast (2020) 17, xiii
Believing Youth Movement (Yemen) 97
Bennett, Naftali 147
Benomar, Jamal 100, 107
Biden, Joe
on Iraq 234
on Syria 134, 144
bin Laden, Osama 169
Black September (Jordan-PLO conflict) 30
Bolton, John 197
Brahimi, Lakhdar 227
Bremer, Paul 210
Bush, George H. W. 161
Bush, George W.
agreement to end Iraq War 217
"Marshall Plan" for Afghanistan 161

division and inability to form
united front, Syria example 131
economic conditions 6, 9, 48–9
external factors 10–15
future prospects 35–7
historical overview 1–2, 7–10
internal factors 7–10
legitimacy, lack of state x, 8–9
nationalism 7–8, 11, 22
Oman, socioeconomic drivers 27–8
populism 62, 96–9, 102, 142
socioeconomic conditions 6, 68–9
Syria, governance 128
Yemen, economics 90, 91–7, 99
dual sovereignty. *See* civil wars,
resolving
al-Dulaymi, Adnan 213
Dunbar, Charles 78

economic development. *See* drivers of
conflict
Egypt
Bedouins, discontent among 32
Islamist movements in 31–2
nationalism 65
role in Yemen 65, 121 n.3
separate peace with Israel 13
Eisenhower Doctrine (US policy) 66
engagement, foreign. *See* external
involvement
engagement diplomacy 239–55
Afghanistan example 251
applications and overview 239–41
challenges and recommendations
242–4, 249–53
direct *vs.* indirect efforts 245
externally led diplomacy 253–5
with governments and rebels
248–9, 252
outcomes, possible 241–2

peacekeeping 256 n.9
tools and strategies 244–8
Yemen Group of Ten as model for
122 n.24
See also civil wars, resolving
external involvement
in Afghanistan, high level 26
in Algeria, low level 26
challenges and responsibilities
41–2, 243–4
direct intervention
approach 81
early engagement,
importance of 250
effects of military aid 45–7
history and overview
59–60, 239–40
importance of timing 242–3
indirect approach 81–2
in Libya 179
multilateral diplomacy 268–9
peacekeeping missions 51
preventing conflict
recurrence 48–51
risks of democratization 49
role in conflict resolution 45–8
in Sudan 23
in Syria, failed 128–31
See also stability, domestic
extractive systems, political and
economic 90

Farouk (King of Egypt) 31
Fatah (West Bank), role in "Black
September" conflict 30
Fatah-Hamas Civil War
(Palestine) 21–2
fault lines, ideologies
and conflict 9, 63, 65–6
al-Fayyad, Mohammed Ishaq 225

foreign engagement. *See* external involvement

Free Syrian Army (FSA) 129

Free Yemenis 92

Gaddafi, Muammar
  leadership and overthrow of 177, 178, 183
  The Little Green Book, 181
  overthrow of King Idris 180

GCC (Gulf Cooperation Council). *See* specific conflict names: external involvement

GCC Initiative and Implementing Mechanism (Yemen)
  Hadi attack on 121 n.9
  implementation and opposition 100–2
  National Dialogue Conference 100–1, 106–7, 115, 117, 119, 120
  Saleh signs 100
  See also Yemen Civil War (2014–)

Geneva 1 communiqué on Syria 128

geographic divisions, imposed
  colonial period 11
  effects on domestic conflict 23, 24–5, 28, 102, 117
  Islamic groups' goals regarding 72
  legitimacy, lack of state 8–9
  regional dynamics 13, 59–60

geopolitics. *See* civil wars, geopolitics of

Ghani, Abdul Aziz Abdul 95, 100

Ghani, Ashraf 153

al-Ghashmi, Ahmad 93, 94

Gorbachev, Mikhael 157

Griffiths, Martin 104

Grundberg, Hans 109, 114, 115

Gulf Cooperation Council. *See* specific conflict names: external involvement

Hadi, Abed Rabbo Mansour 121 n.9

al-Hakim, Ammar 228–9

Halabja genocide, Iraqi Kurds 19, 209

Haqqani Network, in Afghanistan 158–9

Hashid tribal confederation (Yemen) 93, 101, 108, 122 n.26

al-Hashimi, Tariq 218

Hayat Tahrir al-Sham (HTS, Organization to Liberate the Levant) 141–2

Hifter, Khalifa
  attempted overthrow of GNA 177–8, 197–8
  role in Libyan Conflict 184, 267
  suspends government 187–8

al-Hilal, Abdul Qadir 96

historical case studies. *See* case studies, historical

Holder v. Humanitarian Law Project (US Supreme Court ruling) 250

al-Houthi, Abdul-Malek, Sa'dah War agreement 105

al-Houthi, Badr al-Din 97

al-Houthi, Husayn 97

Houthis (Yemen)
  2014 conflict and 101–2
  cross-border missions 111
  emergence of 96
  Peace and National Partnership agreement 107
  potential for negotiations with 263
  rise of 97–8
  Saleh partnership with 101–3, 104
  See also Zaydi Shi'a tribes (Yemen)

role in Libya 197
Syria, policy in 247
See also specific conflict
names: external involvement
United States Supreme Court, *Holder v. Humanitarian Law Project* 250
UNRWA (UN Relief and Works Agency for Palestine Refugees in the Near East) 21–2
USS Cole, 2001 attack on 113

West Bank (Fatah), role in "Black September" conflict 30
Western Sahara. Morocco-Polisario Front conflict 34–5
Williams, Stephanie Turco 179, 198

Yemen
effects of Soviet collapse 78–9
external impacts on stability 107–13, 117–19
extractive political and economic system 90, 93, 96–7, 115
fault lines of conflict 90, 91, 92, 96–8
Group of Ten 122 n.24
tribal identity-based nationalism 92
Yemen, Republic of (RoY)
buildup to 1994 civil war 94–5
coalition government formation 95
end of Cold War 78
unification failure and consequences 93–6, 119–20
unity agreement, motives and terms 93–4
Yemen Arab Republic (YAR, North Yemen)
establishment of 92
power structure in 92–3
tribal dynamics 93

Yemen Civil War (2014–)
Arab Spring and 99–101
economic collapse and war economy 113–14
external mediation efforts 100–2, 104, 106–7, 112, 114–15, 122 n.24
history and overview 89–90
Hodeida Port, role in 104
Houthi-Saleh partnership 101–3, 104
influences of Saudi Arabia-Iran regional rivalry 107–8
Iran involvement in 110–11
JCPOA 111
origins of 90–91, 121 n.9
Peace and National Partnership Agreement 107
PNPA and 102, 107
recommendations for future 116–19
recommendations for settlement 116–20, 263
requirements for settlement 91, 119–20
Riyadh Agreement 103–4
Russia and US involvement 111–13
Saudi Arabia involvement 108–9
Southern Transitional Council 103
transitional government, weakness of 101–2
transitional government failure 103
UAE involvement 107–8, 109–10
US involvement 112–13
See also GCC Initiative and Implementing Mechanism (Yemen); Saʿdah Wars (Yemen, 2004–10); Yemen instability
Yemen instability 89–122
1962 uprising 17–18, 90